EYES ᵀᴼ SEE

EYES to SEE

CARL GALLUPS

Critically Acclaimed Bestselling Author

FOREWORD BY TOM HORN

STUNNING REVELATIONS FROM THE WORD OF GOD THAT
HELP MAKE SENSE OF OUR EPIC, PROPHETIC TIMES

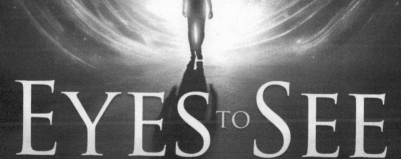

EYES TO SEE

IS OUR WORLD READY FOR THE
COMING VISITATION?

Defender
Crane, MO

Eyes to See: Stunning Revelations from the Word of God That Help Make Sense of Our Epic Prophetic Times

By Carl Gallups

Defender Publishing
Crane, MO 65633

© 2024 Defender Publishing
All Rights Reserved. Published 2024.

Printed in the United States of America.

ISBN: 978-1-9480-1478-6
A CIP catalog record of this book is available from the Library of Congress.

Cover design by Jeffrey Mardis
Interior design by Katherine Lloyd

Dedicated to Haddon and Abel

I had no idea that a couple of "little guys" could bring
such unfathomable joy and hilarity into my life.
Boy, was I mistaken!
I thank the Lord Jesus Christ for both of you.

Other Bestselling Books by Carl Gallups from Defender Publishing

Yeshua Protocol
(November 2022)

Glimpses of Glory
(March 2022)

The Summoning
(January 2021)

Masquerade
(March 2020)

The Rabbi, the Secret Message, and the Identity of Messiah
(February 2019)

Gods of the Final Kingdom
(July 2019)

Gods of Ground Zero
(October 2018)

Gods and Thrones
(October 2017)

Most of the world would rather scream with their eyes shut tight than listen with their eyes wide open.

—Piper Kirstie[1]

Eyes To See is essentially Part II of Carl's previous work titled *Yeshua Protocol*.

However, it is not necessary to first read *Yeshua Protocol* in order to thoroughly enjoy and understand this one from beginning to end.

We recommend that you eventually read both, in that they highly complement each other and bring forth a number of independently glorious revelations. Enjoy!

—Defender Publishing, Crane, MO

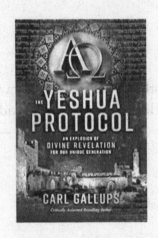

CONTENTS

PART THREE:
UNDERSTANDING THE REASONS

PART FOUR:
THE TEMPLE CORRELATION

PART FIVE:
THE TREE OF KNOWLEDGE

PART SIX:
TIPPING THE HOURGLASS

PART SEVEN:
SEEN AND UNSEEN

PART EIGHT:
FIRST THINGS

PART NINE:
THE DECISION

FOREWORD

Carl Gallups has done it, yet again! He's taken several complex theological and prophetic matters and made them understandable, enjoyable, and a delight to share with others.

I've known Carl for many years, and have published a number of his revelatory books. He has a gift for making these disclosures intimately relevant to our lives and to the prophetic times in which we live.

Eyes to See is no exception. When Carl first submitted the manuscript draft to Defender Publishing for potential publication, I was thrilled. I wrote him immediately and said, "Wow, Carl! I can't wait to read this finalized book!"

Rest assured, you're in for a whirlwind excursion of biblical unveiling. Enjoy the adventure!

—Tom Horn (February 28, 1957–October 20, 2023),
CEO of SkyWatch TV and Defender Publishing

A NOTE
FROM THE AUTHOR

If you've read any of my other books, you'll already know I often construct a much larger scenario as I move along. That fact most likely arises from the years prior to my ministry calling wherein I was deeply immersed in a decade-long law enforcement career.

Step by step, piece by piece, I am weaving together my case—collecting the evidence—praying that you, "the jury," will be convinced that I've carefully and contextually researched the matter to the point of rendering a proper verdict.

In the meantime, after being blessed to have authored a number of books, I've also learned that while people insist on a factual work, they also want an enjoyable read—one that's even entertaining and, at times, gripping. For a long time, I've endeavored to incorporate all those qualities into my writing, including organizing the information in short, understandable chapters as well as presenting a few sections of interesting and easy-to-read, immersive narrative. I pray you'll enjoy the results as you read this book.

My greatest desire is that you will come to see several marvelous truths from the Word of God magnified in the world around you... illuminated in such a way as to bring the highest glory to our Lord and Savior, Jesus Christ—*Yeshua HaMashiach*.

Thank you for taking this journey with me.

PART ONE

SEEING

Jesus said, "For judgment I came into this world, that those who do not see may see, and those who see may become blind." Some of the Pharisees near him heard these things, and said to him, "Are we also blind?" Jesus said to them, "If you were blind, you would have no guilt; but now that you say, 'We see,' your guilt remains." (John 9:39–41)

1
THE TIME MACHINE

*The enemy—Satan and his demonic horde—did not fully
understand what was happening right in their midst.*

As you flip over the last page of this chapter, you'll slide back in
time almost two thousand years. Through your mind's eye, you
will enter the city of ancient Jerusalem and walk those streets with
Yeshua and His disciples.

After reading the series of those novel-like chapters and the staggering revelations embedded within them, we'll dive right into the Word
of God and into the midst of the prophetic events of our own rapidly
changing world. We'll also unveil additional disclosures of incredible
biblical insight, including the latest dependable historical, archeological, and scientific discoveries that serve to bring the Bible into a realm
of brightly illuminated relevance.

Beginning with the first chapters and continuing right up to the
very last words, we'll weave all of those elements together into a tap-
estry of connected knowledge that will bring you into an incredibly
magnified focus upon the prophetic times in which we live. I'm convinced those revelations will help you to more effectively apply the
Word of God to the day-to-day journey of your walk with *Yeshua
HaMashiach* (Hebrew for "Jesus Christ"). In other words, the further
we go down this road together, the more personal this journey will
become to you.

BACK TO THE FUTURE

Our adventure begins within the historical age when the Roman
Empire ruled a large swath of the ancient world. It was the strongest

and most technologically advanced civilization the planet had known until that time.

But those were also the days in which the Jewish ruling elite were suffocating their own people with their Scripture-nullifying traditions, and burdensome regulations—mostly for the sake of retaining their own prestigious positions of authority among the people, while holding on to their delicately privileged standing with the Roman government.

What's more, it was the time in which the Romans had perfected the ancient form of punishment known as crucifixion. According to the National Institutes of Health (NIH), that pervasive first century horror was the most brutal and humiliating form of death known to humanity. A number of experts in such matters maintain that this gruesome fact is still true.[2]

It was during that prophetic period of history, when God would fulfill the grandest part of His glorious Word. The Word, who is Yahweh Himself, had become flesh, in the person of Yeshua. This, of course, was the beginning of the ultimate overthrowing of Satan's kingdom (John 1:1–14).

The Apostle Paul, writer of almost half the New Testament documents, strikingly emphasized that world-changing event.

But when the **set time had fully come**, God sent his Son, born of a woman, born under the law, **to redeem** those under the law, that we might receive **adoption to sonship**. (Galatians 4:4–5, NIV; emphasis added)

OUR TOUR GUIDE

The specific timeframe into which we will land is but a mere pinpoint on humanity's storied timeline—comprising only a handful of months in total. But as we step into that era, we'll experience the events as revealed through the eyes of the Apostle John, the "disciple whom Jesus loved" (John 13:23).

John's words are presented as though he is recalling the events, then describing them through the filter of his own experiences—particularly in light of his constantly shuffling emotions, eternal lessons of mind-bending truth, and the wagonload of agonizing doubts that accompanied those monumental occasions.[3]

These were the last months that sealed the planned fate of Yeshua, through His horrific crucifixion—*our Salvation*. To this day, the entire planet is still staggering from that divinely appointed clash of the unseen realms that took place on Golgotha's cross and at the garden tomb. In the coming pages, you'll be there "in person" as the days leading to that event unraveled at breakneck speed. That ferocious spiritual collision also foreshadowed what was yet to come, in the ultimate *day of evil*.

Finally, be strong in the Lord and in his mighty power. Put on the full armor of God, so that you can take your stand against the devil's schemes.

For our **struggle is not against flesh and blood**, but against the rulers, against the authorities, against **the powers of this dark world** and against the spiritual forces of evil in the heavenly realms.

Therefore put on the full armor of God, so that when **the day of evil** comes, you may be able to stand your ground, and after you have done everything, to stand. (Ephesians 6:10–13, NIV; emphasis added)[4]

Sadly, most of the world, along with sizable portions of today's institutional church, is oblivious to the grand demonic delusion that's currently happening right in our midst...the most prophetic times since the First Coming of Yeshua. The Holy Spirit-led correction of that eternal heartbreak is largely what this book is about.

However, before you can most fully understand it, you have to feel it, smell it, experience it...and *see it*. But to do that, you have to be there.

Now the adventure begins.

BACK TO
THE FUTURE

For our light and momentary troubles are achieving for us an eternal glory that far outweighs them all. So we fix our eyes not on what is seen, but on what is unseen, since what is seen is temporary, but what is unseen is eternal. (2 Corinthians 4:17–18)

There is a chain connecting the sin of humanity and its woe, but the links are not traceable by the human eye...but its works have led to the manifestation of the works of God in the divine plan of redemption. It is so in the instance of the man who was born blind. The blindness of this beggar will have its result, and therefore in the divine counsel had its purpose, in the light which will dawn upon the spiritual as well as upon the physical blindness, and from Him (Jesus Christ) will dawn upon the world.[5]

2

ASTONISHINGLY
STRANGE

*"I've tried everything else! Who knows?
Maybe this will work!"*

I was standing right beside Yeshua at the moment it happened. On that day, I witnessed something utterly impossible! We all did. Me...Peter, James, Matthew, and the rest of the Twelve.

Even this many years later, I realize we were spectators of the most incredible miracles the world had ever seen. And we just happened to have front-row seats! Even then, we still didn't know the full importance of what was taking place—not until much later.

I'll start my recollection by looking back to a particular Sabbath day in Jerusalem.[6]

It was early fall, soon after the great Feast of Tabernacles, also known as Succoth, the last of the Seven Feasts of the Lord.[7] The temperature was unseasonably warm, and the Pharisees were on our heels again—this time with rocks in their hands. So we darted through the narrow streets of that ancient city until we were saturated in sweat.

The massive crowd, which only a few moments before had been intently listening to Yeshua teach in the Temple courts, unknowingly prevented the ones who clutched those murderous stones from gaining access to us. The religious authorities were desperately trying to get their hands on us, their eyes ablaze with seething hatred and their hearts on fire with searing, murderous rage.[8]

"Make way! Make way! *We demand it!* Clear the way...*now!*" They shouted their commands as they shoved their way through the masses, kicking out of the way several roaming street dogs as they went. The bulging veins of their foreheads, appearing as though they would pop at any moment, signaled their seething hatred for us.

Thankfully, their efforts were futile. The hordes of people were too densely packed, and we had already leapt down from the speaker's area before Yeshua's attackers could get near us. Before the gaggle of Pharisees knew what happened, we were gone.

We escaped from the immediate vicinity and blended into the crowd as we scampered among the throngs still swelling the city streets. Powerful aromas of the open marketplace wafted through the air; the sizzle of food cooking over oakwood fires, the heavenly scent of baking bread, and the sight of freshly ripened produce were comforting distractions. We were finally safe, for the time being. At least it felt that way—and it *smelled* that way, too.

So far, so good.

THE HOPELESS SOUL

A bit later, we stumbled upon a blind beggar in the streets of Jerusalem.[9] At least we *thought* we had merely "stumbled" upon him. We would later discover this was no accidental encounter at all. Yeshua hinted to us that our rendezvous with this man had been planned from *the beginning* of time itself.[10] In actuality, we hadn't yet understood the truth of that much bigger picture—the eternal nature of it all. In fact, at the time, we couldn't have even begun to comprehend such a thing…not for a while.

But what a pitiful sight the man was! To be honest, there were many other people in varying degrees of similar crisis scattered throughout the streets of Jerusalem. Each hoped that they, too, might get a few coins tossed their way so they could eat another scanty meal. But this particular person was different. He was known, among many in the city, to have been blind since the day he had drawn his first breath of life. Poor fellow! How miserable he must have been. None of us could even imagine living such a depressing life.

Our hearts ached for him from the moment we saw him. He could do little else than sit there, every day, in public places and plead with those who passed by…hoping to somehow stir the compassion of others to help supply his daily sustenance. This was the totality of his so-called life, and apparently it was all his existence would ever be. That's what we assumed. But we would soon witness a drastic turn of events.

As we eased up to the man, Yeshua exchanged a few tender words with him. That's when we saw the beggar clearly. The sockets where his working eyes should have been were grotesque. It appeared as if eyes had, in fact, been there at one time, but now the entire area was disfigured; the eyeballs seemed to have shriveled, and the places where they should have been were matted over with scar tissue.[11]

A few moments later, Yeshua stooped down and gathered up a bit of dirt in His palm and spit into it. He stirred the solution with a finger of His other hand, swirling it around to make a sticky paste. With the man's permission, Yeshua tenderly applied the clay-like substance to the area of his disfigurement.

Just then, the man perked up a bit. Yeshua had leaned over and whispered something else into his ear. After a brief exchange between the two, the blind man stood and began to amble his way toward the popular, superstition-laden Pool of Siloam, tapping his walking stick as he went, like he had probably done ten thousand times before. Only this time, he had a real purpose in his steps. He was on a mission.[12]

Click. Tick. Click. Tick. Click. Tick.

Sporting his newly muddied eyes, he swept his walking stick back and forth in front of his steps, searching for obstacles that might be in his path. But he never even stumbled. Instead, he steadily made his way to the waters of Siloam's pool.[13]

That's when it happened.

A few seconds after scooping some water from the pool and splashing it in his eyes, he began shrieking. "I can see! I can see!" Dozens of stunned onlookers rushed toward him. "My life has been made new!"

he screamed. "I can see! I can see all of you! *I see! I see! I see!* I see you, and you, *and you!*" He pointed his finger at individuals in the crowd, seeming to desire to prove that he could actually see each of them.

I almost choked on the knot that welled up in my throat as I watched what was playing out in front of me. My eyes began to pour water; I could barely breathe. I fell to my knees and began sobbing like a child, my chest heaving as I continued trembling. *What had I just witnessed?*

CONTEXT

Before I tell you the shocking "secret" that Yeshua later revealed to us about the healing and the resulting outrage, I'll retell the saga by going back to what led up to this day. I'll take you to the events that unfolded several weeks before the blind man's eyes were opened. It's all intricately connected to the bigger picture of what you will soon get to experience for yourself. You'll see!

The fuller perspective that I'll bring, perhaps, will also help you to "see" the truth in the same way we were made to understand it… gradually, yet powerfully. It was a discovery that floored us all, and one I'll never forget.

This is why I can't wait for *you* to also discover the depths of what actually happened over the course of those history-altering days. More than likely, the revelations will *not* turn out to be what you might be expecting at the moment!

3

THE FESTIVAL

*This was yet another infuriating fact for the Pharisees and other
religious authorities to have to stomach.*

The story really began to develop at the beginning of the fall Feast
of Tabernacles, just a few weeks before we wound up in Jerusalem, while we were still near Lake Galilee. During that time, we
were entering the last handful of months of Yeshua's earthly life and
ministry.[14]

In truth, none of us understood that important detail. But, looking back, we should have known. Yeshua had done everything but
draw us a map and paint a picture of what He was up to. However,
we were still in the process of developing our own spiritual vision. So,
at the time of the festival, we were yet to fully understand everything.
But we would soon take a giant leap forward in that regard!

Thankfully, Yeshua was patient with us.

But then again, *He always was.*

GOING UP TO JERUSALEM

Previously, we had been ministering throughout the broader region
surrounding Capernaum, several days' journey north of Jerusalem. It's
a beautiful area, and Capernaum is one of the larger towns located on
the western shores of Lake Galilee.[15] The most popular route used for
travel from there to Jerusalem required a journey of about three days
on foot—through Samaritan territory.[16]

But even that relatively short distance could prove to be dangerous. Bandits sometimes turned up along the most traveled paths,
waiting to ambush straggling travelers. Occasionally, there were even

politically motivated ruffians to contend with, most often involving the Samaritan population. And we would have to travel right through that area—one most Jews routinely avoided.

There are also the dangers that come with extreme weather shifts, and the hazards presented by the often-grueling terrain itself. And none of those concerns even included the rarer, but still possible, lion or bear attack.[17]

Because of those concerns, groups of caravans were forming, allowing for a greater measure of traveling safety. A number of those clusters were already on the road headed to Jerusalem and the ancient Temple Mount, the city's centerpiece.[18]

LET THEM ACKNOWLEDGE YOU!

Several members of Yeshua's wider circle of relatives, including the larger group of constantly growing "disciples," were urging Him to go up to Jerusalem for the feast as well.[19] They were certainly in awe of Him because of the widely known miracles He had performed and the incredible teachings He had shared for almost three years. However, they had not yet made the giant leap of calling Him the "long-awaited Jewish Messiah." That revelation was still well beyond their understanding.

Besides, making such a claim was not the safest political position to take at the time—not by a longshot. At this point in His ministry, some of Yeshua's relatives were still waiting for Him to be publicly recognized as Messiah by the Jewish leaders themselves before they said anything of the sorts.[20] If that happened, they thought, it would be much safer for them to join in with the growing public accolades. In their minds, there would be no better time for that official recognition to take place than at the Feast of Tabernacles, the most well attended Feast day of the year. If it was going to happen at all, they reasoned, that would be the absolute best occasion.

However, instead of joining them, along with the other convoys, Yeshua said, "You go on ahead. I'm not going to attend the feast until the proper time. That will be a moment I set for Myself, a time that will make the greatest impact for the Kingdom mission. My occasion to be acknowledged has not yet fully developed...*but it will come*, I promise. When it does arrive, you won't be able to miss it!"[21]

It seemed Yeshua was always speaking in riddles. He had a certain glint in His eyes as He said these things to them. After He had answered them, He simply turned and walked away, going about His business, mingling with the crowds that continued to gather.

We remained in Capernaum for a while longer, until the day before the great feast was already underway in Jerusalem. It was during that time when Yeshua had instructed us to follow Him there. So we set out on our journey toward the Temple Mount. We had no idea what an unfathomable experience that would prove to be.

THE HOLY CITY

We arrived in Jerusalem a little more than three days later, during the middle of the feast. At Yeshua's direction, we went straight to the Temple courts where the bulk of people had assembled. It would be the perfect place for Him, once again, to teach among the crowds.

We were no strangers to the scene. Whenever we had been there in the past, the Pharisees and Sadducees had often made a concerted effort to badger us. This time would be no different. In fact, their agitation of us would intensify. But, once again, this was where the people would be expecting to hear from Yeshua. So He would do what He frequently did when He was there: Instruct the crowds with an almost unbridled passion.

Yeshua was now a well-known figure throughout Judea, Galilee, the Decapolis region, and well beyond. In fact, by this time, a large number of people were coming to Jerusalem on the major feast days in the very hopes of seeing Yeshua and hearing Him explain the mysteries of the Kingdom of Heaven. And of course, many of them were counting on witnessing Him perform more miracles. There was *always* that!

But one thing was certain. The religious authorities could not have imagined the turn of events that were about to take place during this last and greatest Feast of the Lord for that year.[22]

4

AT THE TEMPLE

It soon became evident that a number of the people were audibly making known their belief in Yeshua as the potential Messiah.

As we made our way toward the teaching area at the Temple, we heard the expected murmuring and saw people pointing at us. We also spotted the obligatory entourage of Pharisees and other leaders among the Jews as they headed our way. There was no doubt as to why they had shown up in such large numbers.

As the people gathered, the Jewish rulers, with a note of envy in their hushed tones, mumbled to each other their collective apprehensions. Finally, one of them softly spoke what the others were thinking, "How is it that this man has so much learning? How does he so deeply comprehend the intricate connections of God's Word like this, especially when he has never studied formally—*as we have*?" The rest of them acknowledged their concerns by nodding their heads in affirmation, attempting to console each other with the truths their compatriot had spoken.

Seeing their indications of agreement, the man continued, crooking his mouth sideways as he intended to keep his whispered concerns among themselves, "We have spent, *and still spend*, most of our waking hours studying the details of God's Word, yet this man comes out of an obscure little village in the hills of Galilee and teaches as though he is the final authority in holy matters. How does he draw these immense crowds? Why don't this many people come to *our* teachings? Who does he think he is? What kind of bewitching power does he wield over the crowds?" The old Pharisee was visibly incensed.

This was not Yeshua's first time teaching and performing miracles in and around Jerusalem and the Temple Mount. So, once again, the tension quickly escalated.

But Yeshua knew the inmost thoughts of the perplexed religious leaders, even as they whispered their concerns to each other. He astonished them by immediately, and publicly, answering their assumed-to-be private questions. "My teaching is not only Mine," He exclaimed, "but it is of Him who sent Me. If anyone's genuine desire is to do God's will, he will know whether My teaching is from God or whether I am speaking only on My own authority." Before the authorities could assess what they had just heard, Yeshua continued, raising His voice so all could hear.

"Think of it," He challenged. "The one who speaks only on his own authority seeks his own glory; but the one who seeks the glory of him who sent him is true, and in him there is no deception, or glory-seeking." The Jewish rulers glanced at each other. The looks on their faces said it all: "How did he know that we had just been privately speaking of these very things?"

As they pondered this matter, Yeshua continued speaking, "Has not Moses given you the law? Yet often you egregiously violate the very commandments he gave to you. For example, some of you standing right here in front of Me are literally plotting to kill Me."

At this, some in the crowd gasped and cried out to Yeshua, "Are you going mad? Do you have a demon? Who is seeking to kill you? Why would you say such things?"[23] A trace of derisive laughter and murmuring could be heard rippling through the throng.

Yeshua answered: "I did one miracle, not long ago, here in Jerusalem, on a Sabbath day, and some of you saw it, or at least heard about it. A number of you still argue among yourselves about that healing. You debate whether it should have been done in the first place! Some say I violated the Sabbath. Others say I deserve death for such a flagrant 'violation' of the rabbi's sabbath rules!"[24]

Yeshua paused to let the gravity of His words sink in before venturing on to what He would say next:

"But consider this…Moses gave you circumcision, although in reality that law was in effect long before Moses—because it had been given to Abraham by God Himself. But here's the problem: If the prescribed time for circumcision happens to fall on a Sabbath day, then you are willing to make all manner of allowances for that ritual to be fulfilled. Is this not so?"

A number of the people shook their heads in agreement. The religious elite, however, just stood there…looking at Him, holding their collective breath.

"Yet circumcision has nothing to do with healing a person's entire life, it has nothing to do with making a person whole again!" Yeshua explained. "So then, why are some of you angry with Me because on that Sabbath, when I was last with you in Jerusalem, I made a man's body whole? Instead of celebrating the man's wholeness and his life returned to him, you are angry *with Me* that I did what no one else, not even the authorities standing among you, had been able to do! Was not God glorified in that demonstration of His love and power? Was not God Himself among you on that day?"

The people stood dumbfounded.

"I tell you the truth. Miraculous things are coming to pass and will continue to happen right before your eyes!" Yeshua said, "yet you *don't even see* what's really taking place among you!" He quickly glanced across the crowd.

"Do not judge by mere physical appearances alone," He continued, "but judge also with right judgment, with spiritual judgment! Then you will have the capability of seeing everything else that's happening around you as well, especially concerning the Kingdom of God and its presence that is now, most assuredly, among you!"

One person in the crowd began making his opinions known to those standing around Him, "If they were truly seeking to kill Him, why is He still here, speaking openly and in this authoritative manner, yet they are saying nothing at all to stop Him? Listen to how He speaks! Listen to the claims He's making! Could it be the authorities know this really is the Messiah? Are they afraid of Him? Look at how the people love Him!"

Still another one argued, in a much louder voice, "We know where this man comes from, and when the true Messiah appears, not a soul will know where He originated!"[25]

As Yeshua's eyes swept over the now-hushed crowd, they rested mainly on the Pharisees. The atmosphere grew thick as the friction warmed. Looking directly at the religious elite, Yeshua suddenly spoke again: "You know Me, and you know from where I have come. But I have not arrived here of My own accord. He who sent Me is true, and Him you do not know. I know Him, for I come from Him, and He sent Me."

At that point, a growing number of people in the crowd were audibly making known their belief in Yeshua as the potential Messiah. Suddenly, an anonymous shout could be heard above the others.

"When Messiah appears, will He really be able to show us more signs and wonders than this man has done? I think not! The Law and the Prophets are clear, telling us wonders that Messiah would do. This man has done them all! This must be Him! This *has* to be the Messiah!"

With that, a roar of general consent rumbled through the mass of humanity that stood before Yeshua. Even so, most still strained to hear His every word above the noise.

As they frantically moved among the people, the Pharisees overheard a few groans of disagreement at the unknown voice's claim, but a greater number of others muttered words of enthusiastic approval to those who were near them. And some of those who had agreed even began to shout out their belief that Yeshua *was Messiah*, making sure they were heard above the crowd.

That's when the chief priests and Pharisees sent for the Temple officers. They were adamant that Yeshua should be arrested immediately. To their minds, He was walking dangerously close to the realm of blasphemy, because He was not rebuking the crowd's claim of His messiahship. Besides that, this mere son of a carpenter from Nazareth might manage to start an insurrection, thus bring down the wrath of Rome upon their heads. Most particularly in jeopardy were their own cherished positions of honored power over the people. So, obviously, this currently heating situation could not be tolerated!

"I will be with you a little longer, and then I am going to the One who has sent Me to you," Yeshua declared to the people, as He was still primarily focused upon the religious leaders among them. "At that time, you will seek Me, but you will not find Me. Where I am going, you cannot come."

The authorities again collectively expressed their deepest concerns about Yeshua, but still quietly, among themselves, "Where does this deranged man intend to go? Does he believe we'll be unable to find him?" Others among them wanted to know, "What does he mean, 'You will seek me and you will not find me,' and, 'where I am you cannot come'? What? Is he going to kill himself?"

Eventually, the Temple officers arrived and positioned themselves in strategic locations around the growing group of spellbound listeners. Yet, in spite of the officers' presence, Yeshua continued teaching as if they weren't even there…or as if He *wanted* them there. As if He had *hoped* they would be there!

The people's focus, whether they agreed or disagreed with the idea that this man could be the Messiah, remained frozen on the One before them. The religious leaders continued to glare at Him, the look on their faces oozing the unbridled jealousy that frothed and boiled in the depths of their souls.

Soon, it became apparent that the people's reaction to Yeshua's teaching was varied. Many believed, but some were still confused and others were even resistant.

Still, so far, the Temple officers had done nothing about taking Him into custody. Just a short while later, everything would become much more tense.

5

LIVING WATER

The Pharisees and Sanhedrin members were enraged.
If this was not abject blasphemy, what was?

The next day was the eighth and last day of the Feast of Tabernacles. We had just made our way back into the Temple courts when Yeshua got up before the gathering crowds and began to teach, again.

This time, however, He opened His message by startling the religious elite and, at the same time, thrilling many who had gathered in His presence. He spoke of unbridled Messianic hope, a message they had been longing for.[26]

It was in that moment that Yeshua declared in a booming voice, "If anyone thirsts, let him *come to Me* and drink. Whoever believes *in Me*, as the Scripture has said, 'out of his heart will flow *rivers of living water.*'"

Those thunderous words had an indescribable effect on the crowd. They held such sway with the people because one of the most celebrated parts of the ritual of the great feast consisted of a daily, festive *parade of the water*. And that ceremony, on this last day of the Feast, had just concluded. [27]

WATER LIBATION

The water libation was hugely popular because it was the long-cherished ceremony of commemorating the "living water" with which God had physically sustained the lives of His Exodus people as they sojourned in the wilderness almost 1,500 years ago.[28]

Not only that, but the official rabbinical interpretation of the day regarding the deep-seeded symbolism of the water ritual also connected it with the gift of the Holy Spirit. Their interpretation expressly declares, "Therefore, for this reason, this place is called the house of drawing, because from here is drawn the Holy Spirit. As it is said, 'with joy shall ye draw water out of the wells of salvation'." [29]

THE CEREMONY

Therefore, the excited throngs would join in each day during the week of the Succoth Feast with a procession of white-robed priests winding down the gravelly trail from the Temple courts to the Pool of Siloam. And there, with a golden vase, they drew sparkling water from that famous spring.

The priests would begin their chant of worship as they traveled back up the path toward the Temple, where they reentered the gates amid joyful singing and outcries of praise from the people. The priests then poured out the retrieved water on the western side of the altar of burnt offering.

At the time all this was taking place, another priest poured out a drink offering of wine. And on the eastern side of the altar, the people, with great reverence, joined in and recited the words of the much revered *Hallel*.

In unison they chanted:

Praise the LORD! Praise, O servants of the LORD, praise the name of the LORD! Blessed be the name of the LORD from this time forth and forevermore! From the rising of the sun to its setting, the name of the LORD is to be praised!

Tremble, O earth, at the presence of the Lord, at the presence of the God of Jacob, who turns the rock into a pool of water, the flint into a spring of water![30]

Think about the power of the moment! On that day, at the conclusion of the last celebration of the water parade, Yeshua stood there and proclaimed everything they had just done was, believe it or not, about *Him*! And around Him were multitudes of people who, for seven consecutive mornings, had participated in chanting the words of that prophecy!

Though the vast majority of the people didn't understand it at the time, the genuine satisfaction of their spiritual thirst stood right in their midst—in the person of Yeshua. And at that very moment the ancient striking of the rock and the streams gushing forth in the desert would be intimately present in their minds.[31]

Furthermore, everything happening in that parade of celebration also brought to mind the Exodus wilderness life, with its forty years of dwelling in tents and being nourished by the manna from Heaven. Again, so many in the crowds, just days before, had heard Yeshua proclaiming that the manna also represented His life-giving sustenance.[32]

For everyone who had spiritual discernment, Yeshua was proclaiming that the true source of living water (and the giving of the Holy Spirit of God) was now at hand. And they were looking right at Him![33]

THE BLASPHEMY

In that moment, and within that context, Yeshua exclaimed in yet another thunderous voice, "If anyone thirsts, let him come to Me and drink! Whoever believes in Me, as the Scripture has said, 'Out of his heart will flow rivers of living water!'"

When the people heard Yeshua speak those words, someone in the crowd cried out, "This really is the Prophet!" That's when exuberant shouts of praise burst from the midst of the throngs, the sounds of it wafting in the air and fluttering through the streets of the surrounding city.

But another one in the crowd said, "No! This man *is the Messiah*! The anointed one of God, sent to save us from Rome!"

Still another one in the crowd shouted, "But is Messiah really to come out of Galilee? We can hardly believe this! After all, has not the Scripture most assuredly declared that Messiah will come from the offspring of David, and from Bethlehem, the village where David was?"[34]

So, even then, there was division among the people about His identity. Some of them wanted Him arrested. Most were considering the possibility that He was in fact the Messiah—and they openly said so. But, still, no one laid a hand upon Him. Frankly, I was shocked that had not yet happened.

The Pharisees and other Sanhedrin members were furious. If the words Yeshua had spoken and the reactions those words invoked among the crowd were not words of abject blasphemy...then what were they? And now everyone had heard Him commit this grievous sin. Still, most of them didn't even challenge Him!

Sensing the brewing theological storm, the Temple officers approached the chief priests and Pharisees to try to calm them as if, at this point, that endeavor was even possible.

Instead, the religious rulers turned their anger toward the officers. "Why did you not bring him to us?" they demanded to know. "Why did you not arrest him on the spot?"

"No one has ever spoken like this man!" the commanding officer responded. "Everybody says so! It's incredible! Just look at this crowd!"

The Pharisees' eyes widened, and their faces turned a deeper shade of furious crimson. "Have you *also* been deceived?" the leader accused them all. None of the guards replied. They simply stood there, struggling for an answer.

The elder Pharisee continued to rail at the officers. "Have any of the Temple authorities, *or even we*, believed in this one from Nazareth? No! We haven't! Not one of us! But this crowd obviously doesn't know the law, or how to properly rebuke a heretic. Well...*they are accursed*! Every last one of them!"

One of the most illustrious Sanhedrin members, the respected Pharisee, Nicodemus, was present among the group of rulers. Having secretly visited with Yeshua before this day, he pleaded with his cohorts:

"Does our law judge a man without first giving him a hearing, and learning what exactly it is that he does?" he asked them. "Should we not invite him to speak to us in private?"

Nicodemus continued with his hands folded in a prayer-like posture, "He is an intelligent man. He is a gracious man. I'm certain He would respond in a positive manner if we were to approach Him in this way. As you know, I've conversed with Him not too long ago!"

A particularly furious leader among them spoke up, "Are you from Galilee *too*, Nicodemus?" he asked. "Search and see that no prophet arises from Galilee! You must be speaking in jest—suggesting that we should invite *him* to speak to *us*!"[35]

During this time, the crowds began to disperse. The evening was approaching, and Yeshua and the rest of us had, moments ago, begun to make our way to the Mount of Olives. By the time Nicodemus finished his plea among his peers, we were already outside the city gates.

So, at that hour, each of the ruling elite finally departed to his own home. *But they had another plan.* The plot had been previously agreed upon, just in case the day ended as it had.

They had set a trap for Yeshua. They were certain it was a snare from which Yeshua could not possibly emerge unscathed. They were now ready to launch it. "This can't possibly fail!" they had agreed.

They would soon find out how badly mistaken they had been.

6

CAUGHT!

She had come within seconds of a horrible death.
And now she was in the hands of this man called Yeshua.

Early in the morning of the next day, we came back to the Temple and went up to the teaching area. After the heated exchanges of yesterday, a huge crowd had already gathered. Yeshua took His position on the platform, sat down, and began to teach. I glanced around at the still swelling throng.

Not long after He started speaking, a commotion erupted among the massive gathering. Startled by the noise, we scanned the crowd and saw a gaggle of Pharisees approaching. They were manhandling a horribly disheveled woman who obviously was their captive. They ploughed their way through the people, who dutifully parted to make a clear path for them. The entourage headed straight for us, making their way in such a manner so as to take a position squarely before the people. The poor, weeping soul in tow was clearly in a state of heart-wrenching distress. She seemed as frightened as a caged cat that had just been plopped down into a pit of ravenous wolves.

The oldest among the Pharisees spoke up, looking around at the crowd to ensure they saw what would happen next. "This woman!" he shouted for all to hear, "We caught this *filthy* woman in the very act of adultery...just moments ago! We saw her with our own eyes!"

The crowd let out a collective gasp as the black-robed ones suddenly heaved the woman to the ground at the feet of Yeshua. He rose from His seat of teaching and stood glaring in the direction of the wicked hypocrites in front of Him. The woman landed beneath Him with a sickening thud, causing a cloud of dirt to rise around her.

Yeshua's eyes were still fixed upon the frauds standing in front of Him. They simply glared back at Him, the air growing heavier with the sense of impending doom. *What is coming next? This can't turn out good*, I thought. I caught myself holding my breath.

The woman shrieked a terrible cry as she hit the ground. Her hands were bound, and now her palms and elbows were skinned and bleeding. She was visibly humiliated and had been spun into a heightened sense of terror, fearing certain death was just around the corner.

The eldest Pharisee challenged Yeshua. With contempt dripping in every word he spoke, "*Good teacher*, as I've already announced, this woman has been caught in the act of adultery. There can be no argument with that fact. We have plenty of witnesses." The other ornately robed sycophants agreed in unison.

"In the Law," the elder continued, "which we are most certain you are familiar with…Moses commanded us to stone a vile and despicable woman such as this. So what do you say? We now implore you: Give us your answer! We are waiting for your *wise* response."

The woman, face buried in her hands, was bent over in the dirt, heaving out her pitiful weeping. Surely, she thought there was now no escape.

Of course, we knew these despicable men, in the name of religion, had arranged this spectacle to test our Master in the presence of His huge audience. Peter, James, and I were more than ready to brawl, if necessary. So were several others among us. But when Yeshua looked at us, His eyes said, "No. Don't do it. Not now. You'll ruin everything. This day *had* to come…" We had seen that look before, several times.

It was becoming so obvious. The religious elders were forever looking for an official charge to bring against Yeshua. They wanted Him disgraced. They wanted Him arrested. And most importantly… they wanted Him dead! And now, they thought they had found their moment. They couldn't have been happier with themselves, and their faces revealed their arrogance.

JUDGEMENT WRITTEN IN THE SAND

It was in that moment that Yeshua knelt and began writing in the dirt.
We stood dumbfounded. What an odd reaction! The woman was cry-
ing, face down in the dirt, and the Pharisees were still ranting. In fact,
a couple of the men were beginning to gather stones. All the while,
Yeshua was scribbling something in the dust...as though He didn't
even hear them.

The Pharisees, sounding like a jury of squawking crows, continued
expressing their disdain for Yeshua. "What are you going to do about
this?" the elder demanded, as he pointed to the crumpled up sniffling
woman. "What is your verdict? The people want to know! And they
want to know *now*!"

In the middle of their raging...Yeshua stood back up. Calmly.
Resolutely.

He nodded His head downward, toward the words He had just
scratched in the dust.

That's when He said to them, with a knowing expression upon His
face, "Let him who is without sin among you be the first to throw a
stone at her."

He glanced back down at His writing.

They knew He wanted them to look at it.

7

THE FINGER OF GOD

*Still horribly traumatized by what she had been forced to endure
at the hands of the Pharisees, she continued to weep.*

As I remember that moment when Yeshua was writing in the dirt, I can't help but think: *If those Pharisees had only realized!* They were looking at the same fingers that had etched the Word and the Law upon the stone tablets at Sinai...the same hands that formed the frame of Adam from the clay of the earth. Yet they were secretly plotting to kill Him! At the moment, however, I could only watch it play out...in awe.

OUR INMOST BEING

The elder Pharisee nudged closer to Yeshua and looked down. He scanned the words that were now etched in the loose earth. His face first grew red with embarrassed horror, then whitened, as the blood appeared to drain from His face.

He snapped his head and looked back up at Yeshua. "How do you know these things?" he snarled in a carefully hushed tone. "How is this even possible? These are intimately private matters! *Who are you?*"

Yeshua almost indiscernibly shook His head in acknowledgment of the question. The gesture indicated that, by now, the Pharisee ought to know just how He knew all this "secret" information. Then Yeshua elevated the challenge, continuing to gaze hard into the elder Pharisee's eyes. "Once more, I will say to you and your hypocritical entourage," He said. "He who has no sin in his own life, throw the first stone, and we'll get on with it. But if a single stone is thrown, I'll instantly read what I've written, and I'll do it in the biggest booming voice I can muster, so that all who've gathered here this day will hear it!"

Yeshua again pointed downward to His writing, this time using His right index finger, as a judge might point toward the accused standing before him in court.

The old Pharisee stood frozen in fear. He looked around at the crowd and his cronies with eyes that indicated he was now the *caged cat*.

Yeshua bent down yet again and scrawled something more in the dirt. At this, the older Pharisee turned on his heels toward the others who were with him. "Let's go!" he commanded. "Quickly! Put your stones down...now! Before he ruins us all! I'll explain everything later! Leave this disgusting woman with him! He can deal with her now... she's his responsibility!"

The men complied with their leader's barked-out orders and began to amble away one by one, the older ones first, followed by the younger.

REVELATION

We later discovered that Yeshua had scratched each of the Pharisees' *names* in the earth. And, next to each name, He had also scribbled a concise list of some of their own sins, recent and from years ago—sins that no one had known about at the time, except for them...and, somehow, except for *Him*! Among the sins listed were some that even involved the very sin they had accused the woman of committing.[36]

Revealing to the rest of us what He had done, and to our further shock, Yeshua privately reminded us of certain passages found in the scrolls of Jeremiah and Isaiah.

In that moment, we began to understand. During our upbringing in the synagogue, we had heard those Scriptures several times before that day. But on that day we began to understand what the events of that moment were about.

Yeshua then quoted the prophet Jeremiah, emphasizing certain words—words that caused us to "see" and understand what had just happened:

The heart is deceitful above all things, and desperately sick; who can understand it? "I [YAHWEH] search **the heart and test the mind**, to give every man according to his ways, according to the fruit of his deeds...."

O [YAHWEH], the hope of Israel, **all who forsake you** shall be put to shame; **those who turn away from you shall be written in the earth**, for they have forsaken the [YAHWEH], **the fountain of living water.**[37]

Next, He recited a portion of the scroll of Isaiah.

Behold, Elohim **is my Yeshua;**[38]
I will trust, and will not be afraid;
for Yahweh is my strength and my song,
and **He has become my Yeshua.**
With joy **you will draw water from the wells of Yeshua.**

There it was! In the context of that full passage, the prophet Jeremiah had initially spoken of the Lord's judgment upon ancient Israel. The ancient Israelites had rejected the ways of the Lord and had forsaken the fountain of living water—God's forgiveness and His hand of protection.

The Lord told His people—through Jeremiah—that because of their unrepentance and their refusal of His living water, He had written their names in the dirt. It was a sign of judgment and a demonstration that He knew their thoughts and their hearts. He knew their ways. Therefore, if they didn't repent, their names would be remembered no more, especially as the winds of judgment descended upon the earth from the heavenly realms. Their names would be blotted out forever, like the long-forgotten lives and memories of the lost souls in the days of Noah and the days of Lot.[39]

Undoubtedly, the eldest of the Pharisees would have been intimately familiar with that passage. That's why they were the first to vacate the premises. Yeshua chuckled as He told us what He'd done,

and why the oldest of the Pharisees had chosen to leave first: "I made
their lists a bit longer and more detailed than the lists of the younger
ones!"

Moreover, just the day before, Yeshua had proclaimed that He
alone was the fountain of the true *living water*. As you will remember,
He had done this on the last day of the feast for the crowd and the
rulers of the Jews to hear. Yet, the Jewish religious class of the ruling
elite had still rejected Him—repeatedly, in spite of all He had miraculously done.

Then the Pharisees had seen their names and their secret sins
written in the dust by Yeshua's hand, legible for all who cared to see!
They had been flabbergasted. So they filed out, leaving His presence
as quickly as they could. The words of Yahweh had just been made
alive—again—in their midst.

THE WOMAN

Now, as most of the people were dispersing from the Temple area, the
Pharisees had already vanished.

After a while, we and only a few of the remaining crowd were left
alone with the woman. Still horribly traumatized by what she had
been forced to endure at the hands of the Pharisees, she continued to
weep. She had, after all, come within seconds of a horrible death.

"My dear woman," Yeshua asked her, with a touch of tenderness
in His strong voice, "where are your accusers now? Has no one con-
demned you?"

"No one, Lord!" she replied, fearfully looking around, obviously
stunned by what was happening. "They've all left! But...how? *Why?*"

"Neither do I condemn you," Yeshua said to her as He bent down.
"You may go, and from now on sin no more. That's all you need to
know." Cupping her face in His hands...He smiled.[40]

We gathered around and helped the woman to her feet, quickly
untied her hands, and began to examine her wounds. She stood there
sniffling, and at times a relieved giggle would rise up in her voice as

she pushed tears from her eyes. She was free! She had been rescued from certain death! Her murderous persecutors were long gone, having quickly left in public humiliation.

As we continued to minister to her needs, Yeshua walked a short distance away. He stopped. He looked down at the dirt, the writing still there.

With his right foot, I saw Him wiping away the Pharisees' names and the lists that accompanied those names. *What an act of grace and mercy.*

But there was still more to come. Things were about to heat up quickly.

8

WHERE IS
YOUR FATHER?

*Those cawing human crows had a glint of pure evil
in their eyes when they asked the question.*

We left the scene of the travesty of that *almost-stoning* event in a spirit of relief and celebration. We were beginning to understand several important links.

Yet our comprehension would become even clearer, right up to the day the blind man's eyes were opened with Yeshua's spittle and mud. And on that specific day would come the biggest revelation of all.

But I'm getting ahead of myself; we're not there yet in my recounting of those days. First, let me tell you what happened next!

THE EVENING SERVICE

Later on, in the evening[41] of the early-morning incident involving the adulterous woman, we went near the treasury area of the Temple, adjacent to the Court of the Women.[42]

Once again, Yeshua instructed the gathering throngs as they came back to the nightly teachings. And once again, along with the crowds came the Pharisees. They were always present when Yeshua interacted with the masses. It seemed their hypocrisy knew no boundaries.

Those religious thugs were constantly aware of our location. Watching and analyzing His every word. Forever looking for a way to accuse Him of some imagined heresy.

✦✦✦

Let me give you the context of what happened next. Back on the evening of the middle of the Feast—when Yeshua had first arrived to teach in the Temple courts, and on each of the five successive nights thereafter, the Court of the Temple had been illuminated by four large, golden candelabras. Their brilliant lights shone throughout the city. It was a gorgeous sight to behold!

Dancing, singing, and music had continued through the entirety of every night until the break of day. The brilliant lights of the mammoth candelabras were historically linked with the imagery of the *pillar of fire* which had guided those who walked in darkness during the ancient Exodus wandering.[43]

But on that last night of the feast, unknown to most that had assembled, the true Light of Heaven would be in His own Temple. And He would be speaking the words of light and life to His own people. That is, all those who were spiritually attuned to His words and presence—all who could truly "see."

It was at this moment that Yeshua roared out His first declaration of that last evening. And with those words, yet another frenzy erupted among the Pharisees…and even among some of the others in attendance.

"I am the light of the world!" Yeshua proclaimed. "Whoever follows Me will not walk in darkness, but will have the light of life!" Many in the crowd applauded. Some were ecstatic. Others were waiting, watching to see what would happen next. The One speaking had already claimed to be the true spring of the water of life, and now… *this!*

The Pharisees at the front of the crowd were the first to challenge Yeshua. "*Ah ha*! Now you are bearing witness about yourself, yet again; Your testimony is therefore not true!"

They snarled out their response to His declaration, pointing their fingers at Him and stomping their feet in disgust as they drove home their point.

"Even if I do bear witness about Myself, My testimony is true," Yeshua replied, for I know where I came from and where I am going, but you do not know where I come from or where I am going."

He paused to let His words sink in. The atmosphere fell silent, but not for long....

"You judge according to the flesh—by the authority of your own rules, your fabricated traditions, and your Scripture-nullifying teachings," Yeshua continued. "However, I judge no one in that manner. But when I judge, my judgment is true. For it is not I alone who judge, but I and the Father who sent Me."

"You take that back!" the leader of the Pharisees shouted his outrage for all to hear as the tension grew. "Your claim is bordering on blasphemy! You are not the judge of anyone! Only Adonai Himself is judge of all!"

"In your Law it is written that the testimony of two people is true," Yeshua countered. "I am the one who bears witness about Myself, and the Father who sent Me bears witness about Me."

"Where is *your* Father?" one of the men asked, a glint of pure evil in his eyes. The Pharisees had obviously been plotting again. And, as it turned out, *they were!*[44]

This is when I knew real trouble was about to boil over. I knew what Yeshua's response would be to the question. Those cawing human crows surely were not going to like His answer! In fact, it would only enrage them more.

9

VILENESS
PERSONIFIED

*We had secretly figured that something like this
would happen one day.*

"Here's the problem," Yeshua began by answering the Pharisees' malicious inquiry. "You know neither Me nor My Father. If you knew Me, you would know My Father also. You wouldn't have to ask the question."

The religious rulers simply didn't understand that Yeshua was speaking to them about Yahweh being *His Father*. To me, it was unbelievable that they didn't comprehend this fact, but the truth of their misunderstanding was becoming increasingly obvious.[45]

Yeshua continued, "When you have lifted up the Son of Man, then you will know that I am He, and that I do nothing on My own authority, but I speak just as the Father taught Me. And He who sent Me is with Me. He has not left Me alone, for I always do the things that are pleasing to Him."[46]

At that moment Yeshua dropped another boulder of biblical truth, "Truly, I say to you, everyone who practices sin is a slave to sin. The slave does not remain in the house forever; but the Son always remains, He always has a place in the Father's house. So if the Son sets you free, you will be free indeed."

Before the indignant contingent could respond, Yeshua cut them off. "Yes. *I know!*" He asserted, "I know you claim to be the offspring of Abraham, yet you seek to kill Me because My word finds no place in you. I speak of what I have *seen* with My Father, and you do what you have *heard* from your father."

One angry Pharisee replied with tightly pursed lips, "Abraham *is* our father!" Rage boiled over in the hot broth of his words. As he spoke, he jabbed at the air with his finger.

THE ACCUSATIONS AND LINKS

Yeshua sighed and then spoke again, a note of calm sorrow in His voice. "If you were Abraham's *legitimate* children," He said, "you would be doing the works Abraham did, but now you seek to kill Me, a man who has told you the truth that I heard from God. This is not what Abraham did."

Yeshua didn't stop there. "You are of your father the devil," He said, "and your will is to do your father's desires. He was a murderer from the beginning, and does not stand in the truth, because there is no truth in him. When he lies, he speaks out of his own character, for he is a liar and the father of lies. But because I tell you the truth, you do not believe Me."

Then the unthinkable happened.

"*We* are not the ones who were born of sexual immorality!" the enraged leader said flat out, with no mistaking what he was getting at. "*We* are not the ones who are 'illegitimate!' But we're not so sure about you!"[47]

Again I saw the hatred in their eyes as they hissed out those words. "We have but *one* Father—even Elohim!" they insisted.[48]

In front of the entire crowd, they had backhandedly accused Yeshua of being born from an illegitimate union and of having more than one "father."[49]

♦♦♦

I tilted my mouth toward Peter's ear and said, "That's what the ordeal with the woman caught in adultery was all about, earlier this morning! It was about our Lord's mother—and the rumors that have surrounded His birth since His earliest days in Nazareth and the region of Galilee!"

Peter's eyes widened and he nodded his agreement. He, too, was beginning to understand the matters beyond what we had merely seen with our eyes.

We had imagined that something like this would happen one day. In fact, several contemptible accusations along these same lines had already been lodged against Him before that day. After all, Yeshua had been reared in Nazareth, a tiny farming village in the Galilean hill country. Right after He had begun His ministry in Galilee, the religious elite among the Jews had thoroughly investigated His origin. They often questioned His legitimacy in public. That night during the feast, they had done it again, much more directly.[50]

But remember! On this very morning, the Pharisees had hurled the adulterer into the dust, at our feet, demanding that Yeshua issue the order to stone her to death on the spot!

Could it be that the spectacle the Pharisees were so anxious to confront Yeshua with on this morning was designed with that fixation? Was the whole debacle really about the issue of Yeshua's legitimacy? Were the religious elite hoping He might react with a public display of sobbing emotion, facing the pressure of having to order the woman's death sentence?

Could this be why, this evening, in front of the crowds, the Pharisees had returned with such ferocity? Maybe they had shown up among the huge crowd for the distinct purpose of continuing to accuse Yeshua of being been born in "illegitimacy."

Surely those religious clods heard the gossip passed around in Nazareth for the last thirty years regarding Yeshua's mother and Joseph, and the allegations they had suffered early in their relationship. They would have also likely heard of how, soon after the sordid accusations, the young couple departed to Bethlehem, a journey conveniently arranged by the taxation registration "circumstances" of the day. Also, they surely would have discovered that Mary and Joseph had not returned to Nazareth until Yeshua was four or five years old. By now, all of us knew those things, and we knew the Pharisees at least possessed some knowledge of those facts as well. How could they not?[51]

The similarities were simply too eerie not to consider. The evil in the Pharisees' hearts ran deep. Nothing was beyond the vilest imaginable treachery when it came to their hatred of Yeshua.

However, in a few days, as the next regular Sabbath approached, we would finally make the vital connections. What we had been a part of, over the last week or more, would begin to link together into one gigantic revelation that Yeshua would lay out before us.

It would be a disclosure designed to turn back on the teachings of the Pharisees themselves, and openly reveal their blatant hypocrisies. The revelations would be impossible to dismiss other than through the blindness of their own hearts. Soon they would witness a stunningly divine disclosure of truth for which they would be held eternally accountable.

And think of it! The entire affair would prove to revolve around a nondescript blind beggar in Jerusalem, with Yeshua making mud for the man's eyes. That day was quickly approaching.

What Yeshua had planned was absolutely brilliant!

But then again, we're talking about Yeshua. So why wouldn't it be?

10

THE ESCAPE

He had just declared He was somehow equal to God

That final night of Yeshua's preaching sessions in the Temple courts had culminated with the Pharisees insisting upon pushing the emotion laden notion of His "questionable" lineage. They had wanted to know exactly what He meant when He spoke of "His father"—the identity of whom was always in serious doubt, as far as the Pharisees were concerned.

They just couldn't let it go. They apparently thought that, by this specific line of discourse, they were dragging Yeshua ever deeper into their net and into yet another snare—hopefully an inescapable one. But the opposite was true, as all of us—not only the disciples, but also the Pharisees themselves—would find out, on a soon coming and divinely particular Sabbath day in Jerusalem.[52]

GREATER THAN ABRAHAM

But for now, let me quickly take you back, once again, to that last night in the Temple courts. This was a real turning point wherein everything else is headed.

The Pharisees set forth their final arguments with vigor. Yeshua's responses to their contentions simply threw more dry kindling on the already hotly burning fire of their increasing fury.

The leader of the gang of religious leaders launched right into their agreed-upon invectives: "Tell us *Teacher*. Are you greater than our father Abraham? *Be careful with your answer*! Remember, Abraham and all the prophets died! Yet you claim He 'saw' you—and you saw him?

41

Exactly *who* do you make yourself out to be? What kind of delusional self-glory are you trying to persuade us to believe?"

"If I glorify Myself," Yeshua answered, "My glory means nothing. My Father, *whom you claim as your God*, is the one who glorifies Me."[53]

There. He had declared point blank that the same God they claimed to worship as their own was also His Father and the ultimate authority of everything He said and did. Their mouths hung open in amazement when He answered them. If they had been able to find their words, they most likely would have collectively screamed, "*How dare you!*"

But, before they could utter a sound, Yeshua continued.

"You do not even properly know that same God," He said, "nor do you genuinely serve Him in Spirit and in Truth." A good number among the crowd gasped again as He leveled this heavy accusation.

Then, Yeshua followed up His shocking declaration with yet another one: "But, unlike you, *I do know Him*—fully, and intimately!"

He continued, "So, if I were to say that *I do not know Him*, I would be a liar...like you! But I *do* know Him and I *keep* His Word. Your father Abraham rejoiced that he would see my day. He saw it and was glad."

"What!?" the Jewish rulers retorted with unrestrained ire, "You are not yet fifty years old, and you have *seen* Abraham? This is even a more outrageous claim!"

They looked at the crowds that were standing behind them and repeated, "This is blasphemy upon blasphemy! This is despicable talk, the talk of a madman! His state of delusion is nothing less than demonic possession!"

Yeshua paused, then answered, "You are eternally mistaken. I do not have a demon. But I can tell you this: Truly, I say to you, before Abraham was, *I am.*"

As far as the religious elite were concerned, Yeshua had finally crossed the line into utter sacrilege. He had declared He was somehow equal to God by hinting that He had an eternal nature, especially by using the specific words "I AM," which only further emphasized His claim. I don't think anything else He said could have made Yeshua's critics any angrier.[54]

It was then that the Pharisees picked up stones. They intended to kill Him and, most likely, to kill the rest of us as well—just for being associated with Him. Instead of allowing that to happen, we quickly removed ourselves from the Temple area. As you know, this wasn't our first time to make such a speedy exit. We knew exactly what to do and how to do it.

In spite of being skilled in the arts of making ourselves scarce, we still barely escaped with our lives that night. But, because of the enormous size of the crowds on the Temple grounds and throughout the city itself, and along with the cover of the quickly darkening evening, we simply disappeared from sight. Of course, it could have been that Adonai blinded their eyes to our presence. That's what I believe, anyway.

Afterwards, and for the next several days, it seemed to the rest of us that Yeshua was purposely laying low, only to appear again in a most public way. As a matter of fact, that's exactly what happened. And it wouldn't be long before we would find out why.

Now that you have the complete context…let's go back to where I first began my account. That is where the entire ordeal comes together with a thunderous clap of revelation!

11

A PRESCIENT SABBATH

*A miracle had been wrought
right under their noses.*

When we first encountered the blind man, and before we spoke directly to him, we pulled Yeshua aside and privately asked Him a question. We so longed for Yeshua to finally resolve this matter of rabbinical interpretation for us.

Peter was the first to speak up, as he often was. "Rabbi, who sinned?" he asked. "Was it this man himself, or his parents, that he was born blind?"

We shook our heads in agreement, because we all wanted the Teacher's insight on the matter. After all, we had been taught in our synagogue lessons and our Jewish homes from the time we were children that physical calamities were often handed down because of the parents' sins—as well as because of our own decisions, of course. So which was it, in this case?

This was a complex issue, and we were hoping our Teacher might enlighten us. Sitting before us was this pitiful blind man, a perfect case in point.[55]

Yeshua's answer was jarring. "It is not that this man has sinned, or his parents," He said, "but that the works of God might be displayed in him. We must be faithful with the works of Him who sent Me... while it is day. Because night is coming, when no one can work. As long as I am in the world, I am the light of the world."

When He again declared, "I am the light of the world," our thoughts went back to just a few nights ago when we had been in the

Court of the Women at the Temple. In the moment, on that day, we had begun to feel that we were part of something much bigger than our own meager lives.

Yeshua turned from us and approached the blind man. His reply caused us to mumble among ourselves. I quietly asked our entourage, "Was this man really born blind for this very moment? How are we, of all people, the ones chosen to perhaps witness a miracle the world had never seen before?" They shrugged their shoulders. They were just as dumbfounded as I was.

Looking back, I am now convinced that this was *exactly* what Yeshua had been declaring to us. Sometimes I have to force myself to take a breath when I contemplate the unsearchable depth of these truths.

After Yeshua anointed the man's shriveled, malformed eyes with the clay-like concoction of spittle and dirt, He leaned in toward his ear and softly said, "Now, go, wash in the pool of Siloam."

THE SILOAM CONNECTION

The Pool of Siloam was situated at the southeast corner of Jerusalem in the Kidron Valley, just a short walk from where we were standing. It was even a place spoken of by the ancient prophet Isaiah.[56]

The word "Siloam" derives from a word meaning "sent." The same word was frequently used by Yeshua…to describe *Himself*. For the last several days, He tirelessly tried to explain to the Pharisees that He, too, had been "sent"—from the Father of all Creation. Over and over, He utilized that word to describe His own heavenly mission.

Now, He matter-of-factly commanded the man, with the concoction of mud and spit on his eyes, to go to the pool called "*Sent.*" Yeshua was building His case, point by point. Doubtless, the rationale was about to be presented to the religious rulers of the Sanhedrin, starting with the Pharisees.

But this was only the beginning! There was much more to come.

OBEDIENCE THROUGH FAITH

We stood in amazement as the blind man simply, and without hesitation, obeyed Yeshua's command to do this strange action set in motion by the One "sent" from above.

The man's countenance visibly changed as he ambled toward the pool. His face now beamed with a childlike anticipation until he eventually reached the water's edge, finding its borders with the tapping of his stick. He continually apologized as he bumped and prodded his way through the still-growing crowd around the pool. Upon reaching the famous waters, he finally stooped over, methodically feeling his way as he went down on his knees.

In a few more moments, he was lying on his belly, touching the ground in front of him with gnarled hands to make certain he was able to find the water. It was obvious this wasn't the first time he had dipped himself into this pool; he seemed to know just how to do it. He reached into the edges of the pool with cupped hands and dashed the water onto his face, directly into his eyes, just as Yeshua had instructed.[57]

At the sensation of the cool liquid upon his face, the man smiled, tears trickling down both cheeks. Jubilant, he raised his head and slowly turned it from side to side—as though he were a small child gazing at a newborn puppy for the first time.

Then it became obvious...he was seeing *everything*! He soaked up the sights like a parched desert wanderer who had mercifully stumbled upon a spring of icy water.

"I can see! I can see!" he shrieked, as he sprang to his feet. "I have eyes! Working eyes! Eyes to see!" I could barely believe what I was beholding.

The man darted into the bedazzled crowd, sobbing uncontrollably. His tears splattered into the dust as he danced in celebration among the onlookers, and he dropped his cane to the ground, realizing he no longer needed it. Many who were watching began to revel with him; some even openly wept, their thoughts racing: *How could this be? A* man with shriveled and useless eyes since birth can now suddenly see with new and perfectly normal eyeballs? And all this from the application of clay upon his diseased eye sockets? This is utterly impossible! You could see those musings in the expressions on their faces!

The news of what they were witnessing rumbled up and down the village streets like thunder. The formerly blind man cried out over and over again, *Baruch Hashem Adonai!*—"Blessed be the name of the LORD!" His life had been completely transformed in one glorious, indescribable instant. And, for that matter, so had ours!

Eventually, the man plopped down in exhaustion. He cupped his head in his hands and his sobbing slowed as questions whirled through his mind: *What happened to me? How did this happen? Who is this one called Yeshua, who worked this impossible miracle? Why did this happen to me, of all the beggars in Jerusalem?*

And…Where is this One who healed me? Why is He not here now… with me?

*And, and, and…*his questions seemed endless.

He would later tell us these things about that day, and especially the shock of the moment in which he first began to see the world around him. But by the time the riotous celebration had gotten heavily underway, we were already exiting the scene. We simply *had* to leave the multitudes and the ruckus.

We knew the Pharisees would hear of the "impossible" healing and would soon hunt us down with a vengeance. How could they account for this miracle, one that had happened right under their noses? No one could deny it—and they would have to try to explain it…somehow.

Would Yeshua never cease to amaze and confound those around Him?

But before that day was over, even *we* would be in for several more earth-shattering surprises.

12

QUESTIONS

Why was the bizarre method of dirt and spit used to heal a man's congenital blindness—a seemingly impossible feat?

Sure enough, just as we had anticipated, the Pharisees appeared in the distance with their furious entourage just now coming into view. They were frantically searching for us, zigzagging through the crowds. The ones leading the gaggle of black-robed potentates stopped in their tracks, occasionally grabbing stragglers by their sleeves, trying to determine if they had seen us somewhere among the crowds. After a moment, they spotted us, and pointed in our direction! Thankfully, once again the tightly packed multitudes hindered any kind of speedy approach toward us. We picked up our pace and put more distance between us and the Temple crowds.

We shuffled along, keeping our heads as low as possible and our eyes straight ahead so as not to draw undue attention. We were still stunned by what we had witnessed. Yeshua had not yet explained to us why He had healed the man in such an odd manner. We would find out shortly.

UNPRECEDENTED

Not once in history had the peculiar procedure of applying dirt and spittle been heard of as a cure for blindness, much less for one *born* blind. Yet, *we had seen it!*[58]

Even Peter, the often contentious ringleader of our inner circle of the Twelve, turned to me and muttered his thoughts about the events in an uncharacteristically humble tone. "John! How can this be?" he asked. "We've seen Yeshua restore sight to the blind before. Don't get

48

me wrong; those were amazing miracles, no doubt! We've even seen
the rabbis themselves apply various concoctions to wounds and sores,
and even to the eyes, to help cure disease and irritations.[59] But we've
never seen this done to one who has been blind since the very day he
came out of his mother's womb—and with such horrible disfigurement. I don't think it's *ever* happened before—anywhere!"[60]

I just shrugged. How could I argue? Peter was right. *Again.* [61]

Just when we thought we had seen Yeshua do everything…*that
was when* He would carry out even more astounding actions in our
presence. To be sure, we were getting used to Yeshua's surprises. But
this particularly unexpected spectacle, besides being downright astonishing, was also confusing.

Why didn't Yeshua just speak and decree the man's sight to be
restored, like we'd seen Him do before? We had also seen Him do that
kind of thing—by simply issuing a command—when He instantly
calmed the wind and the waves in the midst of a storm. Or why didn't
He maybe just touch the poor fellow's eyes, as we'd also seen Him do?

And why did Yeshua send the man to the Pool of Siloam? Yeshua
had never suggested the waters there might have *healing powers*. The
way He methodically went about curing the man's blindness made it
seem as though Yeshua had been making some sort of grand statement.
But what exactly was that statement? And for whom was it intended?

Then, as if He once again knew our thoughts, soon after the turmoil subsided, Yeshua pulled us aside and explained what we had
witnessed.

It was as though He had arranged this flabbergasting event before
the beginning of time itself. He told us how He used the entire incident
to address some of the Pharisees' most vile accusations about Him. He
had also purposely worked the miracle in a very specific manner, a way
that would completely confound them…unless they were willing to
acknowledge who He really was.

As He unveiled what He had done, the experiences of the last weeks
began to flood through our minds. We were beginning to connect the

stunning spiritual revelations. What Yeshua did and the exact way He
did it were nothing short of wisdom straight from Heaven's Throne!

If the Pharisees didn't "get it" by now, there appeared to be no hope
for them.

13

THE LEGITIMATE ONE

*They have no excuse for not seeing who I am
and who has genuinely sent Me.*

It didn't take long before the Pharisees pounced on the poor fellow.
The man and his parents were summoned by the religious council to give an immediate account of what had happened to their son. The religious leaders were frantic to discover exactly who had "done this thing"—and on the Sabbath, no less! They already had their suspicions...but they had to be certain.

THE TEACHER

In the meantime, we were alone with Yeshua. During those moments of relative solitude, He opened our spiritual eyes to what had taken place over the last several days, culminating in the healing of the blind man.

Yeshua started by reminding us about some of the finer points of the highly revered, but often oddly crafted, rabbinical laws. That body of "law" was a sacrosanct collection of orthodox teachings that had been orally handed down for many generations—a legal compilation that was frequently expanded. By the beginning of Yeshua's ministry, the codification of those teachings had become as important, or even more so, than the Word of God itself. There were many thousands of those manmade, suffocating laws.[62]

Yeshua had frequently confronted a number of the rabbis about those "laws" with unmistakenly direct accusations. "You hypocrites!" He had said on one instance. "You nullify the genuine Word of God by holding to your made-up traditions! In this way, you appear righteous to others, but within your hearts, you are full of hypocrisy and lawlessness!"[63]

Right then, however, at Yeshua's instruction, we were sitting on the ground in front of Him awaiting the enlightenment He promised.

Peter, sitting next to me, nudged me with his elbow, telling me to move over to give him more room. I snorted, and then slightly adjusted myself to accommodate him. With a wink in my direction, then a subtle grin, Peter indicated he was satisfied with the extra room I allowed and appeared confident that he was still the self-appointed leader of the Twelve.

Once we were settled in, Yeshua began by reminding us that among the traditions and rabbinical laws He had frequently railed against, was one that directly related to the attempted healing of eye problems... *on the Sabbath.*[64]

"For one thing," Yeshua said, "to use spit and dirt mixed together in a healing event of this nature, according to the religious rulers, involves the work of *kneading*. And kneading of almost any material on the Sabbath is strictly forbidden by the rabbis.[65] But, oddly enough, it's not forbidden by the Law and the Prophets! That burdensome tradition was long ago invented and refined only by the rabbinical elite."[66]

Yeshua had sparked a lot of memories. I vaguely recalled some of those laborious instructions from my many years of regular synagogue attendance. But they certainly were not the kind of teachings we would have committed to our memory.

What Yeshua said next astonished us.

THE DISCLOSURE

"Now I'll tell you what I've been laying out right in front of the Sanhedrin elite over the last number of days, along with the rest of the Pharisees and the people in general.

"It was all one grand lesson," He continued, eyes sparkling, "that is, for any who have the eyes to see!

"What I did *today* with our friend who was born blind was to magnify My entire teaching. That one simple deed alone is certain to infuriate the Pharisees beyond measure, because it goes right to their man-made Sabbath laws and...*so much more*."

He paused. Then, looking around at all of us He said, "Believe Me when I tell you this!"

We nodded, acknowledging His assertions. I leaned toward Him, making sure I would hear every word He said next. I didn't want to miss a thing.

"You'll remember," Yeshua continued, "the rabbis have incessantly attempted to provoke Me about My birth, genealogy, and overall 'legitimacy.' You'll also remember this happened on several different occasions over the last few days alone, not to mention the Pharisees' not-so-subtle references to their seditious conjectures about My birth in the presence of other crowds."[67]

We all, again, concurred. Of course, we remembered. Over the last several days in particular, those allegations seemed to have grown more pointed.

"Well," He went on, "that's exactly what the situation with the woman 'caught in adultery' was about. The Pharisees had hoped to rattle My anger over the matter of My mother's divine anointing and her appointment from Heaven through the angel Gabriel."

Now it was my turn; I lightly poked Peter's ribs with my elbow, indicating, "I told you so!"[68]

Yeshua went on. "You'll also recall that, after the event with the woman, as we were discussing the lineage of Abraham, they declared they were not the 'illegitimate' ones. Their inflection more than insinuated that *I was the one* who was illegitimate."

Clearing His throat and shifting His position a bit, Yeshua continued. "They refused to 'see' who My Father really is, and why I work the miracles I do," He said. "Each of My miracles is meant to glorify the Father and His Kingdom. They have no excuse to not see who I am and who has genuinely sent Me. They have not seen or heard of anyone before Me who could work these wonders, nor can they replicate those works themselves."

Yes! I remember thinking. *How could we not have recalled these scriptural facts? More importantly, how could it be that the Pharisees, the exalted "teachers" of Israel, could still not see them by now?*

But the deafening thunderclap of the next revelation was only seconds away!

14

THE BOMBSHELL

It is the Truth that declares,
"I am who I say I am."

Yeshua continued with His riveting explanation. "Instead of inquiring more about the true Kingdom work and exactly why I have been sent to them by the Father," He said, "the ruling elite have falsely accused Me of many things. They have even charged Me with having a demon."

Yeshua paused for a moment to let that truth sink into our hearts, then went on. "So...I used their own words, their own fables, their own ridiculous rules against them today. And I did it for everyone to see. I also did it on the Sabbath—deliberately."

His point was beginning to take shape in my mind.

"And now they have no answer," He said. "They have no excuse. There is no path they can take on which they can talk their way out of what happened today. They can either accept or reject what they have seen as my final declaration. To reject it means they will have to reject their own teachings and fables—the notions they have used for ages to control the people. The decision is now theirs. I assure you, they know it. I also assure you that they hate Me for it."

With that, Yeshua had our complete attention! However, I felt as though He was again speaking to us in some sort of grand parable; His words seemed a bit veiled, so I spoke up. "Lord, please explain this mysterious teaching!" I said. "What are the rabbinical teachings and fables that You are speaking of?"

THE FOLKLORE THAT CONDEMNED

Yeshua smiled at me and continued. "Here's the explanation, John," He said. "The rabbis have an ancient myth among themselves—one they often elaborate upon in their closest circles, and sometimes they even teach it in the synagogues.

"That myth declares that only a *legitimate firstborn son of a birth father* has miraculous healing properties within his spittle. They believe and teach that the firstborn son's spittle can bring healing to various ailments of the eyes.

"Furthermore," Yeshua continued, "they also teach that this marvelous power does not come from the mother's side, only from the father's side—but, again, only if the son is the legitimate firstborn of that father. If that son is only the firstborn of the mother, but of *another* father, then his spittle has no power! It's *their* story. It's their tradition! It's their own folklore. And all the rabbis are aware of it."[69]

Yeshua scanned each of our faces, enjoying our reaction to what He laid out before us. We sat flabbergasted.

"More than likely," He said, "those Pharisees assumed I was not aware of their fanciful tale. Today, however, they know differently! I have used their own words and teachings against their arrogance…and in judgment of their foolishness."[70]

Yeshua's countenance saddened as He spoke those last words, shifting position again so He could comfortably continue. He then leaned toward us, and His eyes suddenly brightened.

"Now, think of it!" He said. "If they refuse to believe My miracles have come from the genuine Father of all Creation and were made evident in the presence of throngs of people, then what will they have to say about a miracle wrought in a manner backed by their own legends?"

This was really beginning to come together now. I couldn't wait to hear the rest!

"Today, in this very moment," Yeshua said, "those same men are examining a man who was born blind, but who can now see! They cannot believe that instant healing has happened."

My own eyes were beginning to "see"!

"And how did this unprecedented wonder happen?" Yeshua asked us.

Answering His own question, He went on. "It happened," He said, "because the genuine *firstborn, legitimate* Son of Heaven and the *authentic* Son of God, spoken of by the prophets, mixed His own spittle with the same dust of the earth from which those sanctimonious Pharisees earliest parents were first created![71] Then, that clay mixture was applied to the eyes of a man—not one with a mere infection, but one who was blind from birth—the healing of which is an absolute impossibility, humanly speaking"—He paused, then picked back up, "—unless, that is, they are willing to *see* the truth before them. It is the Truth that declares...*I Am Who I say I Am*, and that *I have been sent by the Father of all humanity.*"

Andrew spoke up first. "Master!" he said. "It makes perfect sense now! And so do the Pool of Siloam, and Your declarations about being the Light of the World, and the Living Water, and writing the sins of the Pharisees in the dirt!

"These were all a part of what You were building up to, weren't they? They were meant to reveal to the Pharisees who You really are... but only if they could 'see' it with repentant, humbled, and willing eyes!

"Am I right?"

Yeshua beamed. "Yes, Andrew!" he said. "You have spoken well! As you are well aware, the Pool of 'Sent' is central to the Feast of Succoth's celebration. It is the pool of 'living waters' in the eyes of the religious elite and to the people. That is why *I sent* the blind man there...further punctuating who I AM. And I did it all by doing what the Scriptures clearly say...that only the Creator and His legitimate Messiah can open the eyes of the blind.[72] By those Scriptural teachings, as well as by their own fables, I have given them one more chance to 'see'!"

At this, Yeshua stood up from His cross-legged seated position and said, "Wait here for Me, I still have something else I need to do. It's important, and I must do it alone."

As He left, we agreed that we now understood the happenings of the day, as well as what had gone on during the Feast of Succoth. All of this had been unfolding before us over a number of days. I'm just thankful we were given the ability to take it in and to understand it— especially after what happened next.

We spent the better part of the next hour discussing what Yeshua had shown us. But...there was still more to come.

15

INSPECTION

They still couldn't acknowledge what was right before them.

While Yeshua had been telling us the mysteries of exactly what He had done, the Pharisees were frantically trying to find the underlying cause of the miracle. They were mostly concerned that the entire city was already spreading the details of what they had seen and heard.

Some of the people knew the once blind man was saying his healer made mud as an eye ointment. Those same people also knew this specific procedure had flatly gone against the laws of the Sabbath.

The people were also aware that if anyone of them had known about this "unlawful healing," they were to immediately report it to the religious authorities. In this case, not only did they know about the healing, but they also knew the man claimed Yeshua was the one who had healed him!

So, they grasped the man by the arm and hauled him into the Pharisees for questioning. By fulfilling this solemn duty, they figured they would stay in the good graces of their religious overlords and not lose their coveted membership and places of prominence in the synagogues.[73]

Now standing before the convening body of Pharisees, the religious leaders began to interrogate the frightened man. "Tell us, how exactly did you receive your sight?"

"He put mud on my eyes, and I washed, and now I see," the man answered, looking them in their eyes. That's really all I can tell you." So far, even in his state of apprehension, he remained calm.

Several of the Pharisees spoke up at once. "This Yeshua fellow is not from God!" one said. "This is clear," chimed in another, "because he does not keep the Sabbath!"

Yet another interjected, "Wait. Wait. Think about it! Then how is it that a man who is such a *Sabbath sinner,* as you say, can do such miraculous signs?"

The men argued among themselves, with the healed man standing right in their midst. They obviously didn't care that his life had been restored, or that he could miraculously see. All they seemed to care about was whether the healer in this situation had broken one of their coveted laws. They cared most about their prestige among the people and how they would explain this obviously "impossible" miracle.

After a moment or two of heated discussion, the men turned their attention again to the blind man. "What do *you* say about him, since he has opened *your* eyes?" asked one of the leaders.

The man shrugged. As he spoke, he sounded as if he were asking a question, rather than giving a straightforward answer. "Rabbis, I don't know. I *really* don't know! Perhaps He is a prophet?"

How should I know about this healer? the healed man thought to himself: *I still, to this moment, have never laid my "seeing" eyes upon Him!*

Growing more and more humiliated in their situation, the Pharisees gave orders for the man's parents to appear before them as well. It wasn't long before they were rounded up and escorted to stand in front of the ruling elite.

When the healed man's mother and father arrived, one of the Pharisees asked, "Is this your son, who you say was born blind? How then does he now see?"

His father answered, "We know for a fact that this *is our son*—as do all the people of our neighborhood—and that he was indeed born blind. We are offended that we would even be asked these questions. But *how* he now sees we do not know, nor do we know who opened his eyes. Ask him! He is a full-grown man, obviously of substantial age.

And, once again, I wish to emphasize that absolutely everyone in our area of the city knows him! He will speak for himself."[74]

The man's father answered in this manner because he and his wife feared the ones they were responding to. Some time back, the Pharisees, along with the Sanhedrin, had made it public knowledge that anyone who confessed Yeshua to be Messiah would be banished from the synagogue...permanently.[75]

Once again, with visibly mounting frustration, one of the Pharisees turned to the healed man. "Give glory to God by admitting the one who restored your sight is a sinner!" he demanded.

The once-blind beggar answered, his gaze directed to the floor. "Whether He is a sinner or not, I simply do not know. I don't even know who He is. But one thing I do know..." he said this as he slowly raised his head and looked squarely at his judges "...is that though I once was blind, now I see!" Through his newly bolstered courage, he asserted, "Of that, there can be no doubt!"

The men pummeled him with questions once again, voices elevated and at times speaking over each other. "But *how did He do it*?" "Tell us!" "What exactly did He do to you?" "How did he open your eyes?"

"I have told you already," the man replied, "and you would not listen. Why do you want to hear me say the very same things again and again? Do you also want to become His disciples?"

The man grew angrier—angry at the obstinacy of the self-righteous men seated before him. It was obvious they had no explanation for what had happened to his eyes and how he had been made to see. But none of this was *his* fault! Why was the weight of this entire matter being laid upon *his* shoulders, as though, somehow, *he* had done something dreadfully wrong, as if he himself had violated their precious Sabbath rules?

But one of the Pharisees reviled him again. "*You* are his disciple!" the loudest of the group said. "But *we* are disciples of Moses! We know God has spoken to Moses, but as for this man, we do not know where he comes from!"

The formerly blind man, now bolder than ever, answered, "*Well, well!* This is an amazing turn of events! You do not know where He comes from, yet He opened my eyes! He has done something to me that has never happened before, in the entirety of history! And you don't even know where He comes from? This is quite a startling admission you make!"

At this, the Pharisees grew even more agitated. But the man continued to speak, answering their questions with words they didn't want to consider.

"We know God does not listen to sinners," the healed man said, "but if anyone is a worshiper of God and does His will, God listens to him. Never since the world began has it been heard that anyone opened the eyes of a man born blind. Not even in our Scriptures! Not one instance of it! If this man were not from God, He could do nothing! Yet…here I stand before you, as a witness to what He has done!"

The men began to scream at him again, "*How dare you!* You were born in utter sin; steeped in it from the beginning of your life! How else could you have been born blind? And *you* would dare try to teach *us?*"

Then, calling their security force, they cast the man from their presence and declared him to be barred from synagogue services from that day forward.[76]

The former blind man had spoken accurately to his judges. But they had ignored the facts in favor of their own laws, protecting their own distinction and their power over the people.

They still wouldn't acknowledge what was right before them.

16

FOUND

Unbeknownst to the "unseeing" ones at the time,
Yeshua's turned back was the worst expression of the judgment
of Heaven's throne they could have received or even imagined.

Yeshua was headed straight to the man as these judgments were being leveled against him.

As He walked, Yeshua heard the people murmuring that the Pharisees had just now cast the man and his parents out of their tribunal, and out of the synagogue. Yeshua groaned in righteous anger, knowing He still had a task to complete.

Even though He had healed the man, the spiritual blindness of the Pharisees made their hearts harder than ever. In their rage, they had taken their own embarrassment out on the poor fellow—a man who had done nothing but allow Yeshua to recreate his eyes and restore the coveted sight that would forever change his life.

Yeshua, being who He was, knew exactly where the man was, so it wasn't long before He was face to face with him. Of course, the man had no idea who stood before him. Not yet anyway.

Yeshua looked at him and nodded a friendly *hello*.

The man returned the gesture and continued walking, heading toward his home and his parents. Yeshua stopped him in his tracks with a simple question, "*Please*. Let me ask you something important." The man looked at Yeshua in wonderment.

"Do you believe in the Son of Man?" Yeshua asked.

The man made a quick assessment of the person standing before him. There was something comforting about His presence. He felt no

63

immediate threat from Him. This definitely was not one of the Pharisees, or one of their cronies.

"Yes. I do believe in the Son of Man," the healed man answered the stranger. "Has He come? Is He here? Why do you ask me this? Do you know Him? Please tell me who He is, sir, and where I might find Him, so that I may believe in Him!"

Yeshua said, "You have already seen Him, my friend!"

"What!?" the man exclaimed. "I've already seen Him? Was He in the crowd that saw me celebrating?"

"As a matter of fact," Yeshua replied with a huge smile, "it is He who is now speaking to you. You are looking at Him…with your own eyes!"

"Yes!" the man cried, his vocal praise attracting the attention of the Pharisees just entering the area where Yeshua and the man were standing.

"Yes, Lord, I believe! I recognize Your voice, now that You have spoken more to me! *Yes!* There can be no doubt! No one could have done such a thing to me unless He were the Son of Man!" Yeshua embraced the man as several tears seeped down His own cheek.

Then, almost uncontrollably, the man dropped to His knees at Yeshua's feet. He wept in great, heaving sobs…pouring out glorious tears of joy. He worshipped Yeshua as one would only worship God Himself.[77] Over and over the man asserted, "Adonai, *I believe*… Adonai, *I believe*…!"

Yeshua spoke again to the man, "For judgment I have come into this world, that those who do not see…may see, and those who *think* they see…may become blind." Yeshua glanced in the direction of the Pharisees as He spoke.

The Pharisees heard all these declarations. And they had heard enough.

"*What?* Are *we* also blind?" the leader of the group demanded. Their question dripped with condescension.[78]

"We see just fine, and with our own eyes! But…we certainly *do not believe* you are the Son of Man, or that your 'father' is the God we worship! We still don't know who your father is! *Is it because you don't know?* You are nothing more than a blasphemer...with a demon that has driven you mad! And most likely, you are nothing more than an *illegitimate one.* That's who you are!"[79]

At this, Yeshua said, "Oh, if only you were still *blind*, with no knowledge whatsoever of the truth. Then you would have no guilt; but now that you wholeheartedly assert, 'We see,' even after all I have shown you, and all I've worked among you in your presence...then your guilt remains. My healing of the man born blind, with spittle and mud, by your own stories and customs, testifies against you! So, yes... you are *still blind*, whether you acknowledge it or not."[80]

They looked at Him as though He were crazy, although they knew what miracle He had wrought—and by it, they knew what message He sent them. But apparently, none of that mattered. Their hatred still blinded them all.

Heartbroken, Yeshua spoke again, "I am now going to tell you an eternally lasting truth. *Please* listen with your hearts and see with your eyes...eyes that are opened by the Spirit of God."

Before any of the men could object, Yeshua continued, "He who does not enter the sheepfold by the door but climbs in by another way, that man is a thief and a robber. But he who enters by the door is the shepherd of the sheep. To him the gatekeeper opens. The sheep hear his voice, and he calls his own sheep by name and leads them out. When he has brought out all his own, he goes before them, and the sheep follow him, for they know his voice. A stranger they will not follow, but they will flee from him, for they do not know the voice of strangers."

He paused, looking into their souls. How dark their blindness was! It was obvious they still didn't understand what He was saying.

So Yeshua spoke again, trying to reach them by expanding upon the truth He had just laid out. "Listen carefully to Me," He said. "Please hear My words. *I am the gate for the sheep*. All who came before Me are thieves and robbers, but the sheep did not listen to them. I am the door. If anyone enters by Me, he will be saved and will go in and out and find pasture. The thief comes only to steal and kill and destroy. I came that they may have life and have it abundantly."

Still no apparent understanding was seen in their faces. Yeshua was determined they would have no excuse from this point forward.

"*I am the Good Shepherd.* The Good Shepherd lays down His life for the sheep. He who is only a hired hand does not own the sheep, so when he sees the wolf coming, he leaves the sheep and flees; the wolf snatches them and scatters them. The hired hand runs because he cares nothing for the sheep. But I am the *Good Shepherd.* I know My own, and My own know Me, just as the Father knows Me and I know the Father; I lay down My life for the sheep.

"I have other sheep that are not of this fold. I must bring them also, and they will listen to My voice. So, there will be one flock, one shepherd. For this reason, the Father loves Me, because I lay down My life that I may take it up again. No one takes it from Me, but I lay it down of My own accord. I have authority to lay it down, and I have authority to take it up again. This charge I have received from My Father."

When Yeshua had stopped speaking, it was clear there was still division among the religious leaders. Most of them agreed that he must have a demon and now accused him of being insane.

Yet, some argued that someone who could open the eyes of the blind surely wasn't one stricken with a demon, nor was He insane!

Ah! A few were beginning to see!

However, after saying these things, the One who had previously written their names in the dirt and catalogued some of their secret sins simply turned His back…and walked away.

Yeshua's turned back was the worst expression of the judgment of Heaven's throne those arrogant ones could have received, or even imagined. However, that truth had now completely escaped them.

But the choice had been theirs. After everything they had witnessed over the last several weeks, they still purposely elected *not to see.*

PART THREE

UNDERSTANDING THE REASONS

Where then does wisdom come from?
Where does understanding dwell?
It is hidden from the eyes of every living thing.
(Job 28:20–21, NIV)

17

HEAVEN'S SNARE

But we impart a secret and hidden wisdom of God, which God decreed before the ages for our glory. (1 Corinthians 2:7)

Through Yeshua's very presence, as well as His precisely timed miracles and divinely formed parables, we now understand He was always engaged in the process of balancing every single movement of the universe necessary to carry out Heaven's plan of redemption.

However, that monumental balancing act would sometimes include rearranging and manipulating the physical elements as well. He demonstrated that power by turning water into wine, speaking words over a few loaves of bread and a small catch of fish to provide a gigantic meal for over ten thousand people, and halting the wind and waves during a violent storm with His simple command. That's not to mention that He raised certain people to life again—in front of witnesses.

And even now Yeshua had opened the eyes of a man *born* blind. In all these acts, Yeshua had commanded the very elements of the cosmos itself. He was accomplishing things only God Himself could do. Yet the eyes of those who possessed blackened hearts refused to see.

> For **by him all things were created**, in heaven and on earth, visible and invisible, whether thrones or dominions or rulers or authorities—**all things were created through him** and for him. And he is before all things, and **in him all things hold together.** (Colossians 1:16–17, emphasis added)

Through it all, Yeshua was relentlessly determined that Satan would not thwart His plan…the divine strategy that would take Him to the cross of Golgotha. He went to that cross on purpose, *for us.*

However, at the same time, Satan, in his arrogance, eventually came to believe getting Yeshua on that cross was the result of his own diabolical scheme. Therefore, since Satan was now under this particular delusion, everything had to fall into its proper order, according to Heaven's secret plan. And it did. Flawlessly. Right down to the second. *Every. Single. Time.*

Yeshua made certain of it.

One might not see these truths simply by reading a passage or two here and there in the New Testament. But by looking at the bigger picture in context, with the corresponding biblical truths from both the Old and New Testaments attached, there can be no doubt. Yeshua was working Heaven's plan. At the same time, Satan was kept largely in the dark regarding the specific details of that plan.

> All things were made by him; and without him was not anything made that was made. In him was life; and the life was **the light** of men. And the light shineth in darkness; and **the darkness comprehended it not.** (John 1:3–5, KJV; emphasis added)[81]

When everything had been completed, even the angels in Heaven ultimately understood the glory of what they had not known beforehand (1 Peter 1:12). The entire kingdom of darkness would also stand in astonishment over the deep and public humiliation in which they and Satan would now have to wallow.

> Having canceled the debt ascribed to us in the decrees that stood against us. He took it away, nailing it to the cross! And **having disarmed the powers** and authorities, He made a **public spectacle** of them, **triumphing over them** by the cross. (Colossians 2:14–15, BSB; emphasis added)[82]

Through the cross of Golgotha, Satan's kingdom would be on its way to total annihilation.[83] The "serpent's" head would be *crushed* (Genesis 3:15), and Heaven and earth would eventually be brought together again, under one head, the rightful owner—Yeshua (Ephesians 1:9–10).[84]

No passage of Scripture more succinctly states the foregoing truths than the following:

> Yet among the mature we do impart wisdom, although it is not a wisdom of this age **or of the rulers of this age**, who are **doomed to pass away. But we impart a secret and hidden wisdom** of God, which God decreed before the ages for our glory. **None of the rulers of this age understood this**, for if they had, **they would not have crucified the Lord of glory**. (1 Corinthians 2:6–8, emphasis added)

THE HEART OF THE MATTER

Verse 8 of 1 Corinthians 2 is the crux of our examination. Consider the context of what those words are really declaring, "None of the *rulers of this age* understood this, for if they had, *they would not have crucified* the Lord of glory."

Here's an academic oddity: One would be hard-pressed to find a plethora of scholarly material that even ventures to suggest the phrase "rulers of this age" has anything to do with Satan and his demonic minions at all. But I am convinced the scholars who hold to this interpretation are simply mistaken, almost shamefully so.[85]

They are not faulty because I say so, but because the Word of God says so. We discover this by looking at the context and myriad corresponding verses of Scripture, as well as the original Greek language.

However, in spite of this theological misstep by many, I can also attest that several reliable scholars *do* understand that the designation of "rulers" in 1 Corinthians 2 includes Satan and his demonic realms. You can read several of those at this endnote.[86] As you'll see in the next

couple of brief chapters, there simply can be no other credible interpretation of the matter.

David Guzik's *Enduring Word Commentary*:

> Are the rulers of this age men or demonic powers?
>
> This debate goes all the way back to the time of Origen and
> Chrysostom. On the surface, it seems clear that **the rulers of
> this age must refer to human rulers**, because only they didn't
> know what they were doing when they incited the crucifix-
> ion of Jesus. **However,** one could say that **demonic powers
> were ignorant of what would result** from the crucifixion of
> Jesus—the disarming and defeat of demonic powers (Colos-
> sians 2:15)—and **had they known they were sealing their own
> doom** by inciting the crucifixion, **they would not have done
> it.** (emphasis added)[87]

Context

The entire implication of the passage in 1 Corinthians is that somehow the "rulers of this age" were duped through their own spiritual
blindness, and they subsequently lost their bid for domination of the
earthly realm. As stated in the last several chapters, Yeshua's greatest
goal was to *defeat Satan* by going to the cross. The "age" Paul is speaking of is none other than humanity's entire existence in this fallen
world, right up to the return of Yeshua HaMashiach.[88] More on that
later.

But for now, let there be no misunderstanding. Yeshua didn't go to
Golgotha's cross to merely defeat the Sanhedrin Council or the Sadducees and Pharisees as a group. Neither did He go to the cross to only
destroy the power of the scribes and rabbis, or even the governmental
complex of the Roman Empire itself.

His death was affected for the ultimate purpose of defeating *Satan's
manifold power and his entire kingdom on earth*—every last vestige of

it! (See Hebrews 2:5–18). Yeshua had come to reverse the curse of the Garden of Eden—that was the mystery hidden in God and revealed in His Son—the Word that had become flesh! We know these truths because Yeshua is identified in Scripture as the "Lamb who was slain from the foundation of the earth" (1 Peter 1:20; Revelation 13:8; 1 Corinthians 2:7).

> [The Apostle Paul says] though I am the very least of all the saints, this grace was given, **to preach** to the Gentiles the **unsearchable riches** of Christ, and **to bring to light** for everyone what is **the plan of the mystery hidden for ages in God**, who created all things, so that through the church **the manifold wisdom of God might now be made known** to the **rulers and authorities in the heavenly places.** (Ephesians 3:8-10, emphasis added)

So, in order for Yeshua to sacrifice Himself on the cross, Satan couldn't be allowed to even come close to knowing that action was the precise way Yeshua *would* defeat him. Otherwise, Satan would have tried to stop it with all his might. There's simply no other way to see it.

Further, as we'll discover in the next couple of short chapters, the Scriptures clearly portray that it *flatly was* Satan who actually thought *he* was the one who had orchestrated Yeshua's crucifixion. That fact doesn't make sense unless he simply didn't know the crucifixion itself would be the undoing of his stolen kingdom.

18

RULERS OF THIS AGE

It's as though the Holy Spirit's inspiration of Scripture did not want us to miss this vital piece of information.

Just who were the "rulers of this age" spoken of in 1 Corinthians 2:6–8?

This phrase encompasses two biblical categories of entities. One group includes the political and religious leaders who arranged for Yeshua to be crucified. The Scripture states the matter concisely:

> Concerning Jesus of Nazareth, a man who was a prophet mighty in deed and word before God and all the people, and **how our chief priests and rulers delivered him up to be condemned to death, and crucified** him. (Luke 24:19–20, emphasis added)

We also find another set of rulers mentioned in the Scriptures; their identity is truly without question and directly related to the answer we seek:

> Put on the whole armor of God, that you may be able to stand against the schemes of the **devil**. For we do not wrestle against flesh and blood, but against the **rulers**, against the **authorities**, against the **cosmic powers** over this present darkness, against the **spiritual forces of evil in the heavenly places**. (Ephesians 6:11-12, emphasis added)

> …to bring to light for everyone what is the plan of the mystery hidden for ages in God, who created all things, so that through

the church the manifold wisdom of God might now be made
known to **the rulers** and **authorities in the heavenly places**.
(Ephesians 3:9–10, emphasis added)

It can't get much plainer than that, can it?

SATAN'S ALIASES

Satan is also presented in the Scriptures as being the "ruler" of the fallen
earth age. His demonic hosts are called "rulers" as well. Of course, as
the supreme "ruler" of our fallen realm, Satan certainly exercises his
diabolical power over human rulers as well.

But "ruler" is not the only title Satan has been given in this regard.
He is also called by several synonyms. It's as though the Holy Spirit's
inspiration of Scripture did not want us to miss this vital piece of
information.

Have a look at those corresponding titles. They appear in the English
translations as "ruler," "god of this age," or "prince of this world."

The **god of this age** [Satan] has blinded the minds of unbelievers, so that they cannot see the light of the gospel that displays
the glory of Christ, who is the image of God. (2 Corinthians
4:4, NIV; emphasis added)

[Yeshua declared] Now is the judgment of this world: now
shall the **prince** [also translated "ruler"] **of this world** be cast
out. (John 12:31, KJV; emphasis added)

[Yeshua declared] Hereafter I will not talk much with you: for
the **prince** [also translated "ruler"] **of this world** cometh, and
hath nothing in me. (John 14:30, KJV; emphasis added)

[Yeshua declared] Of judgment, because the **prince** [also
translated "ruler"] **of this world** is judged. (John 16:11, KJV;
emphasis added)

Wherein in time past ye walked according to the course of
this world, according to the **prince of the power of the air,**
the spirit that now worketh in the children of disobedience.
(Ephesians 2:2, KJV; emphasis added)[89]

THIS AGE

Now compare 2 Corinthians 4:4 and 1 Corinthians 2:8 with Ephesians 3:8:

> None of the **rulers of this age** understood this, for if they had,
> they would not have crucified the Lord of glory. (1 Corinthi-
> ans 2:8, emphasis added)

> The **god of this age** [Satan] has blinded the minds of unbeliev-
> ers. (2 Corinthians 4:4, NIV; emphasis added)

> …the plan of the **mystery hidden for ages** in God… (Ephe-
> sians 3:8, emphasis added)

The words "of this age" as they appear in the foregoing texts are
telling. That fact settles the matter of interpretation of the "rulers" that
Paul is talking about in 1 Corinthians 2:8. Satan is the "god of this
age." A "god" is also a "ruler" by any nuance of the definition. Therefore, Satan is at least one of the "rulers" to which Paul was referring.

Also, the word for "age" in the Greek language is *aión*. The same
word is used in all three of the foregoing passages. It is the word from
which we derive the English word *eon*—a term meaning something
like "infinity."[90] Again, this gives a distinctively clear definition to the
"rulers" Paul was referencing—those who, had they fully understood
the eternal consequences, would *not* have crucified Yeshua.

Now that we know who these "rulers" are, let's take a closer look at
the profound understanding the Word of God wants us to *see*.

19

SATAN'S SHAME

*Now to him who is able to strengthen you according
to my gospel and the preaching of Jesus Christ,
according to the revelation of the mystery that was
kept secret for long ages. (Romans 16:25)*

Let's look at two passages making it clear that Golgotha's cross was not a "trap" that Yeshua would be caught in unaware, regardless of what the religious elite and Satan thought. He delivered Himself to Golgotha—before the foundation of the world!

1. "I lay down my life that I may take it up again. **No one takes it from me,** but I lay it down of my own accord. I have authority to lay it down, and I have authority to take it up again." (John 10:17–18)

2. **Concerning this salvation,** the **prophets** who prophesied about the grace that was to be yours searched and inquired carefully, inquiring what person or time the Spirit of Christ in them was indicating when **he predicted the sufferings of Christ** and the subsequent glories. It was revealed to them that they were serving not themselves but you, in the things that have now been announced to you **through those who preached the good news** to you by the Holy Spirit sent from heaven, **things into which angels long to look.** (1 Peter 1:10–12, emphasis added)

Yeshua's planned death on the cross was the best-kept secret the cosmos had ever known! Even the angels around God's throne didn't

know the exact details. Neither did the prophets of old—and they were
the ones who spoke of the matter with supernatural foreknowledge!

THE BETRAYAL

The cross of Calvary certainly *was* the snare in which Satan would
be captured, precisely because Satan thought he was the instigator
of delivering Yeshua to it. He could not have been more mistaken.
Observe the following:

> So when [Yeshua] had dipped the morsel, he **gave it to Judas**,
> the son of Simon Iscariot. Then after he had taken the morsel,
> **Satan entered into [Judas]**. Jesus said to him, "What you are
> going to do, do quickly." (John 13:26–27, emphasis added)

> Then **Satan entered into Judas** called Iscariot, who was of the
> number of the twelve. He went away and **conferred with the
> chief priests and officers how he might betray** [Yeshua] to
> them. And they were glad, and agreed to give him money. So **he
> consented** and **sought an opportunity to betray him** to them
> in the absence of a crowd. (Luke 22:3–6, emphasis added)

Why would Satan possess Judas in order to betray Heaven's Son
to the cross? If Satan was convinced the cross would be his own eternal defeat, no matter what else he might have suspected concerning
Yeshua, why would he do such a thing? Why willfully orchestrate his
own downfall?

The answers to these questions are plain. *He wouldn't have. But
he most certainly did!* Therefore…*he didn't know.* That is exactly what
1 Corinthians 2 says, and what a disturbing number of scholars have
somehow missed entirely.[91]

> None of the rulers of this age understood this, for if they had, they
> would not have crucified the Lord of glory. (1 Corinthians 2:8)

This striking truth changes much regarding how we "see" what the miracles, parables, Yeshua's impeccable timing, and His seemingly coy conversations with those who constantly attacked Him were all about. This passage categorically bolsters the truth of the sovereignty and Lordship of Yeshua. No wonder Satan doesn't want us to "see" it. These words scream to the world, "Satan walked right into Heaven's trap! Now, his fallen and viciously evil kingdom is on the eve of annihilation!"

ANOTHER CONSIDERATION

There is still one question we must ask. Since Satan made such a huge mistake by taking part in delivering Yeshua to the cross, why didn't he have the sense to just examine the Scriptures beforehand? After all, the clues were right there for him to investigate. The answer to that matter is at least three-fold.

First, Satan did not, of course, have the New Testament Scriptures to pore over. The earliest documents were written at least a couple of decades *after* the Crucifixion and Resurrection. Satan only had access to the Old Testament documents. From those Scriptures, he might have been able to discern a few clues, but obviously, he missed the big picture—especially regarding the Crucifixion and Resurrection, the events that would eventually be his own destruction.

Second, Satan did not have the Holy Spirit to guide or illuminate his understanding of the often cryptic Old Testament prophecies. Think of it. Even believers today must still study, pray, and be attentive to the Holy Spirit within us to guide us into the light of genuine truth. Yet, discovering that truth is always the prerogative of Heaven's throne. Satan had none of those tools at his disposal.

When the Spirit of truth comes, he will guide you into all the truth, for he will not speak on his own authority, but whatever he hears he will speak, and he will declare to you the things that are to come. (John 16:13)

Also, as we've seen in 1 Peter 1:10–12, neither the prophets nor the angels around God's throne fully understood all of the details concerning the "Christ event." This didn't happen until those matters had physically played themselves out, right up to the Crucifixion and concluding in the Resurrection.

Satan is a fallen angel. He certainly knows more about the deepest workings of the unseen realms than we do. However, he clearly doesn't know more than the obedient angels surrounding Heaven's throne or the prophets God anointed to deliver the "hints" of what would one day take place.

SILENCE

It's also important to note that after the Resurrection and Yeshua's forty days on earth with His disciples, we do not see anything else about Satan, nor do we read his words in any of the four Gospel accounts. Only after the birth of the Church (recorded in the book of Acts) do we see Satan's activity beginning to pick up again…after the entire Christ redemption event had been carried out.

> [Yeshua] forgave us all our sins, having **canceled the charge** of our legal indebtedness, which stood against us and condemned us; he has **taken it away, nailing it to the cross.** And having **disarmed the powers and authorities,** he made a public spectacle of them, **triumphing over them by the cross.** (Colossians 2:13–15, NIV; emphasis and brackets added)

So, again, since the cross was Yeshua's triumph over Satan, why did Satan take part in orchestrating Yeshua's Crucifixion through his human puppets—the Sanhedrin and Roman officials? The answer to that question, by now, is much clearer. A plethora of renowned biblical scholars agree.[92]

Revised English Version Commentary (Colossians 2:15):

The **"rulers of this age"** are the **Devil and his demons.** Scholars and **Bible teachers are divided** over this point. Many of them say that the "rulers of this age" are earthly rulers such as Herod, Pilate, and the Jewish leaders.... **The reason** for the division is that **the context is misunderstood...**

So the rulers in 1 Corinthians 2:8 **cannot be the earthly rulers.** In contrast, **the Devil would not have crucified Jesus if he knew** that if he did crucify him, then every believer would have the fullness of holy spirit and "Christ in them."[93] (Emphasis added)

By now you probably understand why I took such a firm stance in this regard when we first began this exploration. I laid out the fact that regardless of the relatively large number of scholars who say otherwise, Satan flatly *did not know* the cross of Golgotha would prove to be the demise of his stolen earthly empire.

That secret was sacred. It was secured at Heaven's throne since before time began.

It was guarded...for *our sake.*

20

THE POWER

It is the glory of God to conceal things,
but the glory of kings is to search things out. (Proverbs 25:2)

The fear of a gruesome death by crucifixion was Rome's ultimate grip over the general populace of its day.

The crosses proclaimed to the empire's subjects: "*Don't mess with Rome!* If you do, we will strip you, beat you, humiliate you, crucify you, and make you die the most hideous, shameful death you can imagine. We will make an appalling spectacle of you. We'll impale your loathsome body on a wooden beam and hang it in public places so everyone who passes will stare at your miserable nakedness, and mock it!"

In short, the cross was the most dreaded of all the horrors of that day. But, as it turned out, and as we've discussed, the cross ultimately became Satan's cosmic defeat. Yeshua, by willingly suffering upon that cruel symbol of demonic power, did the unthinkable. He sacrificially turned that horrible symbol of abject cruelty into one of eternal victory over death and the final defeat of the ruler of this fallen world—Satan himself.

Since therefore the children share in flesh and blood, [Jesus] himself likewise partook of the same things, that **through death** [on the cross] he might **destroy the one who has the power of death, that is, the devil**, and deliver all those who through fear of death were subject to lifelong slavery. (Hebrews 2:14–15, emphasis and brackets added)

And now, for almost two thousand years since that day, we have worn jewelry tokens of that cross on necklaces and bracelets, displayed it atop our church buildings and inside our sanctuaries, and depicted it upon pulpits and Bible covers. Many even make the sign of the cross across their chest, or put the sign of the cross on their forehead with ashes, to proclaim its power. We do all of this, and more, to proclaim to the world that Yeshua won and Satan has lost...*forever*. The cross of Yeshua proves it.

The cross is not Yeshua's "shame"; rather, it is the power of God for our salvation. The cross was, categorically, Satan's humiliation. The only reason it became that disgrace was because *Satan didn't know*.

Now we have an enhanced ability to understand the foundational message of the Gospel of Yeshua HaMashiach—the genuine "Lord of all Glory."

> For I am not ashamed of the gospel, for it is the power of God for salvation to everyone who believes. (Romans 1:16)

WHAT ELSE ARE WE MISSING?

With this fresh perspective in mind, let's now probe into several more examples of how today's brand of Christianity sometimes misses other matters of eternal significance, in much the same manner as the Jewish elite of Yeshua's day.

Prepare for your eyes "to see" even more wonders of biblical truth!

THE TEMPLE
CORRELATION

From now on I will tell you of new things, of hidden things unknown to you. They are created now, and not long ago; you have not heard of them before today. So you cannot say, "Yes, I knew of them." (Isaiah 48:6–7)

21

THE NICKNAME

Hear the voice of my pleas for mercy, when I cry to you for help,
when I lift up my hands toward your most holy sanctuary.
(Psalm 28:2)

Within English translations of the Old Testament alone, we find
the word "temple" at least several hundred times. In reality, the
English word "temple" as found in the Old Testament is constructed
from a variety of Hebrew words and phrases in the language of the
original texts.[94]

It's important to know the distinctions between those words,
because they often reveal important clues about the term's significance
that can make a dramatic difference in the depth of our day-to-day
walk with Yeshua.

As we move forward, please don't fret about getting bogged down
in the Hebrew and Greek words themselves. This is not intended to
be a seminary lesson in biblical languages! (And rest assured, it's not
necessary to learn how to pronounce those words, much less memorize
them.)

Rather, the goal here is for you to see the message of this teaching
in a way that will affect your appreciation of who you *really* are in
Yeshua, as well as what is genuinely happening in the midst of our
unbelievably prophetic times. This is something else Satan doesn't
want you to "see."

TWO IMPORTANT WORDS

Among the many times we find the word "temple" in English translations, we are often looking at one of two different words in the

Hebrew language. Following are the Old Testament expressions we'll most heavily focus upon as our exploration begins.

- *Heykal*: This word (pronounced *hey-kawl*) means the actual covering-structure, including the Temple Courts, that once stood on the Temple Mount. It was the stone-and-mortar edifice that housed the *sanctuary*.[95]
- *Miqdash*: This term (pronounced *mik-dash*), means—in its most general sense—the two conjoined rooms inside the *heykal* that were *together* known as the *sanctuary*, or separately known as the Holy Place and the Holy of Holies. The Holy Place was the part of the *sanctuary* that held the lampstand/menorah, the table of showbread, the golden lamp (or candlestick), and the altar of incense. But most specifically, the *miqdash* signifies the innermost sanctuary, or the Holy of Holies, wherein the Ark of the Covenant was placed. The Holy of Holies was separated from the first room by a veil.[96]

SEEING THE DIFFERENCE

Let's look at the nuances of how *heykal* and *miqdash* are used in the Old Testament in order to understand the chief difference between the two. Remember, the reason the *heykal* (the Temple edifice itself) even existed in the first place was to house, protect, and set apart the *miqdash* (sanctuary).[97]

A simple visual we can use to understand the matter is to compare the *heykal* to the entire building complex of a modern Christian church campus. The actual *sanctuary*, however—the structure on that campus wherein the preaching and worship take place on the Lord's Day—would be comparable to the *miqdash*. We can even visualize (for illustrative purposes) that most church sanctuaries are divided into two rooms as well—the *foyer* area where the general congregation can visit, and the *inner sanctuary* where the worship service is held.

But, as you've probably already considered, even *we* use those two

English words, "church" and "sanctuary," interchangeably, and with almost no problem at all. For example, one might say, "I am going to *church* this weekend to sing in the choir during our worship service."

However, the most precise way to say what we are doing would be to say something like, "I'm going to the *sanctuary* at our *church campus* in order to sing in the choir during congregational worship."

Thankfully, in day-to-day speech we don't have to be that specific; we know what we're talking about as we interchange the nuanced meanings of those words and the concepts they stand for. We almost always use them as synonyms. The Hebrew language works pretty much the same way for *heykal* and *miqdash* except for one important detail.

THE MYSTERIOUS NICKNAME

There is a way in which the Hebrew beautifully distinguishes between the two words we've been examining. The *miqdash,* especially the innermost *Holy of Holies*, has a nickname attached to it in Hebrew, one that gives a richer understanding of its unique place within the greater purpose of the Temple structure. The nickname is an ancient and little-known word that's found sixteen times in the Old Testament (ten times in 1 Kings, five times in 2 Chronicles, and once in Psalm 28:2).[98] The word is *debir*, sometimes written as *devir*. Following is its use in Psalm 28:[99]

> Hear the voice of my pleas for mercy, when I cry to you for help, when I lift up my hands toward your **most holy sanctuary** [*debir*]. (Psalm 28:2, emphasis added)[100]

Why would the *miqdash* have a nickname such as *debir*, and what, exactly, does it mean? The answers to those questions are remarkable, and vital to daily life in Yeshua. They are also eternally important to understanding who Yeshua has called *you* to be. And perhaps the most stunning connection will be the revelation of how a particularly

controversial (and often misinterpreted) verse in the New Testament
is to be properly understood. Once you see it, you'll never be able to
un-see it again.

22

THE HOLY WORD PLACE

Therefore the whole of reality that we experience can also be called the Word of God.

We'll first examine what the Hebrew noun *debir* (pronounced deb-eer) means.[101] It can be defined in English in several ways. My favorite is "the holy word place." However, we could also call it "God's speaking place," the "place of the word," or the "place from which the holy word of God flows."[102]

THE *DEBIR*

The *debir* was the sacred place where Yahweh promised to speak with the high priest (originally Moses and Aaron) and where the high priest might also speak with God. From that firsthand fellowship with God, the high priest would communicate Yahweh's commandments to the people. Because of this, the *miqdash,* or the *debir,* is sometimes called the "holy word place," the place where God speaks to His priests and anointed leaders.

[The Lord said to Moses,] There I will meet with you, and from above the mercy seat, from between the two cherubim that are on the ark of the testimony, **I will speak with you** about all that I will give you in commandment for the people of Israel. (Exodus 25:22, emphasis and brackets added)

And when Moses went into the tent of meeting to speak with the LORD, **he heard the voice speaking to him** from above the mercy seat that was on the ark of the testimony, from between the two cherubim; **and it spoke to him.** (Numbers 7:89, emphasis added)

However, we also know from the scriptures that the entire holy place (the sanctuary)—even the part not behind the veil—could also be used as a place where the LORD or an angel of the LORD might speak on God's behalf. In fact, that divine being might even speak to a regular priest, one who was not the high priest.

We find an instance of this illustrated in Luke 1:

Now while [Zechariah] was **serving as priest before God** when his division was on duty, according to the custom of the priesthood, he was chosen by lot to **enter the temple** [holy place–*miqdash*] of the Lord and **burn incense.** And the whole multitude of the people were praying outside at **the hour of incense** [prayer].

And **there appeared to him an angel of the Lord** standing on the right side of the altar of incense. And Zechariah was troubled when he saw him, and fear fell upon him. But **the angel said to him,** "Do not be afraid, Zechariah, for your prayer has been heard, and your wife Elizabeth will bear you a son, and you shall call his name John." (Luke 1:8–13, emphasis and brackets added)

The point is that the entire "sanctuary" (the Holy Place and the Holy of Holies) was referred to as the *miqdash*. But the most sacred use of the word was to indicate the Holy of Holies—behind the veil, in the presence of the Ark of the Covenant and the covering cherubim. This was the truest form of the *debir*—the *holy Word place* of God.

But there's more…

DABAR—*THE VERB*

The Hebrew noun *debir* comes from the verb form of the word *dabar* (pronounced dah-bar), which means "to speak."

At its deepest level, *dabar* means to formalize a name by speaking it, as when Adam named the animals God brought him, and when he named his wife Eve, "the mother of all living."[103] Upon pronouncing these terms, their individual definitions were eternally established. In so doing, those things became "valid" within Adam's realm.[104]

DABAR—*THE NOUN*

Dabar can also be used as a noun meaning "the word." And in the modern Hebrew language it also means "the thing." This is because in the naming of a *thing*, by a word, the authenticity of that *thing* takes on its most significant identification, and even its essence.[105]

For example, God created all *things* by merely speaking His Word. Through that verbalization, God brought forth the whole realm of reality. Consequently, all the created reality we experience daily could also be called the "Word of God."[106]

Imagine! The *dabar* is the spoken word that also brings forth a thing. That sounds a lot like what happened in Genesis 1, doesn't it?

In the beginning, God created the heavens and the earth. The earth was without form and void, and darkness was over the face of the deep. And the Spirit of God was hovering over the face of the waters. And **God said**, "Let there be light," **and there was** light. (Genesis 1:1–3, emphasis added)

Now, let's read the following two New Testament declarations found in John and Colossians in view of what we've just learned. Notice how these passages fit together in perfect agreement.

In the beginning was **the Word**, and **the Word** was with God, and the **Word was God**. He **was with God in the beginning**.

All things were made through him, and without him was not **anything** made that was made...And **the Word became flesh and dwelt among us**, and we have seen his glory, glory as of the only Son from the Father, full of grace and truth. (John 1:1–3, 14, emphasis added)

John 1 is a beautiful representation of the Hebrew term *dabar,* as is the companion assertion of Colossians 1.

[Yeshua] is **the image of the invisible God**, the firstborn of all creation. **For by him all things were created**, in heaven and on earth, **visible and invisible**, whether thrones or dominions or rulers or authorities—**all things** were **created through him** and for him. And he is before all things, and **in him all things hold together.** (Colossians 1:15–17, emphasis added)

What a difference the various shades of meaning of a single word can make! Especially when that understanding helps us to more thoroughly grasp the divinely intended truth of the contextual Word of God.

Next, we'll explore the tradition-shattering discovery of contextual truth afforded to us by the knowledge we have just gained. This is going to get remarkably interesting. I promise!

23

THE GREEK
CONNECTION

*The context in which the words are used is clearly defined
by the text itself...and sometimes by Paul's own
unmistakable explanation.*

When translating Greek New Testament texts into English, we find the English word "temple" used prolifically—much like it is in the Old Testament. However, as in the Hebrew, there are also two different Greek words that are often translated as "temple" in English. Those words are sometimes used interchangeably, in the same way as with the Hebrew. This fact, if not understood by the reader, allows for occasional misunderstanding of vital New Testament doctrinal matters.

The Greek words are *hieron* (pronounced he-a-roan) and *naos* (pronounced nah-os). And, exactly as in the Hebrew language, the first word—*hieron*—refers to the temple edifice itself, corresponding to the Hebrew *heykal*.

The other Greek word—*naos*—primarily applies to the Holy of Holies and corresponds to the Hebrew *miqdash*.

Understanding that the Hebrew *miqdash* is also known by the nickname *debir*, we can accurately claim that the Greek *naos* shares the same Hebrew nickname. For that reason, the *naos* can also be known as "the holy word place." The point to remember is that the Hebrew *miqdash*, along with its Hebrew nickname, *debir*, and the Greek *naos* mean the same thing. Each are synonyms of one another.

THE DIFFERENCE

During Yeshua's earthly life the *hieron* was still standing on the Temple
Mount in Jerusalem. Although, He *did* tell His disciples, just before
His crucifixion, that the magnificent Temple structure would soon be
destroyed (Matthew 24:1–2). That prophesied destruction began in
AD 70, at the order of Rome, less than forty years after Yeshua's cruci-
fixion and resurrection.

However, now that we know what to look for, we can begin to
see several vital nuances when the English word "temple" is used in
translation. Through this insight, we begin to grasp a deeper comprehension of modern doctrinal confusions, as well as a magnified
realization of the prophetic days in which we are living, and what our
part in them should really be.

Here is where the study gets really fascinating.

THE FAMOUS RABBI

By far, the most well-known Jewish rabbi the world has ever known is
none other than the Apostle Paul.

Think about the truthfulness of that assertion. There are currently
2.38 billion people in the world who proclaim to be Christians.[107] That
means that most, if not all of them, are at least familiar with the name
of the Apostle Paul. Not only that, but even out of the non-Christians,
I would venture to say that a vast number of those would have at least
heard of Paul as well. After all, he is the author of almost one half of
the New Testament documents, a huge part of the best-selling book
on the planet—in history![108] The plain fact is that there has never been
a Jewish rabbi known by so many people, and one that has written as
much eternally life-changing material inspired by the Holy Spirit of
God, as the Apostle Paul.

The most important thing to know is that Paul categorically settles
the matter of the interpretation of the "temple" as it is defined in those
two Greek words. Not only does he resolve it, but he also applies his
contextual definitions directly to the days in which we are now living.

Surprisingly, what Paul so clearly declares is often a vastly different thing than what a large sector of today's modern churches teach that it means. Now…*that's* a big deal. Wouldn't you agree?

THE CONTEXT

It's easy to figure out what Paul means by these two words. Paul uses both *hieron* and *naos* within the New Testament books he penned. The context in which the words are used is clearly defined by the text itself…and most of the time the meaning is described by Paul's own unmistakable explanation included within those texts.

Keep in mind that since Paul spoke fluent Hebrew and Greek, he certainly would have been familiar with the Hebrew words *heykal* and *miqdash* that find their Greek counterparts in *hieron* and *naos*.[109]

The larger point is this: In whatever manner Paul defines the *hieron* and *naos* of the last days, it is in that same manner that we are to contextually apply those words as well. In fact, whenever the New Testament as a whole speaks to an Old Testament doctrinal issue, the New Testament holds the *final interpretation* of the subject that came before it in the Old Testament. This is because the New Testament's main message is that now *all things are made complete in Yeshua*. Therefore, whatever Paul has declared concerning "the temple" is the settled truth of the matter, especially if we are going to endeavor to stay within the confines of its truest context.

In "Should we employ the hermeneutics of the New Testament writers?" Dr. Dan G. McCartney (PhD) writes:

> We must rather, like Jesus and the apostles, go on to see and read the Old Testament text in the context not just of the Bible as a whole, but **in the context of redemptive history as a whole.** In particular, we must read the Old Testament with Christian eyes. **Should we employ the hermeneutics of the New Testament writers? Indeed we must.**[110] (Emphasis added; see this endnote for several other scholarly attestations of this truth.)

With these facts in mind, let's now take a contextual look at how Paul defines the words *hieron* and *naos*.

What you'll discover next might shake your biblical understanding a bit, but you will soon see the truth of the matter with your own eyes…and what you'll learn will not simply be my "interpretation" of the matter.

It will be what the Word of God says—in black and white.

24

CLEARING
THE TEMPLE

*Now to him who is able to strengthen you according to my gospel
and the preaching of Jesus Christ, according to the revelation of
the mystery that was kept secret for long ages. (Romans 16:25)*

Paul used the word *hieron* (the Temple edifice itself) only twice, and in only one verse within the pages of all of the New Testament documents he wrote. That word is always translated into the English versions of the Bible as "temple."[111]

> Do you not know that those who are employed in **the temple** [*hieron*] service get their food from **the temple** [*hieron*], and those who serve at the altar share in the sacrificial offerings? (1 Corinthians 9:13, emphasis and brackets added)

The context of Paul's word usage is clear. He is speaking about the entire *temple complex* itself, not singling out a specific room within that edifice.

On the other hand, *nine times* Paul uses the Greek word that is also frequently represented in English translations as "temple." But those instances are translated from the word *naos*. And as you've already seen, the nuanced meaning of that word is quite different than that of *hieron*.

THE FIRST EIGHT

Every one of the nine times that Paul uses the word *naos*, and where they are translated as "temple" in almost all the English translations, are found in *five* different passages written by him. So they are easy to find, and easy to determine the clear context that he defines *naos* to express.

Let's begin our examination by looking at the initial *eight times* that Paul uses the word *naos*. He uses all eight within four distinct passages. We'll look at the ninth use of the word, found in the fifth passage, as we move to the next chapter.

In each of its first eight usages, Paul categorically *sets in stone* the definition of the word within its context. The Greek word *naos* is always the word rendered in English versions as "temple" in these verses.

> Do you not know that **you are God's temple** and that God's Spirit dwells in you? If anyone destroys God's **temple**, God will destroy him. For God's **temple** is holy, and **you are that temple.** (1 Corinthians 3:16–17, emphasis added)

> Or do you not know that **your body is a temple** of the Holy Spirit within you, whom you have from God? You are not your own, you were bought at a price. Therefore glorify God with your body. (1 Corinthians 6:19–20, emphasis added)

> What agreement has the **temple** of God with idols? For **we are the temple** of the living God; as God said, "I will make my dwelling among them and walk among them, and I will be their God, and they shall be my people. (2 Corinthians 6:16, emphasis added)

> So then **you are** no longer strangers and aliens, but **you are** fellow citizens with the saints and members of the **household of God**, built on the foundation of the apostles and prophets, Christ Jesus himself being the **cornerstone**, in whom the whole structure, being joined together, **grows into a holy temple** in the Lord. In him **you also are being built together into a dwelling place** for God by the Spirit. (Ephesians 2:19–22, emphasis added)

There's absolutely no other way to interpret Paul's words about the *naos* (knowing that its Hebrew counterparts are *miqdash and debir*) other than by identifying *naos* as the individual born-again believer, as well as the collective body of genuine believers...*the true Church.*

POINTS OF CONTEXT

So now we have to ask *how* Paul arrived at this definition of the *naos*. Did he simply construct it out of thin air? Did he just make it up? Was it something he merely "wanted" it to be?

Of course not. His stance came from a foundational biblical truth. That fulfilled understanding of the temple was what Yeshua Himself had declared not long before He went to the cross and rose from the grave three days later.

In John 2 we discover that Yeshua was the first one to *define most completely* the word *naos* in its final and fulfilled understanding.[112]

So the Jews said to him, "What sign do you show us for doing these things?" Jesus answered them, "Destroy this **temple** [*naos*, or "holy Word place," or "sanctuary"], and in three days I will raise it up." The Jews then said, ""It has taken forty-six years to build this **temple** [*naos*, or "holy Word place," or "sanctuary"], and will you raise it up in three days?"

But he was speaking about the temple [*naos*, or "holy Word place," or "sanctuary"] **of his body.** When therefore he was raised from the dead, his disciples remembered that he had said this, and they believed the Scripture and the word that Jesus had spoken. (John 2:18–22, emphasis and brackets added)

Have a look at *Ellicott's Commentary for English Readers* concerning John 2:19. Ellicott understood that biblical truth which, sadly, so much of the modern church still appears to be missing.

The **enigma** turns in the present case upon **the double sense** of the word "temple." It meant the sacred [sanctuary] of the Deity, the **Holy and Most Holy place**, as **distinct from the** wider Temple area. But **the true** [sanctuary] of the Deity was **the body of the Incarnate Word**....

The Temple of wood and stone was **but the representa- tive** of the **Divine Presence**. That Presence was then actually in their midst....

He will raise up the **temple of His body** the third day, and in that resurrection will be the **foundation stone** of the **spiri- tual temple** for the world [the church]. (Emphasis and brackets added)[113]

Barnes' Notes on the Bible affirms the same understanding of *naos*:

The evangelist informs us in John 2:21 that by **"temple,"** here, **Jesus meant his body**. It is not improbable that **he pointed with his finger to his body** as he spoke.

The word "temple," or "dwelling," was not unfrequently used...**to denote the "body"** as being the residence of the spirit, 2 Corinthians 5:1. **Christians are** not unfrequently **called the temple of God**, as being those in whom **the Holy Spirit dwells on earth**, 1 Corinthians 3:16–17; 1 Corinthians 6:19; 2 Corinthians 6:16. Our Saviour called his body a tem- ple **in accordance with the common** [New Testament] **use of language**.[114] (Emphasis and brackets added)

There you have it! Our Lord Yeshua called His own body the *debir,* or *the holy word place*...which He most certainly is. What born again believer would argue with this fact? He is the Holy Word that became flesh (John 1:1–14).

The fact is, the "Body of Christ" is comprised of both individ- ual born-again believers, as well as the collective family of born-again believers.[115] That spiritual truth is the source from which Paul gave his definition of *naos*. This understanding is fitting for our times, considering for the last almost 2,000 years, there has been no stone and mortar Temple structure on the Temple Mount.

We, the Body of Christ, are the *only* "new temple" of the last days that is directly defined within the New Testament. *The only one!* A number of respected biblical scholars have shared this same opinion, which was clearly revealed by Yeshua, Paul, and other New Testament writers.[116]

Britt Mooney, author and contributor to *Crosswalk.com*, a conservative biblical commentary and contemporary online scholarship site, asserts this vital truth:

> The short answer is that **nowhere do we see a physical Third
> Temple** being built on this Earth…So why would we make a
> physical Third Temple necessary?[117] There is plenty in the New
> Testament to clearly explain that **the Temple Christ has built
> (and is still building) is an eternal one in the people of God.**
> (Emphasis added)[118]

We are the *miqdash/naos*. We are the *holy word place*.

In light of these disclosures, let's examine the Apostle Paul's ninth and final use of the word "temple."

This is the shocking revelation that the vast majority of today's church doesn't seem to "see." And when they do see it, still a sizable number simply ignore what they see. This was the same shameful sin of the Pharisees regarding Yeshua. They refused to "see" Him for who He really was - because He didn't fit their "traditions."

As you turn to the next page, you'll discover that a huge chunk of today's "church" is no different in its actions than the Pharisees of old, especially when it comes to the idea of "traditional interpretations" that are clearly outside of what the Word of God actually *says*.

25

SEATED
IN THE TEMPLE

*Paul would have been clear in his response to
the church at Thessalonica, and not express his thoughts
in the form of a confusing enigma.*

If you are not already familiar with what we will next uncover, prepare yourself. This illumination will shake your world, especially as it relates to your daily walk with Yeshua.

The final use of the word "temple" by the Apostle Paul in 2 Thessalonians 2:4 is one of the most often misinterpreted passages in the New Testament. Here is the passage that contains that verse in context.

> Now **concerning the coming of our Lord Jesus Christ** and our being gathered together to him, we ask you, brothers, not to be quickly shaken in mind or alarmed, either by a spirit or a spoken word, or a letter seeming to be from us, to the effect that the day of the Lord has come.
>
> Let no one **deceive you** in any way. For that day will not come, unless **the rebellion comes first**, and **the man of lawlessness** is revealed, **the son of destruction** who opposes and exalts himself against every so-called god or object of worship, so that **he takes his seat in the temple of God**, proclaiming himself to be God. (2 Thessalonians 2:1–4, emphasis added)

The interpretation of this verse seems indisputable to many students of the Bible. In fact, those who believe there will be a third

Temple built on the Temple Mount in Jerusalem in the last days point right at this particular verse as their "indisputable" proof of the matter. They often make the point expressing it something like this: It's glaringly obvious the verse states the 'antichrist' figure will take his seat in a last days' rebuilt temple, which would be located on the Temple Mount! How can this verse mean anything other than that?

THE ALL-IMPORTANT CONTEXT

But here's the biblically contextual truth of the matter. It is a fact that in 2 Thessalonians 2:4, Paul makes a dramatic assertion about the antichrist taking his seat in what most English translations call the *temple* of God. But, as we've already seen, Paul has previously defined the "temple" eight separate times. And here, in 2 Thessalonians 2:4, he is using the very same Greek word, *naos*, without ever indicating that he is changing the meaning of what he has already specified it to be.[119]

We also know Paul has already defined *naos* as both born again believers, individually, and the church as a whole. Before we arrive at 2 Thessalonians, Paul never uses *naos* to mean the Temple complex located on the Temple Mount in Jerusalem. *Never.* When considering what Paul means in 2 Thessalonians 2:4, this is a monumental contextual consideration that simply cannot be ignored.

Nowhere in his second letter to the Thessalonians does Paul redefine *naos* to mean the "Temple on the Temple Mount." In fact, not a single New Testament book written by Paul mentions this specific phenomenon even occurring in the last days. If this supposed occurrence was really going to happen, how could the Apostle Paul, who was caught up to Heaven and shown the last days, have missed it? What a monumental omission that would have been!

Therefore, the *naos* of that verse *must* be translated as having the same meaning that Paul has always, and repeatedly, declared. This is a fundamental principle of contextual biblical interpretation, taught in conservative biblical seminaries.[120]

TEMPLE ESCHATOLOGY IS NOT THE ISSUE

Please understand, I am not making the argument one way or the other for an eventual third Temple on the Temple Mount in downtown Jerusalem.[121] Nor am I making an eschatological statement about the "timing of the rapture." This verse in 2 Thessalonians makes neither of those declarations, regardless of anyone's desire to make it fit those non-contextual scenarios.[122]

In truth, Paul meant for his readers to define the word *naos* in this very way. We can clearly observe this fact by examining verses 5 and 15 of 2 Thessalonians, chapter two. They are quoted here from the *Aramaic Bible in Plain English*.[123]

> Verse 5: **Do you not remember** that when I was **with you, I said these things** to you? (Emphasis added)
>
> Verse 15: Therefore, my brethren, **be established** and hold the commandments fast that **you have learned**, whether **by discourse** or **by our epistle**. (Emphasis added)

TODAY'S GREAT APOSTASY

We must also keep in mind, Paul directly identified this "coming of the lawless one" with the *apostasy* or the great *falling away* that would occur in the last days. Now we understand the context of that apostasy has to do with the *church* itself![124]

The apostasy of 2 Thessalonians, about which Paul also warned Timothy, is also concerning the end time "doctrines of demons."[125]

> God's Spirit clearly says that **in the last days** many people will **turn from their faith**. They will be **fooled by evil spirits** and by **teachings that come from demons**. (1 Timothy 4:1, CEV; emphasis added)

Surely, pervasive teachings "that come from demons" in the church of the last days would be an identifier of an apostate church.

In 2 Thessalonians 2, there can be little doubt Paul is addressing the same time period about which he had also written to Timothy. Paul was addressing the apostasy of the last days, sometimes referred to as the "latter times."

> No one should deceive you in any way, because it is not **until the apostasy shall have come** first, and the **man of lawlessness** shall have been revealed—the son of destruction...(2 Thessalonians 2:3, BLB; emphasis added)

THEY KNEW!

If I were to paraphrase, in plain English, what Paul appears to be declaring in 2 Thessalonians 2:5 and 2:15, it might read something like this:

> Don't you remember what I've already taught you on this matter? I have instructed you in my writings, and in my preaching, concerning what all of this means. You know my definition of *naos*, which the Lord Himself declared to be *His own Body*. Of course, *we* are now that "Body." I've often written about the *naos* of God, which is found not only in our own bodies, but also in the collective Body of Christ. *This* is where the flood of false teachings of the last days will occur, and it is where the man of lawlessness will eventually take up his unholy residence in the end times. It will occur within those visible religious institutions calling themselves "the church" of the last days, and within the hearts and minds of people calling themselves Christians!

A number of renowned biblical scholars agree that the genuine "temple" in which the antichrist will eventually "seat himself," is referring to none other than the *apostate church* of the last days. For your

further study, I have provided three academically renowned commentary statements located at this endnote.[126]

At the beginning of this chapter, I made the assertion that Paul
would have been very clear in his response to the church at Thessalonica. He would not have expressed his thoughts in the form of a
confusing enigma. In fact, Paul had devoted much of his ministry to
explaining events of the last days, especially concerning what we're
now examining.

Paul wrote about those truths, consistently expounding on them
within the scriptural documents he circulated among many churches
in the Roman Empire. He defined those words as clearly as possible.

You see, the Temple on the Temple Mount was never meant to
be a symbol of religious power or ecclesiastical preference, or a weight
around the neck of the Jewish people. Rather, it was first meant as a
holy symbol of God's presence among our fallen creation (1 Samuel
2:28), until that Living Word (God Himself) became flesh and dwelt
among us in bodily form (John 1).

Then, when *the Word that became Flesh* was crucified at Golgotha,
rose from dead, and birthed the church by the Holy Spirit...we—
the Household of God (Ephesians 2:19)—became the "Holy Word
Place!" *We* are the representation of Yeshua Himself (1 John 4:17)—at
least in our role as ambassadors of His Word (2 Corinthians 5:20), as
well as His holy witnesses (Acts 1:8), and also a kingdom of His priests
in this fallen world (Revelation 1:6). We are now *the Body of Christ*
(1 Corinthians 12:27)—the *Holy Debir!*

The truth of this vital matter is right before our eyes. It is especially
disconcerting to observe how a great number of God's people still miss
it, especially in the midst of the prophetic times in which we now live.

26

THE RELEVANT WORD

Son of man, you are living among a rebellious people. They have eyes to see but do not see and ears to hear but do not hear, for they are a rebellious people. (Ezekiel 12:2, NIV)

I n light of what we've explored up to this point, hopefully it's much easier to discern what the Holy Spirit of God is revealing to born again believers of the last days. If there were anything the Lord would want our generation to thoroughly understand about our day, I believe it would be the following truths.

THE BIG FOUR

The most obvious—and explosive—prophecies signaling the global events occurring just prior to the Second Coming of Yeshua are clearly laid out within the pages of Scripture. However, few contextual teachings revealing these signs of prophetic fulfillment are even mentioned in pulpits today.[127]

> The **god of this world** has **blinded** the minds of the unbelievers, to **keep them from seeing** the light of the gospel of the glory of Christ, who is the image of God. (2 Corinthians 4:4, emphasis added)

Four of the most significant fulfillments of prophecy are: the supernatural return of the nation of Israel to the Middle East,[128] the unprecedented exponential growth in communication and information technologies,[129] the pervasive global spread of apostasy and cultural pushback to the Word of God[130] and, at the same time, the

109

accelerated spreading of the Gospel to the entire world, a phenomenon that was absolutely unknown before our most recent times.[131]

Consider this fact: Prior to this historical generation, *none* of these
four prophetic occurrences had fully come to pass. Today, all of them
are being realized, and right before the eyes of the world. There can be
no doubt, these days are prophetically unique, and we are now the first
generation in history to be actively watching those precise prophecies
converge.

LOST FOCUS

The prevailing problem of the *visible church* (often wayward denomi-
nationalism and institutionalized "Christianity") is that, for too long,
it has been focused on matters that emphasize growth of membership, perceived political influence, and vastly increasing their financial
assets, almost "at all costs," rather than paying closer attention to the
pervasive apostatizing of the Word of God.

According to the Barna Group's article, *The Bible in America:
6-Year Trends:*

> The steady **rise of skepticism** [toward biblical faith] is creating
> a cultural atmosphere that is becoming unfriendly—sometimes
> even **hostile—to claims of faith**. In a society that venerates **sci-
> ence and rationalism**, it is an increasingly hard pill to swallow
> that an eclectic assortment of ancient stories, poems, sermons,
> prophecies and letters, written and compiled over the course of
> 3,000 years, is somehow the sacred "word of God." Even in just
> the few years Barna has been conducting "State of the Bible"
> interviews, the percent of Americans who believe that the Bible
> is "just another book written by men" increases. So too does
> **the perception that the Bible is actually harmful** and that
> people who live by its principles are **religious extremists**.[132]
> (Emphasis and brackets added)

Almost every God-ordained institution began in the Garden of Eden, or shortly thereafter. Those institutions are now being universally reduced to politically correct travesties of the originals. While masquerading as truth, today's instantaneous information and communication technologies, flooding our world at an alarming speed, are making an absolute global mockery of God's Word.

Consider the fact that practically every nation on the planet struggles to define *marriage, home,* and *family*—as well as the sanctity of life within the human womb. Furthermore, many of these nations, under the demonic leadership of the "rulers" of this present darkness, consistently encourage the redefining of *womanhood, manhood, childhood, the sovereignty of national borders,* and even *gender identification.* When asked to give a definition of what a woman is during her Senate confirmation hearing, the now *sitting* Justice of the current U.S. Supreme Court Ketanji Brown Jackson declared, "I'm not a biologist!" A plain answer was never offered for what should have been considered a simple question with an obvious answer—one we all learned in our third grade science class.[133]

STARING US IN THE FACE

As another example of this travesty, consider the dark chasm of death known as abortion. It has held the shameful position of being the *number one global cause of death* for at least the last four decades, yet very few modern churches address this critical issue. The unprecedented number of abortion deaths stands at about 70-80 million children a year—and that number only takes into consideration the "reporting nations." The truest quantity is probably much higher than that.[134]

Sadly, that astonishing number of abortions are not even counted among the combined *top ten* global causes of death, which stands at around 25 million people, according to the World Health Organization (WHO). The WHO reports the number of dead each year from *all* causes of death, including the top ten, as 55 million, never taking into consideration the 70-80 million babies aborted each year.[135]

To give more perspective to this matter, many have documented the number of people killed in World War II at around 60 million.[136] This means that, *every year*, for decades, abortion has had *more than* a World War II-styled death toll! *Year in and year out!*

Yet, when those of us who know the truth about these matters attempt to point them out in conversations or on social media, we are inundated with the most hateful vitriol imaginable. It's as though many have chosen to strike these truths from their personal reality. It certainly seems a *demon* has crept into the midst of this perversion of truth, don't you think?

MORE HARBINGERS

On top of those previously mentioned collisions of prophetic significance, there is also a rising global epidemic of *mental illness* that's inundating the planet.[137] It's as though we are living in the midst of the world being given over to the "depravity of mind" the apostle Paul warned us was sure to come in the last days (Romans 1:28).

In addition to the mental illness epidemic, and often the dysfunctional effects related to it, *opioid* and *alcohol addictions* are at "epidemic levels worldwide," according to the National Library of Medicine.[138]

When we consider the composite of these prophetic happenings, the 2 Thessalonians 2:4 *naos* connection becomes increasingly more apparent. However, while the Word of God does predict all of these maladies of the last days, in 2 Thessalonians, Paul also foretells of something else in regard to what we are currently experiencing.

Paul prophesied that the "man of lawlessness," or the "son of perdition" (the man who would most likely be preceded by the *spirit of antichrist* as John prophesied)[139] would "seat himself" within the *holy word place* and proclaim himself to be God. In other words, he will function as if he is the "Lord" over a seemingly apostate church in the last days. Now, for the first time since the birth of the church, Paul's prophetic utterances concerning the global defilement of the last days' *true temple* are coming to life right before the eyes of the world.

All of this adds up to an enormous prophetic declaration: what once were mainstream denominations are now collapsing into the mire of the "doctrine of demons," also prophesied by Paul in 1 Timothy 4:1.

The Gospel is being drastically watered down, the preaching of the Word is largely ignored, and in some of these denominations the contextual truth of the Word of God is openly mocked, sometimes even being retranslated to fit the politically correct atmosphere of the day.

A PROPHETIC FORETASTE?

These facts don't even include the prophetically charged event the entire world observed in the years 2020–2021. During that period, for the first time since the birth of the church nearly 2,000 years ago, a global persecution of the church was orchestrated by several world governments. In one voice they began to call for churches to be shut down, and the cessation of singing in worship and the gathering of large crowds. To make matters more intolerable, a number of these "mandates" were under the threat of arrest. Some of the world's leaders, including the City of Chicago Health Department, even threatened to bulldoze the church buildings where the "non-compliant" resided."[140]

In short, we are continuing to experience a relentless, demonic assault on the *holy word place*. And that onslaught is rapidly reaching a global scale. This is a vicious assault of monumental, prophetic proportions upon God's people. To this end, we were "treated" with this ominous *Fox News* headline article on a Sunday morning in late February 2024: "Attacks against churches doubled in 2023, report warns: 'Growing disdain for Christianity': There were 436 hostile acts against Christians in US in 2023, per new report."[141]

Christian persecution today is more widespread than any other time in Church history, and it continues to escalate.[142]

Woe to you, O earth and sea, for **the devil** has come down to you **in great wrath**, because **he knows that his time is short!**"...

Then **the dragon** became **furious** with the **woman** [in this context: the "invisible" church as well as national and spiritual Israel[143]] and **went off to make war** on the rest of **her off-spring, on those who** keep the commandments of God and **hold to the testimony of Jesus.** (Revelation 12:12, 17, emphasis and brackets added)

Furthermore, with the correct contextual understanding of Paul's warnings in 2 Thessalonians 2:4, we should now be able to discern one relevant truth. That truth is: We can no longer ponder this prophesied demonic advance as possibly taking place in a dark and dreary way-off future...because it's happening now, right before our eyes.[144]

Sadly, much of the modern church is oblivious as to what's really going on. They just don't see it.

Next, you'll find out what's driving this onslaught.

PART FIVE

THE TREE OF KNOWLEDGE

Fox News: Harvard physicist searching for UFO evidence says humanity will view alien intelligence like "God" (August 2023).

Harvard professor Avi Loeb predicted that the scientific discovery of an alien civilization—one that may be billions of years old—will prompt humanity to unify...

A worldwide recognition and realization of universal "neighbors" may not shock or terrify. In fact, it might be a profoundly spiritual experience.

"A very advanced scientific civilization is a good approximation to God."[145]

27

ONLY IN OUR DAY

It was only a little over a hundred years ago (as late as 1915)
that some American families were migrating to other
regions of our continually evolving nation in
horse-drawn covered wagons.

I can envision the Apostle Peter slapping his forehead in disbelief as
he wrote the following words in prophetic hindsight.

> For **we did not follow cleverly devised fables** when we made
> known to you the power and coming of our Lord Jesus Christ,
> but **we were eyewitnesses of His majesty.**
> **We also have the word of the prophets as confirmed beyond**
> **doubt.** And you will do well to pay attention to it, as to a lamp
> shining in a dark place, until the day dawns and the morning
> star rises in your hearts. Above all, you must understand that
> no prophecy of Scripture comes from one's own interpretation.
> For **no such prophecy was ever brought forth by the will of**
> **man, but men spoke from God as they were carried along by**
> **the Holy Spirit.** (2 Peter 1:16, 19–21, BSB; emphasis added)

In other words, Peter is saying "Look! It's happening in our generation! Everything the Old Testament proclaimed about the coming of
the Messiah has collided into the midst of our own world! How could
so many have missed it? How could it be that *even we* almost missed it?"

During the early first century, in the days of Peter, John, and a rapidly growing church, numerous Old Testament prophecies were being
directly fulfilled through Yeshua's earthly ministry. So, in real time,

and in the lives of real people who were eking out their existence in the
midst of real life—the world largely missed what had been right before
their eyes regarding the prophetic explosion that was occurring in their
midst. The vast majority of their religious "leaders" missed it as well.
In fact, a number of those professed elites were even involved, directly
or indirectly, in the betrayal and crucifixion of Yeshua![146]

While it's tempting to adopt a judgmental attitude toward the people of the first century, please understand, our generation is doing the
same thing now. That's the reason this book has been written.

The vast majority of the billions of people who populate the earth
today don't seem to comprehend the biblical prophecies that are rapidly developing before them. Most of these prophetic outbreaks have
taken life only in *our* generation, with most of them having occurred
in only the last several decades. Might the lack of "spiritual eyesight"
be related to so many who seem to be missing all this?

UNPARALLELED

The incomparable expansion of technology is one of the strongest
prophetic signs of just how close we are to the return of Yeshua. That
undeniable sharp upsurge began in the early 1950s, only a couple of
years after Israel's miraculous return to the Middle East.[147] I don't
think that correlation is a coincidence, do you?

Following Israel's prophesied return, the upwelling of global knowledge included all manner of nuclear technology, computers, the Internet,
and the advent of information being globally exchanged instanta-
neously, 24 hours a day, not to mention universal cell phone usage, deep
space exploration, satellite warfare, laser warfare, advanced bio-warfare,
drone warfare, satellite communications and weapons guidance, deep-
fake *video and audio*, holographic imaging, virtual reality (VR), and the
dawning of highly advanced artificial intelligence (AI), as well as the
always advancing high speed transportation technologies.

But wait, there's more! We must also consider: biometric identification of human beings, the mapping of the human genome, rapidly

evolving mRNA technologies, sophisticated medical diagnostics, and robotic surgery. There's also Crispr-Cas9 genetic editing, as well as globally pervasive spying and Intel gathering.[148] And we certainly can't forget the advanced quantum physics exploration of CERN and other institutions of physics research that continually attempt to pierce the veil of the multiple dimensions of reality that a number of renowned physicists strongly believe exist.[149]

QUANTUM LEAP

Ponder the following mind-blowing perspectives concerning how quickly all of this is happening.

For the first six to ten thousand years of recorded history, right up until the early 1800s, humanity's only modes of transportation were walking, riding on beasts, and traveling in wagons and carriages pulled by those beasts.

It wouldn't be until almost sixty years after the appearance of the steam driven locomotive in 1825 that the first rudimentary "automobile" was invented, in 1886. It was almost another forty years before the more modern Model-T and Model-A automobiles (with top speeds of 45 mph and 65 mph respectively) became increasingly widespread. All of that occurred just about the same time propeller-driven airline travel was first becoming common. Yet, it was only a little over a hundred years ago (as late as 1915) that some American families were migrating to other regions of our continually evolving nation in horse-drawn covered wagons.[150]

Now, the advent of "driverless" automobiles is looming upon the horizon of our times.

Think about this little tidbit of the "mundane" realities of our lives: Today, more than 115,000 jetliners crisscross the globe every day, at altitudes of 20,000 to 40,000+ feet and average speeds of almost 600 miles per hour. This phenomenon goes on twenty-four hours a day, seven days a week…transporting a mass of people *each year* that adds up to more than half the planet's total population. Hardly anyone even considers the profound nature of what most of the world almost arrogantly takes for granted.[151]

So while today's "enlightened" population openly mocks the Word of God, the biblical predictions concerning each of these things are found within its pages (and in no other "religious book" on the planet), and those prophetic utterances continue to unfold—right before our eyes.

28

SCIENCE FICTION
BECOMES REALITY

*The marriage between these two constantly emerging technologies
might ultimately prove to be prophetically devastating.*

In our current global climate, information, with its various modes
of presentation and consumption, is the most prized commodity to
the vast majority of humanity.

Within the sphere of all these massive techno advancements, our
current tech-giant elites have determined that over 90% of the world's
entire storehouse of recorded knowledge has been generated in only
the last several years of humanity's existence.[152]

The total amount of stored global data was estimated to be 44
zettabytes[153] at the dawn of 2020. By 2025, the amount of data generated *each day* is expected to reach 463 exabytes globally—ten times the
amount that previously took years to store. As a point of reference, all
the words ever spoken by every single human that has ever *lived*, from
the beginning of time until our current day, could easily fit into only
5 exabytes of stored data![154]

ARTIFICIAL INTELLIGENCE (AI)

Even among the scientific elite, most of the modern data storage
technology was considered an impossibility only a few decades ago.
Today this technology is being driven along and made possible by
ever-increasing advancements in the fields of *quantum computing*[155]
and *artificial intelligence*. In December 2023, IBM announced that
its latest advances in quantum computing will soon be able to solve

problems in only *minutes*. They are speaking of computations that would take today's supercomputers *millions of years* to accomplish![156] However, we are just now beginning to understand that the marriage between the two constantly emerging technologies of AI and quantum computing might ultimately prove to be prophetically devastating.[157]

The foregoing concerns are not just the ramblings of a pastor authoring a book titled *Eyes to See*. Rather, they are the concerns of much smarter people than I, people involved in creating, financing, marketing, and deploying this technology.

Consider Elon Musk's warnings in a September 2023 *NBC News* article. Mr. Musk is a prominent name in the fields of AI development, finance, and innovation, yet even he expressed profound trepidation at how these advancements may eventually be used.

Elon Musk: "**The consequences of AI going wrong are severe** so we have to be proactive rather than reactive," Musk told a press gaggle after attending what he called a "historic" meeting. "The question is really one of **civilizational risk**. It's not like… one group of humans versus another. It's like, hey, this is something that's **potentially risky for all humans everywhere**," said Musk. "**There is some chance** that is above zero that **AI will kill us all**. I think it's low. But **if there's some chance**, I think we should also **consider the fragility of human civilization**."[158] (Emphasis added)

Also consider this September 2023 report, cited on several mainstream media sites, concerning a *US Senate AI Insight Forum*.

Leading technology ethicist Tristan Harris spoke with Fox News Digital on the sidelines of the Senate's inaugural AI Insight Forum. Lawmakers **heard from tech giants** like Elon Musk and Mark Zuckerberg, as **well as union leaders** Liz Shuler and Randi Weingarten and experts like Harris and others about where they think AI is headed and how to be best prepared for it.

"When Senator Schumer asked everyone, '**Does the government need to get involved to regulate AI?**' Every single person including **all the CEOs**, Elon, Zuckerberg etc., **raised their hand to say yes.**"[159] (Emphasis added)

By December 2023, Joe Biden's White House issued an unprecedented Executive Order that had many experts in the fields of medicine, manufacturing, and government reeling from the potential risks and even *danger* to the populace at large.

> In an audacious move, the White House recently issued a **staggering 111-page executive order** on Artificial Intelligence.
>
> Typically, executive orders are concise directives, prompting federal agencies to craft specific, detailed regulations. **However, this sweeping document** reflects the worldview that AI **isn't just a technological advancement;** it's an **existential societal threat** and **only the government** holds the **keys to our technological salvation.**[160] (Emphasis added)

As you can see, the tech explosions of quantum computing, which go hand-in-hand with burgeoning AI, are causing rumblings of panic from several prominent tech inventors and AI stakeholders. The technologies of today are historically unprecedented, because they were yesterday's science fiction.[161]

Let me be clear. I'm neither opposed to the reality of advancing technology, nor to AI in general. In fact, I am authoring this book with the use of our latest and most advanced technologies. I'm utilizing a high-speed computer and cloud storage systems, powered by a high-speed Internet connection that enables me to access information storehouses all over the world in mere seconds.

And don't forget, every time we use voice assistants like the currently popular Alexa and Siri, voice-to-text technology, certain features on our cell phones, and even some household appliances…we are using AI. We also currently use many other forms of "weaker AI," and have done so for years. They are called *search engines*. In fact, the collection of weak AI that's been in use for the last several decades is simply too lengthy for me to catalogue in these few pages. But the truth of the matter is that almost all of us are using AI in some form, whether we know it or not. It has simply become a part of what we do, and, in many cases, who we are as a culture.

However, I am also keenly aware of biblical prophecy and the part that integrated technologies play in the last days, and how evil people will deploy those techno wonders for their own villainous desires. Those are the things about which I'm most concerned.

- But [Jesus] replied, "When evening comes, you say, 'The weather will be fair, for the sky is red,' and in the morning, 'Today it will be stormy, for the sky is red and overcast.' You **know how to interpret** the appearance of **the sky**, but **not the signs of the times**. (Matthew 16:2–3, BSB; emphasis and brackets added)
- These are the numbers of the divisions of the armed troops who came to David in Hebron to turn the kingdom of Saul over to him, according to the word of the LORD… Of Issachar, **men who had understanding of the times**, to **know what Israel ought to do.** (1 Chronicles 12:23, 32, emphasis added)

I regularly pray that Yeshua will give me the *eyes to see*, not only so I will not be deceived, but to accurately keep God's people up to date, faithful, and vigilant.

After all, the entire human race has the root of the problem now encoded within the deepest recesses of our own genetics. Our ancient parents ate from the "tree of the knowledge of good and evil," the very thing they were warned not to do. Now look where we are. The proverbial "Pandora's Box" has been laid wide open, and there appears to be no human way to close and seal the lid.

29

APPROXIMATING GOD

Here's the bottom line: Today's technology explosion
shows no signs of slowing down.

US Navy footage showing what appears to be a type of alien technology has, by now, been viewed by much of the world, even by means of several mainstream media sources. A growing number of prominent people are serious about claiming this is nothing short of an alien incursion. In 2023, U.S. Congressman Tim Burchett chimed in.

> Rep. Tim Burchett, who sits on the House Oversight Committee involved in UFO (or UAP's unidentified anomalous phenomena) hearings, said he was shown **classified footage** that hasn't been released to the public. Burchett speculated extraterrestrial life forms could have technology that humanity "can't handle…"
>
> "If they're out there, they're out there, and if they have this kind of technology, then **they could turn us into a charcoal briquette**," Burchett said.
>
> "And if they can travel light years or at the speeds that we've seen, and physics as we know it, **fly underwater**, don't show a heat trail, things like that, then **we are vastly out of our league…We couldn't fight them off if we wanted to**."[162] (Emphasis added)

UFO Official: Alarming Activity 'in Our Backyard'
"Physicist Seán Kirkpatrick, director of the U.S. government's **UFO analysis office**, recently disclosed what he said is **evidence**

of unidentified flying object (UFO) activity **"in our backyard."** Kirkpatrick, who leads the All-Domain Anomaly Resolution Office (AARO), proposed that the source of this activity could either be a foreign power or **extraterrestrial beings.**

"None of the **hundreds of military UFO reports** analyzed by his office **have been positively linked** to foreign activities. Senior defense **officials have also ruled out** the possibility of secret U.S. programs or experimental aircraft…The **prevailing evidence** seems to align more with the startling explanation of **extraterrestrial involvement.**

This revelation reflects a **broader shift** in the **government's tone** on UFO phenomena. Former presidents, senior defense officials, and members of Congress have **departed** from historical practices of **obfuscation and ridicule,** openly considering **extraordinary explanations** for perplexing UFO incidents."[163] (Emphasis added)

Then there was the following report from late November 2023, claiming that a mysterious wing of the CIA currently possesses two completely intact UFO vehicles, among a number of others in lesser condition.

Report: CIA Office Recovered UFO Crashes for Decades

A **secretive** wing of the **Central Intelligence Agency** has been working to recover **"non-human craft"** from crash sites around the globe for decades.

The Office of Global Access (OGA), which is part of the Central Intelligence Agency's Science and Technology Directorate, has been coordinating UFO retrieval efforts since 2003.

"There's at least nine vehicles. There were different circumstances for different ones," one source said. "It has to do with the physical condition they're in. If it crashes, there's a lot of damage done. Others, **two of them**, are completely **intact.**"[164] (Emphasis added)

GODLIKE UNIFICATION OF HUMANITY

At about the same time these imposing claims were being made, the world was also inundated with musings from Harvard Physics Professor Avi Loeb. Dr. Loeb is a physicist who earned his PhD from the Hebrew University of Jerusalem, and the Chief Scientist who heads the *Galileo Project* of Harvard University.[165]

> Harvard physicist searching for UFO evidence says humanity will view alien intelligence **like 'God'**
>
> Harvard professor Avi Loeb predicted that the scientific **discovery of an alien civilization**—one that may potentially be billions of years old—**will prompt humanity to unify.**
>
> That doesn't mean that the realization, on a humanity-wide level, of "neighbors" in the universe would not be a shocking event, Loeb said. In fact, it **might be a profoundly spiritual experience.**
>
> Loeb said that it is conceivable that an **ultra-advanced civilization** may appear to humans to have **godlike powers.**
>
> "You can imagine that the super human civilization that understands how to **unify quantum mechanics and gravity** might actually be able to **create a baby universe in the laboratory**, a quality that we **assign to God** in religious texts…"
>
> "A very advanced scientific civilization is a good **approximation to God**," Loeb said.[166] (Emphasis added)

TO BE CLEAR

I'm not a "back-channel" conspiracy theorist, making the types of claims that even some of our current government officials, physicists, and scientists are making regarding UFOs and aliens being among us. Far from it.

I'm merely pointing out that, for many decades, this possibility has been a concern of a number of well-known researchers, authors, theologians, television programs, UFO symposiums, and science websites. There are even reports from credible sources about Top Secret US military craft being manufactured that are "anti-gravity" stealth aircraft (specifically, the TR-3B Anti-Gravity Aircraft) created from reverse engineering UFO spacecraft.[167] So now, even the global "intelligencia," like a number of others, are publicly expressing their increasing concerns.

I am convinced these "facts" are being spread by agents of deception, and have shared this belief in sermons, radio and TV interviews, my own broadcasts, and in a variety of written material. I am persuaded that this phenomenon is related to the demonic outpouring of the last days, prophesied throughout the Word of God.

> For **false** christs and **false** prophets will arise and perform great **signs** and **wonders**, so as to **lead astray**, if possible, **even the elect**. (Matthew 24:24, emphasis added)
>
> The **coming of the lawless one** is by the activity of **Satan** with **all power** and **false signs** and **wonders**. (2 Thessalonians 2:9, emphasis added)

Could the world truly be on the verge of a *unification* of global humanity that seemingly brings about a "profoundly spiritual experience," one that is "godlike" in its appearance and existence? Think about it; where have we heard this before? In truth, that idea mirrors the 2,000 year old words of Revelation 13, which we are assured will occur in the last days, just before the return of Yeshua. No other book of "faith" on the planet has ever dared to predict such things! Do you see the connections?

WE ARE NOT "IN CHARGE"

In July 2023, former *Fox News* anchor and commentator Tucker Carlson hosted the Family Leadership Summit in Iowa, where several thousand were in attendance.

After interviewing 2024 Republican presidential contenders, Carlson himself spoke about his developing faith when he was interviewed by Vander Plaats.[168] Carlson revealed that even though he doesn't consider himself a "particularly faithful or virtuous person," he began reading through the Bible in February. At the time of the July conference he asserted that he had read the entire Old Testament and was working his way through the New Testament. Carlson then shocked his audience by claiming that during the study of the Scriptures he learned "there are unseen forces acting on people. People, while they have freewill, are not really in charge of the arc of history at all." [169]

He continued, "People's choices matter. You need to do certain things and not do other things. On the other hand, you are not in charge. You are being acted upon by a world you can't see."[170]

Carlson then related that biblical fact to the political realm, saying, "A lot of these [political] issues are symbols of this much larger battle."[171]

Imagine that, by simply reading the Word of God and then opening his eyes to the world around him…Carlson suddenly had the "eyes to see." Once again, no other book except the Bible could do that.

30

GLOBAL MOVERS
AND SHAKERS

*In light of our recent exploration, these warnings don't seem so
innocuous anymore, do they?*

Though many are excited about all this high-tech progress, there is still global concern regarding the fear of runaway technological advances.

The modern equivalent of an "old" nuclear arms race has been sparked by international military powers who are beginning to grapple with the quantum leap of the world's latest tech advancements. Items being seriously discussed today are no longer the stuff of dark and sketchy conspiracy sites; they are now *front and center* in the global halls of government, science, mainstream media, and military research.

Have a look at the following media excerpts, most of them having first appeared as headline articles, that were written while putting this book together.

China, US race to unleash killer AI robot soldiers as military power hangs in balance (October 2023)

AI technology is **the new arms** race pitting the world's powers against each other, experts agree.

China and the U.S. are locked in a race to develop new weapons **controlled by artificial intelligence**, a battle that could determine the **world's balance of power**.

Like the **nuclear arms race** before it, the **AI arms race** comes with **constant dangers**. The report warns of **"killer robots"**—AI weapons such as subs, warships, fighter jets, drones and **combat vehicles** that can operate **autonomously**.

While such technology has the potential to be **a force multiplayer** on the battlefield, its ability to **make decisions independent of human** input also poses serious risks.[172] (Emphasis added)

FBI chief warns that terrorists can unleash AI in terrifying new ways (October 2023)

The chiefs of the **FBI and Britain's MI5** have raised concerns about the **enormous and terrifying potential** artificial intelligence poses **for terrorists**, saying the technology adds "**a level of threat** to that we haven't previously encountered."[173] (Emphasis added)

Former Google Boss Eric Schmidt Raises Alarm on AI Development, Compares to Nuclear Weapons (November 2023)

Schmidt cautioned that **AI could pose a threat to humanity** within the next five to ten years, especially if it reaches a stage where it can make **autonomous decisions**. This estimation narrows down the previously believed timeline of around 20 years, with some experts now suggesting that this **critical point** could be as soon **as just two to four years away**.[174] (Emphasis added)

House hearing on AI deepfakes (November 2023)

"These things are only going to become more prevalent," Mace warned of **AI-generated "deepfakes"**

Rep. Nancy Mace, R-S.C., is calling for solutions to the **wide array of dangers** posed by online content falsified using Artificial Intelligence (AI)—known as "deepfakes."

"These things are only going to become **more prevalent** if we don't start discussing the problem and talking to AI experts on how to address deepfakes now and in the future...

"Ninety percent of AI deepfakes are pornographic in nature," Mace said, listing off the dangers of AI-faked content. "There is a significant amount of child pornographic material…being generated, there's revenge porn.

"And you think about the election next year, and what deepfakes might be generated to come out to sway an election.

"…We have to make sure we have the technology to be able to detect this is fake, you know, and is it going to get so advanced, that we won't be able to detect that it's fake material."[175] (Emphasis added)

Now consider this next "soul-searching" headline, and the potential ramifications of the AI conundrums that it examines.

AI Will Shape Your Soul: But how is up to us. (September 2023)

It's the way these [AI] chatbots do what they do—respond in a friendly first-person voice, reason, make art, have conversation—that distinguishes them from an AI algorithm that mines medical records or a collection of faces….

That's altogether human. No wonder one Google researcher claimed his company's AI was conscious.

The technology, we're told, will get only more advanced. AI chatbots will continue to, as ChatGPT put it to me, "exhibit behaviors indistinguishable from humans."

Since 2016, millions of people have used the AI personal chatbot app Replika to reanimate dead relatives or fall in love with new companions; testimonial articles about "My Therapist, the Robot" and "I learned to love the bot" abound.[176] (Emphasis added)

And then there was this unnerving mainstream media article. "Artificial Intelligence and US nuclear weapons decisions" (November 2023)

The Pentagon announced a new tactical nuclear bomb program on Oct. 27 [2023]. Rep. Mike Rogers, R-Ala., and Sen. John Wicker, R-Miss., welcomed the new bomb because it "will better allow the Air Force to reach hardened and deeply-buried targets" in Europe and the Pacific.

And by the time the bomb is ready after the late 2020s, **AI may have a hand in how and when it's detonated.**[177] (Emphasis added)

What if AI could actually become indistinguishable from a real human, and could accomplish that feat "on its own"? Apparently, these are distinct possibilities according to AI experts.

AI gives birth to AI: Scientists say machine intelligence now capable of replicating without humans (December 2023)

"So in the future, we believe that these, the large and the small [**AI models**], they **will collaborate together** and **then build** a complete intelligence ecosystem," said Chen, a U.C. Davis professor and Aizip co-founder.

"Our technology is a breakthrough in the sense that for the **first time**, we have designed a fully automated pipeline," he said. It **"can design an AI model without human intervention** in the process."[178] (Emphasis added)

Now have a look at what Yeshua Himself told us about the last days. In light of what we've been exploring, these warnings don't seem so innocent anymore, do they?

Men's **hearts [will be] failing them from fear** and the expectation of those things which **are coming on the earth**, for the **powers of the heavens** [demonic and angelic][179] will be **shaken.**[180] (Luke 21:26, NKJV; emphasis added)

For **false christs** and false prophets will arise and perform **great signs and wonders,** so as to **lead astray,** if possible, **even the elect.**[181] (Matthew 24:24, emphasis added)

When it is evening you say, "It will be fair weather, for the sky is red"; and in the morning, "It will be foul weather today, for the sky is red and threatening." Hypocrites! You know how to discern the face of the sky, **but you cannot discern the signs of the times.** (Matthew 16:2–3, NKJV; emphasis added)

For as in the days before the flood, they were eating and drinking, marrying and giving in marriage, until the day that Noah entered the ark, and did not know until the flood came and took them all away, **so also will the coming of the Son of Man be.** (Matthew 24:38–39, NKJV; emphasis added)

PANDORA'S BOX

Today's technology explosion shows no signs of slowing down, and that's not even taking into consideration what's on the horizon, both wonders and evils we have yet to imagine.

In fact, tech is advancing so rapidly that much of the information concerning communication, information, and transportation technology in this book will be obsolete in a few short years, replaced by further advancements. So, if you're reading this chapter years after its original publication, you are most likely being highly entertained by what you're reading concerning our current day![182]

Then again...we are presently living in a world that has already outrageously outdated the world of just a couple of decades ago, just as the Word of God (and only the Word of God) prophesied.

31

UNPRECEDENTED

*Regardless of naysayers' claims, the Bible
did not fail to speak to any of this.*

Consider for a moment that no generation in history prior to ours could have grasped the possibility of the entire planet watching global events unfold in real-time, as foretold 2,000 years ago in various biblical texts. Yet, while we seldom even marvel at this reality, that very phenomenon occurs around the clock, day in and day out.

The images of those day-to-day events are displayed on screens we carry in our hands, mount on our walls, lay in our laps, or sit on our desktops. Sometimes we observe them from digital instruments strapped to our wrists. We are able to keep abreast of those images almost everywhere we go, including when we soar through the skies at 30,000+ feet. We can hardly escape the myriad of "living images" continually streaming before us.

Furthermore, no other generation before us could even conceive the reality of a planet-wide, human identification system, and the technological wizardry required to bring it about. Not to mention a worldwide allegiance to a singular man who, according to Revelation 13–14, will eventually preside over a global government.[183]

The tech systems required for that monumental task seemed unachievable for almost 2,000 years after John wrote those words. We are the *only generation* to possess the technical know-how to do that very thing, and we are currently laying forth the plans to implement those types of global human tracking systems. The technology the Bible predicted is now advancing deeper into the endless abyss of Orwellian scenarios of real-time application, with every tick of the clock.[184]

Today we take for granted what seemed to be purely science fiction just decades ago. This is all a part of our everyday lives, with technology growing by the minute, and we are *the first to see it all.* By the way—think of how many times you read those words as this book progresses!

THE FOUNDATIONAL QUESTION

In light of what we've considered thus far, we now must ask one of the most crucial biblical questions of them all. It's a query that goes straight to the Bible's relevance and veracity: *Does the Word of God truly reveal this unprecedented and exponential eruption of technology that's reshaping the entire human experience?*

If the answer to that question is "no," then consider the ramifications of the necessary follow-up question: If the Bible *doesn't* address these technological advancements, how could we ever again trust the Word of God to be personally relevant?

The short answer is, *we could not.* It would be inconceivable that the Bible would say nothing of such monumental occurrences, as well as their enormous consequences.[185]

I can assure you, regardless of those who doubt it, the Bible did not fail to speak to any of this! The subject is addressed in both the Old and New Testaments. The Bible did not miss it! Rather, *we* are the ones who've been consistently missing what's right before our eyes.[186]

In the next chapter, we'll look at a prime example that Yeshua Himself brought forth about this topic, and how prophecy collides with humanity's last days.

And He told us this phenomenon would occur very soon before His glorious return.

32

THEN THE END
WILL COME

*There can be no doubt, Yeshua's prophecy was about our days
and beyond! His words could be referring to nothing less.*

There is a well-known passage in the New Testament that is irre-
futably aimed at the signs accompanying the end of time and the
promised return of the Son of Man.

In that passage, Yeshua speaks of the technology explosion accompanying the last days. Close attention must be paid to His assertions,
or else the truth of that statement is easy to miss, as so many down
through the ages have. However, for those who have eyes to see it, we
discover a declaration of a certain technical wonder coming to life, and
only in these end times. [187]

Here is Yeshua's prophetic utterance, as found in Matthew 24.

> And **this gospel** of the kingdom will be **preached in the whole
> world** as a testimony to all nations, **and then the end will
> come.** (Matthew 24:14, NIV; emphasis added)

In this statement, Yeshua reveals the fact that monumentally
important technology would burst forth in the days just before His
return. He further indicated that these technological developments
would serve to advance the Gospel around the world. He also proclaimed this unprecedented occurrence would be a definitive sign to
the generation living in the *last days*.

It's important to note that Yeshua's announcement was not a prophecy

137

for *His* time, or even the next few generations following. No, He was specifically referring to *end time* events, occurring just before His second coming. His prophetic utterance is tied to His own words "and then the end will come." Other than the scholarly attestation that follows, I've included six others at this endnote that verify what I have stated here.[188]

Expositor's Greek Testament:

> Matthew 24:14 asserts the same thing with regard to the preaching of the gospel of the kingdom: time for preaching it in **the whole world**, of **all nations, before the end.**[189] (Emphasis added)

As of this writing, we can safely say the "end of the age," and Yeshua's return, have not yet come. Though the New Testament discusses His Kingdom being eventually established on the earth, it has not yet happened, but we are beginning to see His prophecy being fulfilled in our time. And since Yeshua was indeed speaking of "the end," He *had to be* speaking of at least our day, and perhaps beyond.[190]

THE PERVASIVE GOSPEL

Think about the world in which we currently live. Every hour of every day, for the last several decades, the Gospel has been preached in every nation and tribe on the planet.

Essentially, with the push of a few buttons on our digital communication devices, nearly every Christian can share the life-giving message of Yeshua HaMashiach from almost anywhere in the world. No other generation before us has ever experienced this phenomenon. There can be no doubt, Yeshua's prophecy recorded in Matthew 24:14 was about our days and beyond.

Next, let's examine the Old Testament book of Daniel. By applying the same contextual approach we just took with Matthew 24:14, we can discover exactly what Daniel 12:4 was telling us within the similarly coded language of his words.

That passage in Daniel is one of the Bible's most important keys to understanding the world-changing technological advancements of the last days. And, of all things, we find that Yeshua's words in Matthew 24 have a direct connection to Daniel's vision!

33

DANIEL SPEAKS

But you, Daniel, shut up the words and seal the book,
until the time of the end. Many shall run to and fro,
and knowledge shall increase. (Daniel 12:4)

The book of Daniel is the definitive apocalyptic declaration of the Old Testament, in much the same way the book of Revelation is to the New Testament.[191]

For example, a number of the first declarations of Daniel's closing chapter sound almost like they've come straight out of the New Testament, especially from certain parts of the book of Revelation.[192]

Consider the first four verses of Daniel 12:

And at that time shall Michael stand up, the great prince which standeth for the children of thy people: and there **shall be a time of trouble, such as never was** since there was a nation even to that same time: and at that time your people **shall be delivered**, every one that shall be found written in the book.

And many of them that sleep in the dust of the earth shall awake, **some to everlasting life, and some to shame and everlasting contempt.** And they that be wise shall shine as the brightness of the firmament; and **they that turn many** to righteousness as the stars for ever and ever.

And those who are wise shall shine like the brightness of the sky above; and **those who turn many to righteousness,** like the stars forever and ever.

But thou, O Daniel, shut up the words, and seal the book [scroll], even to **the time of the end:** many shall run to and fro, and knowledge shall be increased. (Daniel 12:1–4, KJV; emphasis and brackets added)

Our historical generation is now experiencing the events discussed in the previously sealed scroll of Daniel.

NO LONGER A MYSTERY

Ours is the first generation to realize the mysterious visions in the book of Revelation are either happening now, or will in the very near future. In fact, *all* of the technologies required to bring these things to fruition—either implied, or directly revealed—are right before us.

Consider the prophecies of Revelation 13–14 alone. The entire world will worship one man, and one system. The entire world will not be able to buy, sell, or trade without taking "the mark." These events require super-advanced technology, such as the ability to track everyone's movements, expenditures, bank accounts, food purchases, and so forth. Also consider the assertions made in Revelation about the "beast's" ability to make images "live and breathe," or to "call fire down from heaven."

All of these prophecies require technology that, for the past 2,000 years, was pure science fiction. Only the Word of God contained such seemingly improbable assertions! Yet, we are the first to use all these technologies, and they are exponentially magnifying right before our eyes.[193]

Previous to our historical generation, these events seemed laughably impossible, but now, many students of the Bible agree with the assertions I am making here. Few are laughing now, as we discuss the technological wonders that are part of our everyday lives, spoken of only in the Bible, and unbelievably, over 2,000 years ago!

THE COLOSSAL ISSUE

So here's the question that a number of curious Bible students ask: *Did Daniel's vision reveal today's advanced technology?* It assuredly did, and more than likely went even further beyond! Yet, he was not allowed to disclose the details that John would later unveil in the book of Revelation. In fact, a number of renowned scholars believe the "unsealed" scroll of Revelation chapter 5 is the scroll originally sealed by Daniel.[194]

The purpose of the *coded* language found in Daniel 12 was a message designed to give instruction and inspiration throughout all generations to come, but would only be fulfilled in the last days.

Daniel's mysterious prophecy is happening now, in our lifetime.

34

DANIEL
SAW OUR DAY

What you must realize is that Daniel saw our day.

In analyzing specific words in Daniel 12:4, we can determine the message Daniel revealed, and the relevance of that message to our own historical generation.

First, a quick note to the reader. The extraordinary advancement of end-time technology and its contextual application of Daniel's prophecy was covered in my last book, *Yeshua Protocol*. If you've read that book, you should recognize the information in this chapter as an edited synopsis of that study.

Now, observe the key words of prophecy in Daniel 12 again, emphasized by underlining.

"<u>Many</u> shall <u>run to and fro</u>, and <u>knowledge</u> shall <u>increase</u>." (Daniel 12:4)

UNCOUNTABLE MULTITUDES

Daniel uses the word "many" to the massive number of people travelling around the world in these last days. In the Old Testament text, that word is the Hebrew word *rab*.

Strong's Exhaustive Concordance defines *rab* this way:

Abundant (in quantity, size, age, number, rank, quality), **exceedingly** populous, **to multiply**...[195] (Emphasis added)

In other biblical passages, the Hebrew word *rab* is translated 462 times and often indicates exceedingly large numbers of things. Most of the time the implication is that the number in question is *practically uncountable.*[196]

There is a particularly poignant way that *rab* is used in the very first book of the Bible. The way it is employed in Genesis gives us a clue as to its fullest meaning:

> The LORD saw how **great** [*rab* - globally **ubiquitous**] the wickedness of the human race had become **on the earth** [through an **exponential growth** process, over time], and that every inclination of the thoughts of the human heart was only evil all the time. (Genesis 6:5, NIV; emphasis and brackets added)

CIRCUMNAVIGATING THE GLOBE

In an archaic form of the English language, the Hebrew word *shuwt* is translated as meaning "to and fro." It refers to *travelling about, over long distances*—often meaning to encompass the entire globe, or at least very large swaths of it.[197]

Examples of the use of *shuwt* in biblical passages are as follows:

- For the eyes of the LORD **range throughout the earth** [*shuwt*] to strengthen those whose hearts are fully committed to him. (2 Chronicles 16:9, NIV; emphasis and brackets added)
- And the LORD said to Satan, "Where have you come from?" Satan answered the LORD, "**From roaming throughout the earth**, going back and forth on it. [*shuwt*]" (Job 2:2, NIV; emphasis added)

What you must realize is that Daniel did indeed see our day! He saw the extraordinary rise in travel, communication, and information exchange technologies, and the global chaos that eventually came as a result of them.

KNOWLEDGE AND TECHNOLOGY

The Hebrew word *daath* is translated as the word "knowledge," and is also rich with hidden meaning.[198] Observe a couple of examples of how *daath* is used elsewhere in Scripture.

> In the middle of the garden were the tree of life and **the tree of the knowledge** of good and evil. (Genesis 2:9, NIV; emphasis added)
>
> And [God] has filled him with the Spirit of God, with **skill**, with intelligence, **with knowledge**, and with **all craftsmanship**. (Exodus 35:31, emphasis and brackets added)

The ancient Hebrew text does not use the exact word *technology*, since that word, as we understand it, had not yet been invented. But the word *technology* comes from the word *knowledge*, and you cannot look up the etymology of *technology* without finding *knowledge* in practically every explanation.[199]

EXPONENTIAL INCREASE

Daniel uses the Hebrew word *rabah* in the part of his prophecy that states (in most English translations) "knowledge will increase." *Rabah* is the word translated to English as *increase*.[200] But its actual use in other scripture passages, outside of Daniel, is much deeper than merely "increasing." As an example of exactly what *rabah* means, observe some of the first usages of the word in Genesis. In these verses, *rabah* is translated in English as the word "multiply." *Rabah* always speaks of multiplying through *exponential* increases.

- And God blessed them, saying, "Be fruitful **and multiply and fill** the waters in the seas, and let birds **multiply on the earth**." (Genesis 1:22, emphasis added)
- And God blessed them. And God said to them, "**Be fruitful and multiply and fill the earth** and subdue it, and have

dominion over the fish of the sea and over the birds of
the heavens and over every living thing that moves on the
earth." (Genesis 1:28, emphasis added)

- When **man began to multiply on the face of the land** and
daughters were born to them…. (Genesis 6:1, emphasis
added)
- Bring out every kind of living creature that is with you—
the birds, the animals, and all the creatures that move along
the ground—**so they can multiply on the earth and be
fruitful and increase in number** on it." (Genesis 8:17,
emphasis added)

Daniel clearly stated that in the last days knowledge would flour-
ish, through an explosion of *exponential increase*. To illustrate Daniel's
prophetic accuracy, consider the following.

Bell's Commentary on the Bible (2017)

From the time Christ died to the year 1700, knowledge on
earth doubled. It took 1700 years for all of the previously accumulated knowledge to double on earth. In the year 1900 it
doubled again, only 200 years later. In the year 1950 it doubled again, only 50 years later. In the year 1970 it doubled
again, only 20 years later. **Today information doubles every
2 years.** Prognosticators are pointing to a day **very soon** when
knowledge on earth will double every single day (emphasis
added).[201]

As of the writing of this book, accumulated knowledge is said to
already be doubling every 13 months. However, because of giant leaps
in tech development on the horizon, accumulated knowledge is soon
expected to double *every 12 hours*. I'm convinced Daniel saw it. How
about you?[202]

♦♦♦

THE WORD-SWAP SHOCKER

Now let's do an illuminating exercise in linguistics.

We'll substitute *many, to and fro, increase, knowledge,* and the *time of the end,* as they are found in Daniel 12:4. Each replacement term is a legitimate use of the original Hebrew words, as evidenced from previously cited Scripture. In so doing, see if you notice what a number of current students of the Word are now detecting.

> But you, Daniel, shut up the words and seal the book, until the [days just before the return of Yeshua]. [Vast masses of people] shall [travel throughout the earth], and [knowledge and technology] shall [exponentially multiply]. (Daniel 12:4, brackets added)

Yeshua, of course, knew the truth of Daniel's words, which is why He quoted from Daniel 12 in His discourse on the Mount of Olives, found in Matthew 24. In that sermon, Yeshua pointedly interpreted Daniel to be speaking about the time of the end...*our days.* If you remember nothing else about Daniel 12, please remember this vital truth, so you may relate to others your belief concerning what *Jesus* knew about Daniel's words.[203]

Modern scholars, and God's people in general, have little excuse as to the contextual discernment of Daniel's prophecy. That prophecy and its fulfillment were intended for a specific generation—the generation of the end time.

Our generation.

TIPPING
THE HOURGLASS

Thus says the Lord God, "When I gather the house of Israel from the peoples among whom they are scattered, and will manifest My holiness in them in the sight of the nations, then they will live in their land which I gave to My servant Jacob. They will live in it securely; and they will build houses, plant vineyards and live securely when I execute judgments upon all who scorn them round about them. Then they will know that I am the Lord their God." (Ezekiel 28:25–26)

35

HOLY WAR

The entire planet will be under our law, there will be
no more Jews or Christian traitors. [204]
—*Hamas* Commander Mahmoud al-Zahar

As I was writing this chapter, the world was several months out and still reeling from the October 7, 2023, *Hamas* surprise assault upon Israel. [205] And I imagine the planet will continue to stagger in the midst of that travesty until the coming of Yeshua. I say this because, in the learned estimations of most reliable biblical scholars, this is what the Word of God succinctly declares.

That massive, invasion massacre was the largest single-day murder of Jewish people since the Holocaust, and the most lethal singular day in modern Israel's 75-year history.[206] The horrid ordeal has also been likened, in many ways, to the terrorist attacks leveled upon the United States of America on September 11, 2001. However, statistically, the attack on Israel was 13 times worse than 9–11.[207]

Following are samples of the distressing headlines pummeling the world during the first two weeks after the attack. What you'll read is the rhetoric of which World Wars are born. This is also the contextual revelation of a number of biblically prophetic declarations found throughout scripture.

'Moderate' Palestinian Authority Calls to **Murder Jews**: 'Fight the Jews' and 'Kill' Them All[208] (*Breitbart*, emphasis added)
    Israel is **only** the **first target**, warns **Hamas** commander: Mahmoud al-Zahar: "The entire planet will be under our law,

151

there will be **no more Jews or Christian** traitors."[209] (*Jerusalem Post*, emphasis added)

The Israel-Gaza war could possibly spread to become a wider regional conflict and **drag in more countries** amid the war in Ukraine and other geopolitical tensions, **leading to World War 3**[210] (*NDV-TV*, emphasis added)

Attacks on U.S. troops in Middle East **ramp up** as Israel **conflict escalates**[211] (*Politico*, emphasis added)

Iran Threatens to **Drag the U.S. Into Regional Holy War**[212] (*The Daily Beast*, emphasis added)

Iran threatens Israel over looming ground offensive in Gaza: report - Iran FM **warns Israel of 'huge earthquake'** should Lebanon's Hezbollah get involved[213] (Fox News, emphasis added)

As **Iran threatens preemptive strike**, Biden must deter with total force[214] (*New York Post*, emphasis added)

Iran's Khamenei threatens US as Pentagon readies 2,000 troops for region[215] (*Al-Monitor*, emphasis added)

Iran issues stark warning to U.S. over arms shipment to Israel: Suggests that there may be **adverse consequences** or tensions resulting from such actions[216] (*KITV-ABC News*, emphasis added)

Putin cautions Israel against using tactics in Gaza **like Nazi siege** of Leningrad[217] (*Reuters*, emphasis added)

Israel war: **Kremlin threatens nuclear war** after Biden compares Russia to Hamas[218] (*Washington Examiner—Gazette.com*, emphasis added)

Turkey's Erdogan says Israel's operations in Gaza **'amounting to genocide'**: After slow rapprochement with Jerusalem, **president appears to reverse course**, accuses Israel of 'attacks against civilians'[219] (*Times of Israel*, emphasis added)

North Korea Threatens US for Sending Aircraft Carrier to South Korea[220] (*Bloomberg*, emphasis added)

North Korea raises the specter of nuclear strike over US aircraft carrier's arrival in South Korea[221] (*Associated Press [AP]*, emphasis added)

China Warns Israel Has 'Gone Beyond' Self-Defense in War[222] (*Newsweek*, emphasis added)

Analysis: **China and Russia find common cause** in Israel-Hamas crisis[223] (*Reuters*, emphasis added)

Gaza carnage spreads anger across Mideast, alarming US allies and threatening to widen conflict[224] (*Associated Press (AP)*, emphasis added)

Hamas Official: **We Will Repeat** October 7 Terror Attack **Until Israel is Annihilated**[225] (Breitbart, emphasis added)

Regardless of how this epic international clash turns out in the long run, or what has happened by the time you are reading this book, the entire affair is, at the very least, a prophetic run up to the ultimate return of Yeshua (Ezekiel 37–39, Luke 21, Zechariah 14). It could very well be that all of the biblically foretold harbingers of a coming multi-national war against Israel will converge much more quickly than a sizable number of the world's most renowned prophecy researchers could have imagined.

Since the October 2023 attacks on Israel, a myriad of people want to know exactly how all of these and other recent prophetic events might be linked.[226] With this question in mind, I'll outline several relevant biblical connections over the next few chapters.

Within those pages, you'll discover numerous scriptural links you've perhaps not seen before now. However, when you uncover the links, I believe your eyes will be opened to the stark reality of the eternal depths of the cosmic spiritual warfare in which we are currently engaged…

Just as Scripture has been warning us all along.

36

THE FIRST ONE

The return of Israel to the Middle East is a declaration
found only in the Living Word of God, well over
2,500 years before the event happened.

In the Old Testament, between the books of Deuteronomy and Zechariah, there are almost four dozen locations that speak of Israel's miraculous return to the land in the last days.[227] Many of those prophetic declarations are entire chapters in length.[228]

This biblical fact quite often shocks a number of Bible readers. Most have never considered there were that many specific prophecies concerning Israel's return. Yet, most of the related biblical assertions of the resurrection of the nation of Israel, geared toward a prescient point in history, are very straightforward. And the others are at least indirectly linked to the return of Israel by associational implications.[229]

But here's the foundational fact of the matter. Even *one* prophecy in the entire Bible declaring Israel's return to the land in the last days would be astounding on its own. After all, who would have dared to predict such an outlandish thing, thousands of years before it happened? Who could have guessed it was possible for such a national return to take place?[230] Who but God alone would have even thought to declare such an unbelievable event? *No one!*

Subsequently, one of the most astounding global events the world has ever witnessed was the resurrection of a nation that had been decimated, and its inhabitants scattered to the four corners of the world for over 2,000 years. Never has the world seen anything like it. For years, and even to this day, Israel has been the center of the geopolitical climate, and global news cycle. Not only was its resurrection foretold thousands of years before it happened, but it was also prophesied that the prophetic event would indeed disturb "the nations" to the point of a vitriolic outpouring of hatred against it.

THE FIRST OLD TESTAMENT PROPHECY

Let's examine the *first* prophecy predicting Israel's miraculous return. What is so striking about that initial prophecy is, even before the Children of Israel crossed the Jordan River in order to enter the Promised Land, it was proclaimed by Moses.

We find those words of Moses in the book of Deuteronomy. "But wait," you may ask, "how could that even be possible?" Even though a number of scholars still believe Deuteronomy was not written during Moses' lifetime, the prophecies in the book about Israel's return would still have been penned more than 2,000 years before that historic event occurred! [231]

Though this seemed impossible by human standards, we are the generation that's living right in the middle of the entire event! We are genuinely experiencing the supernatural!

The return of Israel to the Middle East is a declaration made over 2,500 years before the event happened, and it is found *only in the Word of God*. Our world is now within the first generation to see that prophecy literally fulfilled—in strikingly accurate detail. Yet, as is so often the case, a large portion of the world has no idea what they are witnessing.

Either that, or they despise the fact that it actually happened.

37

SO THAT
YOU MIGHT KNOW

*Moses made it clear that Yahweh meant this unprecedented event
to be a sign, not only to the Israelites, but to all the nations.*

Let's follow the amazing progression of prophecies articulated in
Deuteronomy. There, Moses begins by challenging his listeners to
name one example where the Lord delivered a specific people from
hundreds of years of slavery, subsequently turning them into a mighty
nation, a nation through which the Messiah would be brought to the
world.

Following is Moses' challenge...

For ask now of the days that are past, which were before you,
since the day that God created man on the earth, and ask from
one end of heaven to the other, whether such a great thing as
this has ever happened or was ever heard of. Did any people
ever hear the voice of a god speaking out of the midst of the
fire, as you have heard, and still live?

Or has any god ever attempted to go and take a nation for
himself from the midst of another nation, by trials, by signs,
by wonders, and by war, by a mighty hand and an outstretched
arm, and by great deeds of terror, all of which the LORD your
God did for you in Egypt before your eyes?

To you it was shown, that you might know that the LORD
is God; there is no other besides him. (Deuteronomy 4:32–35)

The event to which Moses is referring is on the verge of coming to life as he's speaking those words. Soon the birth of the nascent nation of Israel will take place, beginning at the foot of Mt. Sinai—through the giving of the Law—and eventually culminating with that new supernatural nation thriving in the midst of the land of Canaan.

Moses made it clear, Yahweh meant for this monumental occurrence to be a sign, not only to the Israelites, but to all the nations, until the end of the ages. In other words, Israel's very existence, from the beginning, was to be a perpetual and supernatural signal to the world that Yahweh, not Satan, is the rightful owner of all creation.[232]

DEUTERONOMY 29

Now, let's skip to the end of Deuteronomy.

Between chapters 4 and 29, Moses expounds upon the history of Israel's sojourning in the wilderness. He recapitulates the Ten Commandments in chapter 5, and gives other reminders of their past as well as new instruction and prophecies.

Also, throughout those chapters, he reminds the previously enslaved people that they will soon come into the land of blessing…a land they neither earned nor deserved; a land graciously granted to them by God. Within these declarations, Moses is always reminding them that if they did not live up to the promises and blessings Yahweh had given them, the hand of the Lord's protection would be lifted from them. With that "lifting" would come certain disaster to the nation of Israel. They would be uprooted from their land, and dispersed throughout the nations.

> …All the nations will say, "Why has the LORD done thus to this land? What caused the heat of this great anger?"
>
> Then people will say, "It is because they abandoned the covenant of the LORD, the God of their fathers, which he made with them when he brought them out of the land of Egypt, and went and served other gods and worshiped them,

gods whom they had not known and whom he had not allotted to them.

"Therefore the anger of the LORD was kindled against this land, bringing upon it all the curses written in this book, and **the LORD uprooted them from their land** in anger and fury and great wrath, and **cast them into another land**, as they are this day [slaves in Egypt]." (Deuteronomy 29:24–28, emphasis and brackets added)

As you read those verses of Scripture, keep in mind they were spoken to the people of Israel over five hundred years before the prophecy came to pass! This was undoubtedly a supernatural declaration, spoken in the power of the Holy Spirit through the mouth of Moses, and as history verifies, his prophecy did in fact take place.

And the world has never been the same since.

38

THE HUMANLY IMPOSSIBLE PROPHECY

No other book in the world has been written that speaks
of these unbelievable details of prophecies.

N ow for the granddaddy of all prophecies concerning Israel's
return to their homeland in the Middle East in the last days.

That holy prophecy was given by Moses in Deuteronomy 30. As
you read the following words, remember, this is the first recorded
prophecy about: Israel's first journey into the land, Israel becoming
a mighty nation in the land, Israel's eventual rebellion against God's
commandments, and the subsequent return of Israel in the last days to
the land from which Yahweh had scattered them.

This scriptural prediction seems to be a human impossibility—yet
it's right there in Deuteronomy. Moses' prediction was given to him by
the Holy Spirit, and was not of human design.

> And when all these things come upon you, the blessing and
> the curse, which I have set before you, and you call them to
> mind among **all the nations** where the LORD your **God has
> driven you**, and return to the LORD your God, you and your
> children, and obey his voice in all that I command you today,
> with all your heart and with all your soul, then the LORD your
> **God will restore your fortunes** and have mercy on you, and he
> will **gather you again** from all the peoples where the LORD
> your God **has scattered you**.[233]
>
> If your outcasts are in the **uttermost parts** of heaven, from

159

there the LORD your **God will gather you**, and from there he will take you.

And the LORD your **God will bring you into the land** that your fathers possessed, that you may possess it. And he will make you **more prosperous** and **numerous** than your fathers. (Deuteronomy 30:1–5, emphasis added)

The following are a few samples of respected scholars of our day who understand the contextual nature of those prophetic utterances found in Deuteronomy 30.

Enduring Word Commentary—David Guzik

The **ultimate fulfillment** of this would await **the Twentieth Century**, when **God would regather Israel** in the Promised Land. This **modern regathering** is a larger, broader, more sovereign, and more miraculous restoration than that recorded in Ezra and Nehemiah.[234] (Emphasis added)

Israel My Glory—Kenneth B. Symes[235]

Scripture is clear that **Israel's final reestablishment in the land will occur in close connection with the Second Coming** of the Messiah. It is further evident that the Messiah's Second Coming is tied to the second regathering of Israel into her land (Isa. 11:10–12)...**Israel will be reestablished as a nation** before the beginning of Daniel's 70th week (Isa. 28:15–18, 22). [236] (Emphasis added)

Dr. Constable's Expository Notes

The steps in Israel's experience enumerated here provide an **outline of the history of Israel**, since this is **how things** have happened and **will happen for Israel**. These steps are seven: **dispersion** for disobedience (Deuteronomy 30:1), **repentance** in dispersion (Deuteronomy 30:2), **regathering**

(Deuteronomy 30:3), **restoration** to the land (Deuteronomy 30:4–5), national **conversion** (Deuteronomy 30:6; Deuteronomy 30:8), the **judgment** of Israel's oppressors (Deuteronomy 30:7), and national **prosperity** (Deuteronomy 30:9).[237] (Emphasis added)

Not only has the restoration to the land of Israel happened, but the last elemental prediction found in that passage, concerning the nation being "more prosperous…than your fathers," is also an undeniable reality. Sadly, many have missed this great truth as well, including much of the modern day church.[238]

MORE NUMEROUS

Yet another prophecy about the return of Israel that has become reality is the one concerning Israel's formerly dispersed inhabitants being more "numerous" than ever before. The combined population of both David and Saul's Kingdoms is estimated to have never risen above 6 million, yet today, the number of Israel's inhabitants is nearly 10 million and rising.[239]

Isaiah 49 also prophesied of the *great numbers of people* that would populate the prophetically returned Israel of the last days. In verse 20 of that chapter, Isaiah penned the words "this land is too small" as being a specific complaint of the returned occupants in Israel's last days!

(5) And now **the LORD says,** he who formed me from the womb to be his servant, **to bring Jacob back to him**; and that **Israel might be gathered to him**—for I am honored in the eyes of the LORD, and my God has become my strength—[240]

(6) he says: It is too light a thing that you should be my servant to raise up the tribes of Jacob and to bring back the preserved of Israel; I will make you as a light for the nations, that my salvation may reach to the end of the earth.

(19) Surely your waste and your desolate places and **your dev-
astated land**—surely **now you will be too narrow [small] for
your inhabitants,** and those who swallowed you up will be far
away.

(20) **The children** of your bereavement **will yet say** in your
ears: **The place is too narrow [small] for me; make room** for
me **to dwell in.**[241] (Isaiah 49: 5–6, 19–20, emphasis added)

These words were recorded more than 2,600 years before they came
to pass, yet no other book than the Bible speaks of these unbelievable
details. For example, no mention of these historically proven truths is
made in the Quran, the teachings of Buddha, the Hindu Vedas, the
utterings of Nostradamus, or daily horoscope readings. There's simply
nothing else that even comes close to the uncanny accuracy and the
profound nature of the Word of God.

But there's more. Much more.

39

THE LAST ONE

God's last-days timing mechanism was activated when Israel became a nation in 1948.

The book of Zechariah contains the *final* Old Testament prophecy regarding Israel's return in the last days. Zechariah was written about 520 BC, almost 2,500 years ago, during the Persian captivity of the Israelites, and is the second to the last book of the Tanach, followed by Malachi.

> Thus says the LORD of hosts: If it is marvelous in the sight of **the remnant of this people** in **those days**, should it also be marvelous in my sight, declares the LORD of hosts? **Thus says the LORD** of hosts: Behold, **I will save my people from the east country and from the west country, and I will bring them to dwell in the midst of Jerusalem.**" (Zechariah 8:6–7, emphasis added)

Here's what the highly acclaimed *Keil and Delitzsch Biblical Commentary on the Old Testament* has to say about Zechariah 8.

> The deliverance of the people of God out of the heathen lands did indeed commence with the return of a body of exiles from Babylon under the guidance of Zerubbabel, but **their deliverance out of all the countries of the earth is still in the future.** [242] (Emphasis added)

163

Carl Friedrich Keil and Franz Delitzsch obviously understood that Israel's return would be a literal and future event, even though they wrote this commentary almost 200 years before 1948.[243]

The prophet Zechariah further speaks of this phenomenon in chapter 10:

I will whistle for them to **gather them together**, For I have redeemed them; And they **will be as numerous** as they were before. When I scatter them among the peoples, They will remember Me in far countries, And they with their children will live and come back. **I will bring them back** from the land of Egypt And gather them from Assyria; And I will bring them into the land of Gilead and Lebanon. **Until no room can be found** for them. (Zechariah 10:8–10, NASB; emphasis added)

Following is what a few respected modern biblical scholars have published regarding Zechariah 10.

Enduring Word Commentary—David Guzik (Zechariah 10)
In the 20th Century many Jewish people were **gathered back to the land of Israel**, and in 1948 Israel became a nation again—after more than 2,000 years of not being a nation... The gathering began in unbelief but will end up in belief and trust in Jesus.[244] (Emphasis added)

Evidence Unseen Commentary—James M. Rochford[245] (Zechariah 10)
This cannot refer to the first exile, because this book post-dates the exilic period. Gleason Archer dates Zechariah's book between 520 and 480 B.C. Liberal scholars date this book even later. Also, Zechariah mentions the "far countries"—not merely Egypt and Assyria (c.f. Zech. 12:6). Also, **Ezekiel is normally dated during the exile, and it also predicts the regathering.**

This wouldn't have been much of a prediction, if it was during this period.[246] (Emphasis added)

Then there's this statement from *Gill's Exposition of the Bible*. John Gill (1697–1771) wrote his commentary from 1746 to 1763, and was far ahead of his time regarding the miraculous return of Israel to the Middle East.

Gill says of the prophecies of Zechariah and the last-days return of Israel:

> And **gather them; from the places where they are scattered**, into their land, Hosea 1:10. A **nation shall be born at once;** they shall be multiplied, and not be few, and glorified, and not be small; yea, the **place shall be too [small] for them** to dwell in, Jeremiah 31:18.[247] (Emphasis added)

The same was true of Dr. Arno C. Gaebelein (1861–1945), a world renowned biblical scholar who mastered the Hebrew, Aramaic, Syriac, and Arabic languages. In 1922, Dr. Gaebelien published *The Annotated Bible*, a nine-volume commentary on the entire Word of God.

Dr. Gaebelein also believed that Israel would return to the land, according to the prophetic scriptures which contextually declared that truth. He expected that this prophetic return might happen within his own lifetime, and just missed seeing it by three years.

> I believe that **Israel shall ultimately be gathered again** as a separate nation restored to their own land…[248]
> "These things, which Moses spoke into the ears of the people (Deuteronomy 30) were to come to pass…. 'Then the LORD thy God will turn thy captivity, and have compassion upon thee, and will return and gather thee from all the nations, whither the LORD thy God hath scattered thee' (verse 3). **That will come to pass when this present age closes.**"[249] (Emphasis added)

In the commentary of Dr. John Walvoord (1910–2002), we find another definitive statement of the supernatural return of Israel's presence in the Middle East.[250] Dr. Walvoord is a contemporary of our historical generation, having earned three doctoral degrees in theological studies, and is the past president of Dallas Theological Seminary.

> The partial restoration of the nation Israel to their ancient land in the middle of the twentieth century should be recognized by all careful students of the Bible as a most remarkable event... **The return of Israel** to their ancient land and the establishment of the state of Israel is **the first step in a sequence of events which will culminate in Christ's millennial kingdom on earth.** The present **return of Israel is the prelude** [to that culmination].[251] (Emphasis added)

THE CLOCK IS TICKING

Here's what we've concluded thus far: God's timing mechanism for the *last days* was activated when Israel became a nation in 1948. From the 1500s through the late 1800s and beyond, dozens of biblical scholars have understood the biblical declarations of that great event, and have expounded upon them.[252] Now, the grains of sand have been pouring through to the bottom bulb in God's "end-times hourglass" for decades.

To a number of prophecy experts, those grains of sand appear to be moving with increasing speed. It seems to be that the vitriolic hatred of Israel grows deeper every day.[253]

Which now brings us to the next chapter, and the answers that directly address the increasing frequency of the question: *Why is there so much hatred for Israel, the Jews, and even Christians?*

You're getting ready to encounter several staggering biblical and historical connections that help us to answer that apparent enigma. These discoveries will give increased context and illumination to the prophetic nature of our world. Within that framework, we'll further increase the development of our prophetic "vision," equipping us to live more *intentionally* for the Kingdom.

40

EDEN'S LINK

From Genesis through Malachi and right up to the opening pages
of the New Testament, we can begin to understand the escalation
of anti-Israel sentiment more clearly.

The relentless international hatred of Israel, and the nation's miraculous presence in the Middle East, is often coupled with a general contempt for the Gospel of Yeshua, and its followers and ministers. These factors *are* distinctly correlated, and foretold in the Scriptures (and nowhere else), so let's trace out the biblical explanation of it all.

Not only will we explore the sequence of events in the Word of God, but you will also discover connections to our current times. If you've never considered them before, some of those links will most likely prove to be quite shocking. When we're finished, however, I believe you'll *see* what's really happening—and why most of the world misses the biblical/historical connections.

THE GARDEN FALL

It was in the Garden of Eden where Yahweh confronted Satan, Adam, and Eve with their sin. In that lush paradise, the opening prophecy of the last days was delivered to Satan by Yahweh Himself.

> And I will put enmity between you and the woman, and between your offspring and hers; he will crush your head, and you will strike his heel. (Genesis 3:15, NIV)

What the Lord promised in that declaration was that through the womb of a godly woman would come a male child who would prove to be the demise of Satan's stolen kingdom, and the ultimate doom of Satan himself. Of course, we now know that it was a prophecy of the coming Yeshua HaMashiach…"the Lamb slain before the foundation of the world" (Revelation 13:8).

At that moment Satan knew *why* he was doomed, and *what* was going to bring about his downfall. The problem, however, was that he didn't know *when*, *where*, or exactly *which male* child, or through *which womb* his nemesis would arrive. These unknown facts began to fuel his psychotic path of rage against humanity.[254]

After that Garden pronouncement, Satan began his search for the mysterious child. What an insult this must have been to the *proud one*, to realize a mere "child" would destroy him. The pronouncement obviously infuriated him. Subsequently, the rest of the Old Testament outlines Satan's frenzied quest to find that man-child and completely annihilate Him, before he himself was destroyed by Him. In Satan's overwhelming arrogance, he thought he could thwart God's decree.

FATHER ABRAHAM

Satan eventually got a partial answer to his growing dilemma when he became aware of God's covenant with Abraham.

> Now the LORD said to Abram, "Go from your country and your kindred and your father's house to the land that I will show you. And I will make of you a great nation, and I will bless you and make your name great, so that you will be a blessing. I will bless those who bless you, and him who dishonors you I will curse, and **in you all the families of the earth shall be blessed.**" (Genesis 12:1–3, emphasis added)

Satan finally knew through which "family" of people this mystery child was to come. From this point forward we find Satan laser-focused on the offspring of Abraham—a people who were destined to eventually become the nation of Israel. Thus, very early in human history, Satan's rage began the hunt for a very specific child through the line of Abraham's children.

From Genesis through Malachi and right up to the opening pages of the New Testament, we can begin to understand the escalation of the phenomenon of anti-Israel sentiment more clearly. Satan birthed the fuel of this rage, which continues to escalate to this day. Right up to the first coming of Yeshua he was deadly serious about destroying the "child of his destruction."

Next, we'll look at three specific fields of battle in which Satan, in his arrogance, has unleashed his psychoses of unmitigated fury. Through his various ruses, he's telegraphing his message of intended dominance over the entire planet, all of which are meant to be an affront to the throne of God.

ISRAEL, THE CHURCH, AND THE WOMB

The main last days' stratagem Satan employs is his abject hatred for the *returned nation of Israel itself*. His second front is to target the genuinely born-again people of God—*the true Church*. Further, and particularly devastating, is Satan's destructive focus upon the *"womb of the woman"* in general, (as we've seen in a former chapter of this book—outlining the #1 cause of global death in our day) and the "seed" it produces.[255]

All three of these battlefronts have blossomed into full-blown global scourges, and we are the first generation to witness the carnage and insanity that accompanies each one. Sadly, only a few pulpits in America give these matters even a casual mention, though the planet is currently awash in the blight of their combined existence. Yet, Scripture prophesied each of them, and furthermore, it foretold the world's reaction to them (Luke 17:26–27).[256]

Although every bit of this evil has been lurking in the shadows of humanity for millennia, the church has largely missed the truth of Satan's scheme to hunt down and destroy the prophesied Seed in these areas.[257] Satan has been hiding behind the cosmic curtains of interdimensional principalities, discussed in Ephesians chapter 6, pulling the strings of authority and influencing not only the sin-darkened hearts of powerful people, but also the institutions they control.[258]

Never forget, though, it was through these ancient truths, spawned in the Garden of Eden, that Satan's murder-laden psychosis began.

41

THE GENOCIDE CONNECTION

*Satan thought he had finally destroyed
the ultimate Seed of God.*

Satan had to find and eliminate the singular Seed that could be used to bring about his own destruction, so he went to work on the people of Israel—Abraham's seed. He would eventually arrange for Abraham's descendants, the Israelites, to be enslaved in the land of Egypt.

From Egypt, *Nachash* (Hebrew word for "serpent" or Satan [Revelation 12]) would pull the strings of his puppet, Pharaoh, so that a murderous edict would be issued through him: "Kill all the newborn male children among the Israelites" (Exodus 1:15–20).

Satan believed he might be able to thwart Yahweh's Garden of Eden prophecy with his brutal plot. But in spite of Pharaoh's malicious scheme, God spared a little Hebrew boy by the name of Moses—the one who, in years to come, would be used by Yahweh to lead Israel's deliverance from Pharaoh's clutches.

However, even after the Exodus and throughout the forty years the Israelites wandered in the wilderness, time and time again, neighboring civilizations came against God's people, seeking to destroy the newly emerging children of Israel.

Satan continued to manipulate the emerging world empires toward his diabolical goal, long after Israel was settled in the land. From the beginning of the Assyrian Empire in 722 BC, through the Babylonians and Persians, and then the 449 BC rise of Alexander the Great's

Greek empire, Satan relentlessly endeavored to hunt down and destroy the Seed, along with the entire nation of Israel. *Nachash* continued to manipulate a large portion of humanity with this diabolic goal in mind.

The homicidal pattern of Satan becomes evident when we examine those national histories under the microscope of biblical context. Through those empires, *Nachash* would enslave and hold God's people captive, kill their children, and even attempt to eradicate the entirety of the Jewish nation. With a primary focus on male Hebrew children, Satan would try to destroy *the* male Child through a certain Pharaoh of Egypt, and eventually through Nebuchadnezzar of Babylon. Then, several hundred years later, he would set out to destroy the whole of the Jewish race through a man named *Haman*, the top assistant to the emperor of earth's new superpower—Persia.

But even in the wake of his psychopathic rants, Satan's plan to destroy that one path to the arrival of the Seed was thwarted by Heaven's throne…every single time.

IN SIGHT OF THE GOAL

By the turn of the first century, the Roman Empire had spawned one of the most vicious war machines and far-reaching kingdoms the planet had ever seen. The Jewish people were swallowed up in the global melee that had brought about its brutally violent birth.

Israel's priests and rabbinic officials gained enough power to become comfortable and highly influential by bowing to the new Roman government. They were even assigned their own "king," Herod, who would rule over them within the Roman province of Judea.

King Herod wasn't much more than a political puppet of the Roman government. He was especially susceptible to the demonic powers behind the thrones of his despotic Roman overlords, and was widely hated. The foundation of the arrogant king's infamous reputation came from the depths of his brutality and murderous heart, an especially fertile seedbed in which Satan's diabolic plans could grow.

Thus, this degenerate "leader" of the Jewish people was demonically manipulated into focusing on the little village of Bethlehem, less than six miles from Jerusalem's gates and Herod's palace. It was time for Satan's plan to repeat itself.

Satan tried once more to corner the Seed, readying for the slaughter of the child. To make certain his plan succeeded, Herod ordered the murder of all the male children under two years of age and born in Bethlehem during the same period as the soon-coming "King of the Jews." This newborn Heavenly King was reported to have arrived through the womb of a woman with a lineage tied directly to David's ancient throne.[259]

Once more, Satan's modus operandi was in play: *Kill the children, find the Seed, and destroy Him!* The story is the same, from Genesis to the Gospels…and the vitriolic fallout of that ferocious cosmic warfare rages on today.[260]

BEHOLD THE LAMB

Satan thought he had finally destroyed the ultimate Seed of God—that is, until he received yet another ominous announcement about thirty years after the Bethlehem massacre. From the serene shores of the Jordan River, *Nachash* was soon tuned in to the frequencies of a disturbing decree that was blasted from the lips of a desert preacher. It was a prophetic outburst that rippled through the burgeoning crowds, then ultimately among most of the Jewish population of Galilee and Judea, of the Roman Empire:

Behold the Lamb of God!

Myriads of people from the surrounding regions were pouring into the Jordan River valley to see this spectacle. As they came, throngs of them were baptized by John, in order to begin their journey of repentance and turn back to Yahweh. The prophetic nature of their time seemed to waft through the atmosphere, and they had gathered to welcome what they hoped to be the soon coming days of the long-awaited Messiah, the promised Seed of Abraham.

John the Baptizer shouted the announcement as he pointed to Yeshua, his voice rolling through the desert and across the placid river waters, "Behold! *Here* is the Lamb of God! The One sent from Heaven's throne! The One who has come to take away the sins of the world!"

The serpent was enraged, but now at least he *knew* the "Who" of Yahweh's Garden death sentence that had been pronounced upon him several millennium ago.

And that's when the real war started.

As we now know, Satan ultimately lost that war at Golgotha's cross, and three days later at an empty tomb. He is now fully aware that his end is near. Subsequently he currently has the returned Israel and the genuinely born-again church in his crosshairs.

> But woe to you, O earth and sea, for the devil has come down to you in great wrath, because **he knows that his time is short!**... Then the dragon **became furious with the woman** [Israel[261]] and went off **to make war** on the rest of her **offspring,** on those who keep the commandments of God and **hold to the testimony of Jesus.** (Revelation 12:12, 17, emphasis added)

Israel's chief adversary is Satan himself, who has been operating from that platform since their ancient beginnings. He failed at his first order of business, which was to prevent Abraham's promise from appearing in the first place. Yeshua did in fact come as a "blessing to all the nations," and now Satan is trying once more to prevent Yeshua from coming again.

Satan's greatest desire is to eradicate the Jewish people from the face of the earth. Nachash is furious that it was through them that Yeshua's first appearance on earth set his impending destruction in motion, culminating in His prophetic return of ruling and reigning on earth. That is why anti-Semitism is so widespread, and why even a growing number of mainstream "Christian" denominations now openly condemn the Jewish state's presence in the Middle East, in spite of the nearly fifty biblical prophecies clearly stating that Israel was decreed to be there. Now Israel's status as a nation is a testimony to the world that Yahweh, *not Satan*, is the legitimate All Powerful One.

In short, much of the Old Testament is reliant upon God's promises to Israel; they are central to biblical prophecy. Everything that is currently blooming before the eyes of the world is connected to Israel's role in providing those prophecies, through scripture. And from that ancient nation, today's Church, the Body of Christ, was born—along with the world-changing Gospel message of salvation through Yeshua.

Since we've laid that groundwork, you should now "see" the general story of the Satan-filled global hatred for Israel, the Jewish people as a whole, and the born-again church. We are living in the days of Satan's vicious, final rampage, and he's playing for keeps. This is as real as it gets, and right now it's still his world…but not for long.

Next, you might be particularly astonished as we connect the biblical and historical facts (both ancient and modern) that expose the relevance of all this to our own times. Some of these links are nothing short of stunning.

Buckle up.

42

ASTONISHING CORRELATIONS

The money is given to you, the people also, to do with them
as it seems good to you. (Esther 3:11)

What do the Amalekites (of Exodus), Haman (of the book of Esther), the ancient Persian Empire, and the modern day terrorist organization *Hamas* have in common, and how do they relate to today's global politics concerning Israel? Furthermore, how are they attached to the politics of the United States of America? The foundations of our prophetic days begin to take shape with the answers to these intriguing questions, and provide a much deeper spiritual understanding as to what's really happening.

THE AMALEKITES

Let's go back to Exodus again. After the Children of Israel had departed from Egypt, the Amalekites were the first people to come out in the desert wilderness to try and stop them. The goal of the Amalekites was to destroy *all the Hebrew people*. Does this sound familiar? I'm sure you can guess who was ultimately behind that thought process, an agenda born in the depths of Satan's darkest spiritual realms.

The Amalekite attack upon God's people came in the form of a war, recorded in Exodus 17:8–15, when Aaron propped up Moses' arms and the uplifted staff of Yahweh that he held. Joshua was the commander of the fighting men, and as long as Moses held up the staff, they were winning, but when his arms grew tired, the armies began losing. This was meant to be a sign to God's people that it was not Moses himself that was their "strength," but rather, it was the power of Heaven that would give them victory.

Eventually, the Lord caused the Israelites to prevail over the Amalekites, followed by this declaration:

> **Then the LORD said** to Moses, "Write this as a memorial in a book and recite it in the ears of Joshua, that **I will utterly blot out the memory of Amalek from under heaven.**" And Moses built an altar and called the name of it, The LORD Is My Banner, saying, "A hand upon the throne of the LORD! **The LORD will have war with Amalek** from **generation to generation.**" (Exodus 17:14–15, emphasis added)

Okay. That was interesting, but who were the Amalekites, and how is this knowledge relevant to us? *Hang on.*

ORIGINS

At this point, two very telling passages of Scripture come into play, found in Genesis 28, and in Genesis 36.

> **Now Esau saw that Isaac had blessed Jacob and sent him away to Paddan-aram to take a wife** from there, and that as he blessed him he directed him, "You must not take a wife from the Canaanite women," and that Jacob had obeyed his father and his mother and gone to Paddan-aram. So **when Esau saw that the Canaanite women did not please Isaac his father, Esau went to Ishmael and took as his wife,** besides the wives he had, **Mahalath the daughter of Ishmael,** Abraham's son, the sister of Nebaioth. (Genesis 28:6–9, emphasis added)

Issac[262] was Abraham's "son of the promise," and had two sons, Jacob and Esau. Yahweh would later change Jacob's name to "Israel" (Genesis 35), but Esau proved to be a particularly stubborn fellow. Through a series of unfortunate events, he squandered his birth-right, then became overcome with jealousy toward Jacob and mad at his father Isaac (Genesis 25:23, 29–34; Hebrews 11:20). So, in order to "punish" his father, Esau went straight to the house of Ishmael (Abraham's illegitimate son by Hagar—Genesis 16). In other words, Esau purposely aligned himself with long-standing enemies of Abraham's legitimate family, those from the line of Isaac and of the "Promise of God."

Esau not only married Ishmael's daughter, but also married several Hittite women (the Hittites were a part of the larger Canaanite community), the combined result of which was a good, ole fashioned, Old Testament Hatfields and McCoys!

INTO DARKER DEPTHS

Concerning our current exploration, here's where the plot thickens. In Genesis 36:1–12, we read about one of Esau's grandchildren named *Amalek*. He would become the father of the Amalekites, the clan of Esau's alliance with Ishmael and the Hittite/Canaanite people…all of them were mortal enemies of God's people. In the Desert Wilderness, the *Amalekites* were the first to try and bring about the genocide of the people of Israel.[263]

THE AGAGITES

Now let's delve even deeper into the sordid affair. After the Israelites inhabited the Promised Land and were ruled by a national system of Judges, 1 Samuel 15:8–33 talks of a man named *Agag* who was a later *king* of the Amalekites. His clan of Amalekite descendants would be called the *Agagites*.

So the Ishmaelites, Agagites, Amalekites, and the Canaanites, all longtime mortal enemies of Israel, were related to each other through Esau. Why is it important that the Agagites and Amalekites were all of the very same people through Esau's lineage?

The previous chapter of this book mentioned the Israelites' captivity under the rule of the Persian Empire, after first having been taken captive by the Babylonians. It was under the Persians that a man named Haman comes into the picture. Haman was one of King Ahasuerus' highest officials. In the book of Esther we discover that Haman plotted to convince the king to…here we go again…*kill* all the Jews in the Empire! And guess who Haman was related to? The book of Esther tells us:

> Then Haman said to King Ahasuerus, "There is **a certain people scattered abroad and dispersed among the peoples** in all the provinces of your kingdom. Their laws are different from those of every other people, and they do not keep the king's laws, so that it is not to the king's profit to **tolerate** them. **If it please the king, let it be decreed that they be destroyed**, and I will pay 10,000 talents of silver into the hands of those who have charge of the king's business, that they may put it into the king's treasuries."
>
> So the king took his signet ring from his hand and gave **it to Haman the Agagite**, the son of Hammedatha, **the enemy of the Jews.** And the king said to Haman, "**The money is given to you, the people also,** to **do with them as it seems good** to you." (Esther 3:8–11, emphasis added)

The Agagite/Amalekite people were still at work, guided by Satan, all the way into the Persian Empire and beyond, this time through the Persian official named Haman.

You may be thinking that all this sounds interesting, but what does it have to do with our times, the nations attacking Israel, and the hatred of Israel and the Jews?

Next come the real shockers.

43

THE HAMAN LINK

After the attack on Israel by Hamas, on October 7, 2023,
Prime Minister Netanyahu invoked the metaphor of Amalek.

Following are the ominous biblical links that prophetically attach themselves to our day and beyond—until the promised return of Yeshua.

A VISIT TO CONGRESS

On March 3, 2015, then Prime Minister of Israel, Benjamin Netanyahu, was invited to the United States Congress as a guest speaker. He was invited by then Speaker of the House, John Boehner. The president during that time, Barack Obama, was not in attendance and claimed that he didn't even watch the congressional meeting on television because he had another meeting to attend, a meeting of the European Union.[264]

That very night marked the eve of the *Purim* holiday in Israel. *Purim* denotes the ancient Jewish victory over the genocidal Haman, the Persian official who convinced the King to *kill all the Jews* living in Persia. Today, we know Ancient Persia as *Iran*, so named since 1935.

Netanyahu claimed the deal would release at least 50 billion dollars to Iran. This was originally Iran's money that had been previously frozen (largely because of Iran's practices of hostage taking and state-sponsored terrorism[265]). Netanyahu further maintained that the deal itself didn't eliminate the Islamic republic's ability to eventually acquire nuclear weapons. President Obama was insistent the deal would in fact *take away* Iran's ability to acquire a nuclear arsenal. Netanyahu stringently disagreed.

"This is a bad deal—a very bad deal," Netanyahu told a joint meeting of Congress. "We're better off without it."[266]

Netanyahu insisted that such a deal would more than likely "guarantee" Iran's acquisition of nuclear weapons. He said this was because the bargain allowed the Islamic republic of Iran to keep much of its nuclear infrastructure in place.

> "It will **all but guarantee** that **Iran will get those nuclear weapons**, lots of them," the Israeli leader said. "We'll face a much more dangerous Iran, a Middle East littered with nuclear bombs and a **countdown to a potential nuclear nightmare**."[267] (Emphasis added)

Netanyahu also stated, "Iran's supreme leader...spews *the oldest hatred of anti-Semitism* with the newest technology. He tweets that Israel must be...destroyed." [268]

That evening, in the halls of Congress, Netanyahu said:

> "We're an ancient people. In our nearly 4,000 years of history, **many have tried repeatedly to destroy the Jewish people**. Tomorrow night, on the Jewish holiday of Purim, we'll read the **Book of Esther**," Netanyahu told Congress.
>
> "**We'll read of a powerful Persian viceroy named Haman**, who **plotted to destroy the Jewish people** some **2,500 years ago**. But a courageous Jewish woman, **Queen Esther**, exposed the plot and gave for the Jewish people the right to defend themselves against their enemies."
>
> "**Today** the Jewish people face **another attempt** by yet another **Persian**" **leader** to "**destroy the Jewish people**."[269] (Emphasis added)

After Netanyahu's speech to Congress, the Obama administration rebuked the prime minister, insisting that a deal with Iran would in fact take place by March 31.[270] Once again, the spirit of Haman and the Amalekites is recognized as being in the mix. It seemed the book of Esther was again coming to life, thousands of years after its first occurrence.

NEFARIOUS DATES

Later, just as March 31 was coming to a close, the Obama administration stated the previous deadline would be postponed for a day or so. Then, on April 2, 2015, Obama announced in a Rose Garden ceremony that a deal had been brokered with Iran on the proposed nuclear deal.[271]

A number of prophecy watchers were shocked to discover that April 2 of that year corresponded with *Nisan 13* on the Hebrew calendar.[272] What's so significant about that date of Nisan 13? Have a look at the text of the Book of Esther.

> Then the king's scribes were summoned **on the thirteenth day of the first month [13th of Nisan]**, and an **edict**, according to all that **Haman commanded [was delivered to all the people of Persia]**…Letters were sent by couriers to all the king's provinces **with instruction to destroy, to kill, and to annihilate all Jews, young and old, women and children, in one day** (Esther 3:12–13, emphasis and brackets added)

Think of it! The announcement of Iran's "nuclear deal," releasing tens of billions of dollars to the ancient Empire of Persia, was apparently postponed until the *13th day of Nisan*—the same day Haman's edict to kill all the Jews in the Empire was issued, according to the Word of God! I believe this is no coincidence.

THE OCTOBER 7, 2023, LINK

On October 7, 2023, after the attack on Israel by Hamas, Prime Minister Netanyahu invoked the metaphor of *Amalek*. The liberal mainstream media went crazy, accusing Netanyahu of "genocidal speech."[273]

On October 31, 2023, *The Christian Post* related the following:

> **"You must remember what Amalek has done to you,** says our Holy Bible," Netanyahu said, echoing the words of Deuteronomy 25:17, which states: **"Remember what the Amalekites did to you** along your way from Egypt."
>
> [Esau's son Eliphaz gave birth to a son named Amalek], [Esau was] the twin brother of Jacob, and his descendants are depicted in the scriptures as longtime rivals of the Israelites. In 2021, some military analysts speculated the war against the Islamic State terror group in Egypt was a **reenactment of an ancient biblical confrontation between Israel and the Amalekites...**
>
> Calling the Oct. 7 surprise attack by Hamas "without a doubt rooted in the demonic realm as a **manifestation of the Spirit of Amalek,"** the ICEJ [International Christian Embassy Jerusalem] **cited the book of Esther in which Haman,** an **Amalekite,** [and one of the highest of the king's officials] planned to annihilate the Jewish people only to be thwarted by unceasing prayer and fasting.[274] (Emphasis and brackets added)

THE HAMAN SPIRIT

Regardless of whether or not the Hamas Palestinians are related to the descendants of the oldest biblical mention of the Amalekites (they most likely are not)—it doesn't really matter. The world's hatred of Israel is deeply spiritual in nature. It appears the demonic spirit behind antisemitism in general, and the October 7 attack on Israel specifically, are in fact intricately linked to the ancient Amalekite and Haman spirits, under Satan's authority (see Ephesians 6:10).

As we've already seen, Haman was an important official in ancient

Persia, now modern day Iran, whose military was involved in the plan
to attack Israel on Oct 7. Furthermore, Iran (the home of the original
Haman spirit of the Bible) is believed to sponsor the terror groups
Hamas and Hezbollah, both part of the attack.[275] Their leaders, along
with Middle East Palestinians, are still calling for the destruction of all
the Jews[276]…"From the River to the Sea."[277]

I can see the hand of Nachash all over this, can't you? Satan will
continue the onslaught until the very last.

But the spiritual connections and so-called *coincidences* don't end
there.

44

WORDS
HAVE MEANINGS

*Think of the biblical ramifications
of these historical links.*

The word *Haman* is a proper noun, a name given to the right hand man of the emperor of ancient Persia.

HAMAN

The name *Haman* is only found in the pages of the book of Esther in the Old Testament. That proper noun is used in Esther fifty-four times, and has a specific meaning attached to it. Haman means "enraged," or "turbulent" in nature.[278]

In fact, the duality of *Haman* is that it's both a *name* and a *description* of a person's character and nature. As evident in Esther 3:5, giving the name *Haman* would be similar to parents naming their baby girl *Joy,* because it paralleled her overall expression of life. This is easy to miss if you're not familiar with the Hebrew and Aramaic[279] words found in the underlying text.

> When **Haman** saw that Mordecai would not kneel down or
> pay him honor, he **was enraged** [haman]. (Esther 3:5, NIV;
> emphasis and brackets added)

There are several Aramaic words used in the Hebrew language, *Haman* being one. This is often done in the same way we use our word *shampoo*, a borrowed French word incorporated right into English language speech and writing. In the same way, the Hebrew text in Esther 3:5 reads, "Haman...became *haman*."[280]

Interestingly, the Hebrew word *haman* also corresponds with the Greek word *thumos*, also meaning "to be enraged." It also describes Satan's demeanor in these last days, as he attacks God's people, both Israel and Christians.[281]

> So be glad, heavens, and those who live in them! **How terrible** it is for the earth and the sea, because **the Devil** has **come down** to you, **filled with rage**, [*thumos*] knowing that **his time is short!** (Revelation 12:12, ISV; emphasis and brackets added)

But there's still more.

HAMAS

This may come as a shock to a number of students of God's Word, but the word *Hamas* is also in the Bible.[282]

Hamas is used sixty times in the Hebrew text of the Old Testament, its first usage being found in the opening chapters of Genesis. *Hamas* is a Hebrew word. It translates into English as *violence*, and is listed as one of the reasons God brought the flood to the primeval earth.[283]

> Now the earth was corrupt in God's sight, and the earth was filled **with violence** [*hamas*]. (Genesis 6:11, emphasis and brackets added)

Imagine that! *Hamas* and *Haman* are distinctly and biblically related—at least in their word-meaning associations—and have been so almost since the beginning of time. One word means *enraged* and the other means *violence*.

THE CONNECTIONS

Think of the biblical ramifications of these historical links. On October 7, 2023, the Iran-backed terrorist proxy, *Hamas,* attacked the prophetically returned Israel, claiming they wanted to *kill all the Jews*, repeating what the leaders of Persia/Iran have said for thousands of years, all the way back to Haman.

On top of that, President Joe Biden may have actually funneled tens of billions of dollars to help finance Iran's "nuclear negotiations," according to the detractors of the deal. This money was distributed into the same country whose Ayatollahs and Presidents have called, and continue to call, for the *killing of all the Jews*.[284]

Prime Minister Benjamin Netanyahu of Israel is not the only one to make this biblical/historical connection of the Haman/Hamas terror attack of October 7, 2023, and the true demonic spirit behind it.

As an example, have a look at the following. There are multitudes more like it.

From Haman to Hamas (The Messianic Bible—October 2023)

Iran continues to perform missile tests and develop nuclear weapons specifically to annihilate Israel, and Hamas and Hezbollah continue to amass arms and construct tunnels for terrorist infiltration.

What Haman did not accomplish, the Ayatollah and Revolutionary Guards of Iran have sworn to fulfill. In this way, we see the Book of Esther as not only a historical portrait of salvation but also a prophetic voice of history repeating itself.

With our eyes on current events, we remember the genocidal and petty **spirit of Haman**—who **descended from** the arch enemies of ancient Israel, **the Amalekites**—seeing that **same spirit at work in** the terrorist group and ruling entity of the Gaza Strip—**Hamas.**[285] (Emphasis added)

As we close this chapter, remember Netanyahu's ominous Congressional warnings on March 3, 2015, specifically decrying then-President Obama's release of billions of dollars to Iran for the White House's proposed "nuclear deal." Netanyahu predicted this move would only result in an all-out attack upon Israel by Iran, possibly resulting in a regional or even global war.

Netanyahu's prediction became reality on October 7, 2023.

45

NOW WE
KNOW THE ANSWER

*It truly is a mad, mad, mad, mad—
and highly prophetic—world.*

In the months prior to the October 7, 2023, attack on Israel, then-President Biden, Barack Obama's former Vice President, reportedly released an additional six billion dollars in frozen Iranian cash as part of a prisoner exchange deal.

On October 12, 2023, *The Hill*, a mainstream media outlet located in Washington, D.C., explained:

Opponents of the [Biden Iran deal] think the White House's focus on the specific terms and conditions is disingenuous.

They argue that the bottom line is simple: Iran has access to $6 billion that it did not have access to three months ago.

Whether or not the specific account in Qatar is confined to humanitarian use is **irrelevant**, they contend. If all those funds were used tomorrow for needed medicine, for example, **Tehran would have $6 billion in its regular coffers that it hadn't had to spend.** Therefore, **some or all of that money would be freed up**, possibly to be used for **nefarious purposes**.

"To think that they are not moving money around is irresponsible. **They are moving money around to threaten those they hate.** They **hate Israel**; they **hate America**; they are going to continue to use this," Republican presidential candidate Nikki Haley told NBC's "Meet the Press" Sunday.

189

Florida Gov. Ron DeSantis wrote on social media in the aftermath of Hamas's initial attack that **"Iran has helped fund this war against Israel** and **Joe Biden's policies** that have **gone easy on Iran** have **helped fill** their coffers." [286] (Emphasis added)

Regardless of how all this plays out in political wranglings and international affairs, there are still two biblical considerations to take into account:

- Because of Israel's prophetic return as a nation, whenever they are in the news, and especially when that news involves a vicious attack on them, that event is *necessarily* prophetic. In fact, if one will look closely, and understand this principle of prophetic interpretation, it becomes clear that all these pieces are directly connected: from Sadaam Hussein's launching of Scud missiles into Israel, to the Gulf War, 9-11, the wars in Iraq and Afghanistan, Arab Spring, Netanyahu's Congressional warning to Congress and Obama about the releasing of billions of dollars to Israel's most ancient enemy, all the way up to the Gaza-Hamas terrorist attack on October 7, 2023. It's all about Israel, just as God's Word has told us from the beginning.
- If Israel is attacked by any, or all, of the biblical nations listed in Ezekiel 38, such as Persia/Iran, that too is an event that must be given careful consideration. Persia/Iran has been apoplectic about Israel's presence in the Middle East since the day it was resurrected and reestablished. Persia/Iran is still front and center in their declarations to "kill all the Jews."[287]

Both of those factors, and more, are directly applicable to current world affairs, especially the October 7, 2023, attacks on Israel. Again, by the time you read this book there may be several more links that have also come to light.

It truly is a mad, mad, mad, mad—and highly prophetic—world. As we've previously seen, Satan is the god of this age (2 Corinthians 4:4), and the prince of this world (John 12, 14, 16), and God is in the process of giving the planet over to Satan's depraved mind (Romans 1:18–28). His direct involvement in the disorder of this fallen planet, and his own vicious rule over it, will not end until the return of Jesus Christ…and Satan knows that event is coming soon (Revelation 12:12).

It's coming, even if God's own people are not paying close attention, and whether the world knows it or not (Luke 17:26–27). I pray that increasing numbers of people would receive the eyes to see what's going on in the world, and turn to Yeshua HaMashiach before it's too late. They must hurry; the "doors of the ark" are closing.[288]

Hopefully it's becoming clear that one of the Bible's central story lines is Satan's anger against the Jewish people and the church, born from their midst. The incendiary rage of *Nachash* began in the Garden of Eden, radically intensifying when he discovered the line of Abraham would bring about the destruction of Satan's kingdom. He's been on the cosmic warpath ever since, stealing, killing, and destroying. That's what all this has been about.

The information in the foregoing chapters should help you to biblically answer the questions, "Why is there so much hatred toward Jews and Christians? Why are so many obsessed with destroying them?"

And now you also know—quite pointedly—that this earth is currently *Satan's* world, not ours. The battle is cosmic, vicious, deeply spiritual, and as ancient as the opening verse of Genesis 3.

SEEN
AND UNSEEN

Now faith is the assurance of things hoped for, the conviction of things not seen. For by it the people of old received their commendation. By faith we understand that the universe was created by the word of God, so that what is seen was not made out of things that are visible. (Hebrews 11:1–3)

46

THE LANGUAGE
OF GOD

*In this sense, DNA possesses a form of intelligence that obviously
received its original input code from outside of itself.*

The next two chapters are a synopsis of my introduction to the
basics of DNA found in my previous book *Yeshua Protocol*.
However, this material will serve as an important foundation to the
utterly astonishing new information that comes next. That info will
be a set of dramatic revelations not included in any of my previous
writings. I can't wait for you to see all of this with your own eyes!

These verses from Colossians neatly sum up the biblical worldview
of what we'll explore next.

> Jesus is the image of the invisible God, the firstborn of all cre-
> ation. For by him **all things were created**, in heaven and on
> earth, **visible and invisible**, whether thrones or dominions or
> rulers or authorities—all things were created through him and
> for him. And he is **before all things**, and **in him all things hold
> together**. (Colossians 1:15–17, emphasis added)

THE MANUSCRIPT OF LIFE

As most readers will know, deoxyribonucleic acid (DNA) produces
life, and constantly works to sustain it, and has a language of its own,
apparently from an "outside" source. This fact is according to a number of top DNA researchers, but more on that later.

HGP

The Human Genome Project (HGP), launched in 1990, was a mammoth research effort that became an international undertaking. It was an intensive study spanning thirteen years and costing over three billion dollars to complete. The pursuit was capped off by a White House celebration in June 2000, the same year the *New York Times* published 108 articles related to the Human Genome Project.[289]

The outcome of the colossal undertaking was the detailed structuring and recording of the three billion letters of the human genome. The publication of the first draft was released in February 2001 and completed in April 2003.[290]

The National Human Genome Research Institute (NHGRI) described the journey like this:

> The Human Genome Project (HGP) was one of the great feats of exploration in history. Rather than an outward exploration of the planet or the cosmos, the HGP was an **inward voyage of discovery** led by an international team of researchers looking to sequence and map all of the genes—together known as the genome—of members of our species, Homo sapiens.
>
> Beginning on October 1, 1990, and completed in April 2003, the HGP gave us the **ability**, for **the first time**, to read **nature's complete genetic blueprint for building a human being**.[291] (Emphasis added)
>
> Today, **scientists sometimes refer to this** biological ordering of the genetic code of human beings as **"The Book of Life."**[292]
>
> The complete DNA **instruction book**, or genome, for a human contains about 3 billion bases and about 20,000 genes on 23 pairs of chromosomes.[293] (Emphasis added)

STATEMENTS OF INTELLIGENT DESIGN

Notice the Human Genome Project used the terms *building* and *blueprint*. Those two words are used only in conjunction with the admission of an "intelligence" that is operating outside the actual blue-print and building project. A blueprint always has to be drawn up by an intelligent source, and is prima facia evidence of an intelligent design (and designer).

Following that, the blueprint must be used for the building that is "planned," a process entirely dependent on a source of a specific intel-ligence directing and guiding the process.

On June 26, 2000, Francis Collins, Director of the National Human Genome Research Institute, announced the finalization of the first draft in a key media announcement at the White House. In that broadcast he asserted,

> Today, we celebrate the revelation of the first draft of **the human book of life**" and declared that this breakthrough lets humans for the first time read "our own **instruction book**."[294] (Emphasis added)

It's interesting that Dr. Collins would specifically compare DNA to an "instruction book" that lays out a "blueprint," enabling the car-rying out of the carefully crafted *instructions*. In the secular worldview, that book supposedly occurred by cosmic happenstance, with no intel-ligent input. That assertion, however, is statistically and scientifically impossible, especially if the scientist is following scientific method protocols. A few chapters from now, you'll discover why Dr. Collins was so adamant about calling the human genome the "Book of Life."

Perhaps the label of *The Book of Life* calls to mind Psalm 139:13–17, a piece of Hebrew biblical worship literature that is now almost 3,000 years old:

> For you formed my inward parts; you **knitted me together** in my mother's womb. I praise you, for I am fearfully and won-derfully made. Wonderful are your works; my soul knows it very well. My frame was not hidden from you, when I was

being **made in secret, intricately woven** in the depths of the earth.[295]

Your eyes saw my unformed substance; **in your book** were written, every one of them, the days that were formed for me, when as yet there was none of them. How precious to me are **your thoughts, O God! How vast is the sum of them!** (Psalm 139:13–17, emphasis added)

47

A CODE THAT SPEAKS

*DNA coding produces both life and the biological language
necessary for sustaining that life.*

Your DNA is distinctive from anyone else in the world. This distinctive code knows your past and plots out your potential future, including who you came from and who you might create, as your gender specific reproductive cell joins with that of another human being.

Because of these truths, in addition to being nicknamed the "Book of Life," biologists often compare the human DNA code to a computer language. The similarities between the two are indeed uncanny.[296]

A binary computer code is based on the numbers 0 and 1, but in reality, our DNA code is far more complex than that. Rather, our DNA information exchange process is based on a four-place biological sequencing code that scientists have labeled A T C G. The four nucleotide bases in our DNA code are adenine (A), cytosine (C), guanine (G), and thymine (T).

Those four DNA bases form specific pairs (A with T, and G with C) that, when arranged in certain combinations, determine every single piece of information about who you are. That information is transmitted to all of the *two-trillion* cells throughout your body. Even those trillions of cells implanted within your body, were created by your DNA! Moreover, that very same DNA info exchange process continues to transmit instructions to your cells for your entire life—almost *two-trillion times* every day.

DNA coding produces both life and the biological language necessary for sustaining that life, and that coding process "speaks" and operates by employing a language all its own. All the while, the information necessary to make this happen appears to emerge solely from within itself. In this sense, DNA possesses a form of intelligence that obviously received its *original input* code from outside of itself. A number of highly credentialed scientists now acknowledge that this information had to be purposely inserted from the outside.[297]

AN UTTER IMPOSSIBILITY

Let's simplify this *science-speak*.

The process of life and all its intricate communication arrived in our world with eternal purpose...and an intelligent design to affect those purposes. Secular, evolutionary science, however, would have us to believe it all "just happened," without purpose, and without intelligence. I often use this next illustration to help conceptualize this supposed "impossibility."

Imagine a large meteorite splashes into the ocean, causing a titanic tsunami that comes booming to shore, across miles of coastland beachfronts. What if, after the tsunami washed back out to shore, it turned out that this gigantic wave had left behind, along miles of beach, line upon line of beautiful narratives written in the sand? And, what if each of those prosaic lines contained perfect grammar, faultless sentence structure, and were filled with life changing meaning and awe inspiring communiques?

What if the messages also included specific instructions for building intricate buildings and machines, and even the formulas for creating life itself? Now imagine all of this happened without *any* intelligent input, having *no* initially designed purpose. The beach message was simply a random, uniformed, happenstance caused by a "big bang" meteorite splashdown.

Crazy, did you say? This could *never* happen, not even in a trillion lifetimes, you say? I would agree with you, and any sane person would also agree...that just cannot happen. *Ever.*

The latest biological science, though, has now shown that the code in our own DNA is far more complex than even the hypothetical beach writing scenario. Because as beautiful as that hypothetical beach code might appear, it still cannot think, reproduce, dream, create, express emotion, feel pain or pleasure, or "plan" anything. It has no life within it; it just lies there, displaying a beautifully complex and meaningful message that is soon wiped away by incoming waves. Unless…that writing is *acted upon*—by a person of intelligence.

Yet we are told to "trust the science" and believe an organically written and continually active writing and rewriting of that biological code of three billion letters somehow perfectly combined so we could all uniquely come into being. And it supposedly happened by a mere cosmic happenstance.

Three words describe this staggering proposition: *Not a chance.*

I've now laid out the basic foundation for the shocking revelations to be unveiled in the following chapters.

48

NANO LEVEL
OBSERVATION

For a number of decades, scientists have been able to reliably
"explain" the process of DNA replication—but only in purely
biological and chemically associated terms.

DNA molecules determine which created organism turns out to be a blade of grass, a grasshopper, or a human being.

DNA, along with the instructions it contains, is first passed from adult organisms to their offspring during reproduction. Every living thing on the planet contains DNA.

UNWINDING, UNZIPPING, COPYING,
AND KNITTING

During DNA replication, the DNA molecule *unwinds* so it can be copied. At other times in the cell cycle, DNA also unwinds so its instructions can be used to make proteins, as well as other biological processes necessary for the continuation of the created organism. During cell division, however, DNA is in its compact chromosome form to enable transfer to new cells.

Biological scientists refer to DNA found in the cell's nucleus as "nuclear DNA." An organism's complete set of nuclear DNA is called its "genome."

Throughout the process of replication, double-stranded DNA *unzips* to expose the nucleotides (chemical code language) along its two separate strands. In that procedure, flaps of single-stranded DNA are created. This begins the DNA replication process, which involves the "weaving" of all the proper information back into a usable *chemical message*, a complex and newly created message that is essential for life.[298]

THE UNKNOWN DEPTHS
OF THE REPLICATION ENIGMA

But here's where this matter gets really fascinating. For a number of decades, scientists have been able to reliably "explain" the process of DNA replication—but only in purely biological terms. The description of that biological procedure was essentially reduced to a mere academic exercise that spoke of the numerous interactive "protein globules" or "biological machines" making the overall process possible. Even at that level of explanation, a number of modern students of DNA studies have been gobsmacked concerning the now *observed* reality of its complexity.[299]

Consequently, you'll soon discover that in the last decade or so, that former sanitary, academic explanation has exploded into an entirely different level of understanding. Astronomically so!

Phys.org revealed this fact in a 2017 article:

Microscopes that reveal the hidden complexities of life down to the nanoscale level have shown in exquisite detail how an enzyme involved in DNA repair works its molecular magic.

To get **a closer look**, Hamdan [Samir Hamdan, KAUST Associate Professor of Bioscience] and his colleagues turned to **a sophisticated microscopy technique known as single-molecule fluorescence resonance energy transfer**, or smFRET. This method **repeatedly images** the same area, each time turning on and off different glowing probes that tag different molecules. **Superimposing these images together yields a nanoscale-quality molecular movie** with a millisecond to sub-millisecond temporal resolution.[300] (Emphasis and brackets added)

I have watched a number of these nanoscale-level movies depicting what happens during DNA replication. I have played them for my church congregation at Sunday morning services on several different occasions. Audible gasps can be heard in the congregation when they realize our unformed bodies are literally and continually being "knitted together" in the depths of the "secret place." There certainly are no evolution processes of "imaginary magic" going on inside our DNA. Instead, we are watching intelligence in action, in all its wonder and majesty!

Have another look at Psalm 139.

> For **you formed** my inward parts; **you knitted me together** in my mother's womb. I praise you, for I am **fearfully and wonderfully** made. (Psalm 139:13–14, emphasis added)

No matter how secular scientists try to "sanitize" the indescribably complex DNA process on a purely academic level, for those who have eyes to see, the hard scientific evidence to the contrary is now right before us.

49

MOLECULAR MACHINES

What we are witnessing in these videos, using the latest tech advances to date, is impossible without an intelligent Designer!

The *Veritasium* YouTube channel posted a video in 2022 titled "Your Body's Molecular Machines," which you can watch at the link provided in the endnote reference.[301] That video is only one of a number of the newest-tech nanoscale level movies now available to the public.

Today's molecular scientists agree, this new generation of 3D animation is precisely what they are seeing. The particular video I'm referencing had 4.4 million views as of the writing of this book. Here are some reactions of those who viewed the movie.[302]

A genetics class that I took before **starting medical school** was one of my favorite classes of all time, but I **have never** seen **a 3-D animation of what the molecular machines look like.** This is fascinating. (@grkuntzmd, emphasis added)

One aspect of all this that **I would like to see explored is the why and how of these things actually 'walking' along the strands.** This seems more mechanical in nature (rather than chemical or reactive), so it *begs deeper questions* of the mechanics such as to why did they evolve the process in this way? Do they have joints? Do they carry their energy fuel with them? Can they run out of this fuel and what does that mean for the success of the larger purpose? In my mind, understanding the unique ways our cells communicate (and why they communicate that way) are the **hidden keys to understanding "life."** (@gobeaugo, emphasis added)

And thus I've realized, **the structural difference between a ps4 [PlayStation 4] and a dog is layered mechanical complexity.** The dog is a machine made of machines made of machines that keeps going on in further complexity until you reach the smallest ribosomes shown in this video. Whereas the ps4 on the other hand, is only about two or three layers of machines and is thus around the same complexity as a simple virus. (@ suruxstrawde8322, emphasis and brackets added)

In the time of my lifespan, humanity has gone from Richard Feynman announcing that **nothing in known physics rules** out the **possibility of "nanotech," molecular machines,** to **actually finding** that **nature has already** beaten us to the punch and **invented them.** (@deepfriedsammich, emphasis added)

Endlessly fascinating stuff. I am in **almost disbelief that such order** goes on **inside my cells** to make them **exist** and function and **sustain me.** Just utter wow O_O (@BlinkinFirefly, emphasis added)

I can't imagine how this process could be born from **natural selection [Evolution].** (@EMAN360ELITE, emphasis added)

I like when humans finally caught up to this advanced **biological** process and **had to compare it to machines** that **humans created** that lead to this discovery just to understand it. (@waddee30, emphasis added)

VIDEO TRANSCRIPT AND EXPLANATION

This 6 ½ minute movie allows you to "see" what scientists are observing with their most advanced digital microscopic equipment. The following are transcript excerpts, but you can read the full transcript at the link in this endnote reference.[303]

The bracketed parts of the paragraphs below are my own words, and serve as a summary to a larger portion of information that came before it in the video narration.

These are tiny molecular machines, and they are doing this inside your body—right now...Right now, billions of your cells are dividing, essentially creating new cells...that process (called *mitosis*) requires **an army of tiny molecular machines**... [what you are watching] is a **scientifically accurate depiction of a DNA strand.**

Copying DNA is one of the **first steps** in **cell division.** [What you see now] are the two strands of DNA that are being unwound and separated by the tiny (blue) *molecular machine* called *helicase.* Helicase literally spins as fast as a jet engine!

The strand of DNA on the right has its complementary strand assembled continuously. But the other strand is more **complicated** because it runs in the opposite direction. So, it must be **looped out with its complimentary strand and then assembled in reverse, section by section!**

[The result is a perfectly knitted, looped, and coiled biological information packet—called a "chromosome," one of the largest molecular structures in our body. **It takes many tens of thousands of these seemingly "knowledgeable" molecular machines,** constantly working at unimaginable speeds, to complete the entire process—billions of times a day for the rest of our lives.]

[The video goes on to explain (and visually demonstrates) how this process also depends upon chemical "stop and go" signals that ensure the chromosome is being constructed properly. The signals are sent to the biological "machines."]

When everything is in order, **the "stop" signal is transmitted** by *dynein motors* [chemical "machines" that actually **have legs,** and **feet shaped like little boots,** that **step over and around** other "machines" in the process of carrying out the proper information sequencing! Following is what the narrator tells us about the *dynein motors* you are observing in the video.]

The **dynein motor**—that's **the walking guy** [you're now looking at in the video]. This **is really what it looks like**: it has long **legs** so it **can avoid obstacles** and avoid the kinesins, molecular motors **that walk** in the opposite direction… Personally, **I'm astounded by these tiny molecular machines**, how they're able to routinely and faithfully execute their functions **billions of times over**, inside your body, at this **exact instance.**[304] (Emphasis added)

Is your mind blown yet? Mine *still* is, even after watching the video several times. And so are the minds of those who continue to leave comments on the video, including medical students and other scientists.

How can researchers and most of those commenting under the 3D animated videos of this process miss the obvious truth of what they're seeing? This was all hidden from us until the last few decades, but this information coming to light only in our historical lifetime begs that several monumental questions be addressed.

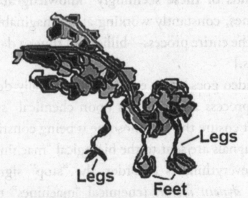

Hand drawing by Carl Gallups
Reproduced from Drew Barry's video representations

Dynein Motor

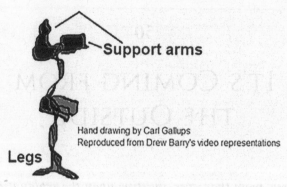

Hand drawing by Carl Gallups
Reproduced from Drew Barry's video representations

Kinesin

To say that what we are looking at is simply a random product of unintelligent, evolutionary processes is akin to the complex beach writing scenario that merely appeared as a result of a tsunami!

Rather, what we are witnessing in these videos, using the latest tech advances to date, is impossible without an intelligent Designer. This could *never* occur through a big bang chemical sludge pond of random happenstance. Not in a googolplex[305] of years.

Just wait, there's even more to unpack on this topic.

We've only scratched the surface.

50

IT'S COMING FROM
THE OUTSIDE

*Now, more than ever, insisting upon the explanation
of "it happened by random evolution" makes one
appear outright foolish.*

I n another YouTube video, posted by *Three Angels Broadcasting Network* (3ABN) in 2019, Tim Standish, PhD of the Geoscience Research Institute is quizzing Ryan Hayes, PhD and Professor of Chemistry at Andrews University.

These two highly accomplished scientists are speaking of the processes involved in the copying of DNA, which, according to them, is a complex and "intelligent" choreography requiring rapid speeds and pin-point precision. They also discuss the sequencing of the essential steps of the life-sustaining information, requiring a copious amount of intelligent data-flow that is definitely not coming from within the mere chemicals of the DNA molecule itself.

Not only does that information operate within the precise DNA arrangement of its chemical "communication" components, but it also operates within each of the tens of thousands of biological "machines" that, trillions of times a day, assist in the replication of DNA within our bodies.

In that 27-minute exchange, Dr. Standish asks Dr. Hayes what his biggest take-away has been about the actual chemical nature of DNA. Following is an abbreviated, in-context, rendition of Dr. Hayes' answer.

210

One of the things that strikes me about **the chemical struc-ture** of DNA is how flexible it is chemically to **allow all sorts of code** and arrangement of its structure…what we call the bases of it, to allow a wide variety almost an infinite number of chemical combinations.

Even as a PhD chemist I am looking at the structure of DNA…and pondering that structure. Once again it struck me that **there isn't anything** about the chemistry that is **driving the arrangement** of the letters and the bases.

So let's say you had a T in the sequence anything could come after it. **There's nothing** chemically that says an A must come immediately after a T or something like that—**they're actually no rules** in the sequencing of it.

Now we know the A and T must match together and the G and the C must match with each other **across the strand**, but **in any order of the rungs** of this ladder they can **come in any arrangement.**

A reluctance of mine was to give up [the chemical intelli-gence theory]. **I wanted** [it to be that human DNA was simply] full of chemicals, and that **we were driven by chemical infor-mation**, but honestly it's **just information that has a chemical component.**

So there isn't a chemical property driving that arrangement. It **has to come from another source.**

I find that **utterly amazing there's nothing that is driving the structure** in the base pairs themselves. There's nothing there that's driving the chemistry. If there was something chemically driving it **we would see patterns.** We would see so many T's and then an A and so many G's followed by a T. But there's no pat-terns, **it is completely random to our eyes.** [306] (Emphasis added)

Dr. Standish responded to what Dr. Hayes had asserted.

I guess that if there were patterns there, then you actually wouldn't be able to code very much information into it. I mean if the letters of the alphabet had to be arranged in just one specific order every time we wouldn't be able to spell millions of different words with it.

And so here we're basically dealing with an alphabet, **a relatively simple alphabet**, with **only four letters**—the A, D, G, and C, and **yet we can come up with**, for all practical purposes, **infinitely different sequences** to code different things into the genome.[307] (Emphasis added)

The program's host, Shelley Quinn, then asks Dr. Hayes if he saw this incredible phenomenon as a "signature of God," a higher intelligence that has to be involved. Dr. Hayes answered:

That's right. If every arrangement is allowed for the codes that are in there, **where did the arrangement come** from that we see? The problem is, when there's **even one letter** that's **wrong** you get molecules and proteins and enzymes that don't work. So the **code fails.**

You need the **correct code** right from **the beginning**, and without it you get failed results - you get **failed** chemicals that **don't do anything.** Or react improperly. You **need a working system** from the get-go.[308] (Emphasis added)

Dr. Standish then joined in:

And you **can't do that incrementally.** You've **got to have** the information **before** you can **keep** the information, so **information technology** is really **built into** our DNA.[309] (Emphasis added)

Dr. Hayes goes on to explain how the present theoretical structure of life, by supposedly random and unintentional generation, is being rapidly amended. This conundrum is being driven by the latest technologies, exposing a much deeper understanding of the DNA replication process.

Dr. Hayes also emphasized the importance of the "biological machines" we examined in the last chapter. He stressed that we now understand those machines to be essential, thoroughly and without question, in order for the DNA to work properly. So now comes the newest heated debate amongst the evolutionary scientists: Which came first, the biological machines that manipulate the DNA into a viable communication device, or the DNA that waited for the machines to evolve so it could then get to work?

In other words, "Which came first, the chicken or the egg?" While they offer *guesses* and *opinions*, to date, no scientist has a scientifically verified solution to answer that question, especially when they leave all possibilities of an intelligent designer out of the equation.

The final analysis of Dr. Hayes boils down to this: DNA and its accompanying biological machine "helpers" did not appear in stages, waiting on each other to burst into existence. Apart from each other, they would never have survived that long. Additionally, they certainly didn't appear together, accidentally, with no purpose whatsoever, and all at once, in perfect working order.

Additionally, what are the origins of this information that guides the activities of the biological machines? How do they "know" what they are doing? Are their activities mere chemical reactions to each other? If so, how do they know what chemical reaction to produce in order to communicate their "information?" The same goes for the information processes that provide almost endless possible combinations of instructions to the DNA molecular structure, and the unimaginably intricate "words and sentences" it forms from only four "chemical letters."

By every definition of the word, it really is *intelligence*, but where does it come from? To say it arose from a random evolutionary process, ultimately deriving from a chemical pond of accidental slush, is incredulous.

THE FOOLISHNESS OF SUPPRESSION

Now, more than ever, an explanation that "it happened by random evolution" appears outlandishly foolish and actually—rather child-like.
Those of us who trust the totality of all these biblical interpretations
and revelations can *see* what's going on. The Word of God told us
thousands of years ago that these days were coming.

For the wrath of God is revealed from heaven against all
ungodliness and unrighteousness of men, who by their unrighteousness **suppress the truth.**

For what can be known about God is **plain to them,** because
God has shown it to them. For his invisible attributes, namely,
his eternal power and divine nature, have been **clearly perceived,** ever since the creation of the world, **in the things that
have been made.** So they are **without excuse.**

For although they knew God, they did not honor him as
God or give thanks to him, but they **became futile in their
thinking,** and their foolish **hearts were darkened.** Claiming
to be wise, they **became fools,** and exchanged the glory of the
immortal God **for images resembling mortal man and birds
and animals and creeping things.** (Romans 1:18–23, emphasis added)

The next chapter will demonstrate the desperation of modern secular scientists, and how they attempt to explain where the intelligent
input driving the entire process of DNA information transfer is being
derived.

This is a major conundrum for them, since they now know the
intricate operating information is not coming from the mere chemicals themselves.

O my people, hear my teaching; listen to the words of my mouth. I will open my mouth in parables, I will utter hidden things, things from of old.... We will not hide them from their children; we will tell the next generation the praiseworthy deeds of the Lord, his power, and the wonders he has done. (Psalm 78:1–4, NIV)

51

EYES WIDE OPEN

*I liken today's DNA conundrum
to our modern sonogram technology.*

In the next chapter you'll observe several intellectual exercises of NIH-published scientists concerning the seemingly unanswerable puzzles of the DNA "chemical information" processes.

But first, let's focus on a foundational introduction to what they have to say in this matter. We'll begin this endeavor by once more highlighting the insightful words of Ryan Hayes, PhD, Professor of Chemistry at Andrews University, also quoted in the last chapter...

So **there isn't a chemical property** driving that arrangement. **It has to come from another source.** [Outside the body] I find that utterly amazing there's **nothing that is driving the structure** in the base pairs themselves. **There's nothing there** that's driving the chemistry.[310] (Emphasis and brackets added)

DNA ULTRASOUND

I liken today's DNA conundrum to our modern sonogram technology. Prior to its invention, and now-ubiquitous availability, evolutionists and secularists assured us that the "matter" within a woman's womb was largely a lump of "biological tissue." We were assured this lump of tissue was not yet a "real" human being.

But with today's ultrasound technology, as well as so much more biological understanding at our fingertips, we know differently. We are the first generation to possess the technology to see a *living child*, moving, playing, smiling, responding to outside environmental stimuli,

216

and even reacting to pain. We are even performing successful surgery on these fetuses, while still in the womb, and saving their lives! It's now glaringly obvious we're looking at a pre-born, human child, and not merely a "lump of living biological matter."

EYES SHUT TIGHT

In 2021, Kirstie Piper, published on an internationally prominent ministry website, stated (concerning seeing her preborn child in an ultrasound imagery procedure):

"For some reason, until **I had looked that baby in the eye**, the reality of preborn life hadn't fully registered with me. The **experience was so eye-opening** that when my boss asked what I thought of the experience, all I could say was, **"Their eyes—I didn't know you could see their eyes!** This is the tragedy of today's political climate surrounding abortion. Most of the world would rather scream with their **eyes shut tight** than listen with their **eyes wide open**."[311] (Emphasis added)

This is basically the same problem that evolutionary biologists have with DNA, once thought to be a mysterious molecular cell containing *chemically communicating* components, that just happened to contain the same "stuff" as all living things. But now, they, and the entire world, has to *look at* what's really happening! So...now they look. But do they really *see*?

WHO IS THE PROGRAMMER?

Following is another way of explaining the DNA conundrum in plain English, from a video now gone viral on the "Engineering Made Easy" YouTube channel. Here is a portion of the transcript of that video, and again, you can read the complete transcript at this endnote.[312]

Dr. Francis Collins, director of the Human Genome Project on this occasion stated, "It is humbling for me, and awe-inspiring, to realize that we have caught the first glimpse of our own instruction book, **previously known only to God**."

A **computer** machine **language**, the binary language, uses **only two letters 1 and 0**. The DNA code uses 4 letters A, G, T and C. In the same way [as our computers communicate] all the functions that are taking place inside the cell of the body are controlled by an incredibly complex and extremely long code written in the DNA, which is placed inside all the cells of our body.

A **computer program** may be **hundreds to thousands of letters** long. But this **DNA code is nearly 3 billion letters** long having a copy of the code placed inside all the tiny cells. Not only this, this code has instructions also for auto-repairing itself.

These all **unbelievably complex functions** are performed by the DNA code at extremely high speed without you even noticing. And this code is not just about its length, the code has to instruct the cell to complete highly complex tasks. So it's obvious that the job to write this program is beyond the limits of a human mind. **No program has ever been written by chance**.

So how can we think that this incredibly long code of 3 billion letters that is unbelievably complex and the densest storage of information in the universe can be written without any super intelligence behind it? **Who is the programmer?**... [As a point of context] A pinhead-sized piece of DNA has the same amount of information as **25 trillion 189-page paperback books**. [313] (Emphasis and brackets added)

With that introduction, you'll now understand the angst in some of the writings of the world's top DNA scientists. Those "academically recognized" research papers were published online and distributed by the National Institutes of Health (NIH).

As you read the in-context excerpts of these otherwise lengthy pieces, notice how they each so desperately try to hang on to the evolutionary explanation for the *miracle* of DNA communication.

One of the problems DNA researchers have is that we are living in the days of DNA "ultrasound" technology! As Drs. Hayes and Stanfield have so eloquently expressed, it has now been proven to be an utter impossibility that these billions upon billions of "instructions" are somehow coming from the chemicals themselves. Rather, the instructions most assuredly are actually coming from an "outside source," and/or were *programmed* by that outside source from the very beginning. Additionally, the programming and information components possess explicitly defined purposes—to create and sustain life!

So, the question they are trying to answer is, from *where* exactly did these intelligently "placed" instructions originate? Dr. Francis Collins, former head of the Human Genome Project (HGP) admits they are trying to answer this without a Creator.

But certainly, the **academic environment** is **not** particularly **welcoming** to open **discussions of** [**faith** in the God of the Bible]. There's a bit of an **unwritten taboo** that you can talk about almost anything else in terms of the search for truth, but maybe **you ought not to talk about religion**.[314] (Emphasis and brackets added)

Get ready to be "scientifically" entertained!

52

STUMBLING
IN THE DARKNESS

The "accidental randomness" of evolution
sure is intelligent, isn't it?

In the next two chapters you'll find excerpts from professional papers written by leading secular scientists, and published by the National Institutes of Health on the NIH website.

In those papers, the researchers attempt to wrap their heads around how the DNA's "chemicals and proteins" are constantly engaged in extremely complex "communications" with each other, with no apparent ability to do so from inside the chemical compounds from which they are made. Remember, these are not rudimentary communications, but rather, they are the most complex and vitally important communications known to exist within the universe!

We'll look at abbreviated declarations and conclusions of the overall research suppositions which started in 1998, and going through the latest papers we have in 2023-2024 (the timeframe of the writing of this book).

ONE IN A MILLION—1998

The first example is written by S. J. Freeland and L.D. Hurst. The NIH published paper is titled, "The Genetic Code Is One in a Million."

> Statistical and biochemical studies of the genetic code have found evidence of **nonrandom patterns** in the **distribution** of **codon assignments**.[315] (Emphasis added)

A one in a million chance, 0.0001% to be exact, is a near statistical impossibility. What the authors of this paper are concerned about is that because of the *nonrandom patterns* in the assignments of information to the components of DNA, there has to be another explanation which evolution alone cannot answer.

Of course, the paper stays true to their latest evolutionary lingo and biases, only to come back to the explanation that, "It happened by evolutionary processes." Laughably, this description is the exact opposite of the meaning of the term "nonrandom."

The Oxford Dictionary definition of nonrandom is, "determined by or resulting from factors *other than chance*."[316] (Emphasis added)

Without God in the picture, it's really the only answer the secular scientists have left, but that doesn't stop them from trying with all their might to redefine words and concepts.

Notice the varied language of intelligent design the authors chose to employ in their quoted admission, using words like *nonrandom, patterns, distribution*, and *assignments*. Each of these terms assign, by definition, a high degree of *intelligence* to a supposed, completely non-intelligent input process.

Look at a portion of the authors' concluding statement:

We thus conclude not only that the **natural** genetic **code** is **extremely efficient** at **minimizing the effects** of errors, but also that **its structure reflects biases** in these errors, as might be expected were the code the product of **selection**.[317] (Emphasis added)

Note once more the obvious language of *intelligent design* they employ. Even within their evolutionary conundrum laden conclusions, they still insist that the intelligent code of the DNA molecule occurs "naturally." The truth of the matter is that only genuine intelligent *input* can produce a code that humans can't even replicate. Even the word "code" speaks of an intelligent design, and according to their paper, *code* is a *language* that produces extreme efficiency, minimizes effects of errors, and reflects biases. If *natural* is defined as "randomly occurring without intelligent input," there is nothing natural about this genuinely intelligent process—even by their own definitions![318]

None of these things would be expected to occur in a nonrandom and "natural" evolutionary explosion that produced a sludge pond of chemicals, which then randomly became an indescribably complex code of life. It is difficult to read their continual double-speak, misuse of English language terminology, and constant scientific contradictions. What's even more embarrassing is the number of people around the world who are fooled by it. They either can't "see it" or they choose not to.

THE UNIVERSAL ENIGMA—2009

The second NIH-published paper we'll examine is titled "Origin and evolution of the genetic code: the universal enigma."

Following is what the authors postulate.

> The **genetic code is nearly universal, and the arrangement** of the codons in the standard codon table is **highly nonrandom.**[319] (Emphasis added)

The authors once again declare that the "code is highly nonrandom." *Highly nonrandom*, by definition, indicates there is a distinctively "intelligent order" that is driving the communication process of a code that even humans cannot replicate. It did not "randomly" burst into existence, it was *coded*. Furthermore, they go out of their way to explain that not only is this code "nonrandom", but it is *highly* nonrandom, thus purposely emphasizing the near impossibility of what they are desperately trying to defend! This makes my brain hurt—how about yours?

The authors go on to claim that the "three main concepts on the origin and evolution of the code are"...

- The stereochemical theory
- The coevolution theory
- The error minimization theory

So let's now take a quick look at the definition of these three "explanations" as to how this "highly nonrandom" code happened to just pop into existence without intelligence.

STEREOCHEMICAL

Interestingly, in 2022, the NIH website published a paper, *Arguments against the stereochemical theory of the origin of the genetic code*, which scientifically disproves stereochemical theory as an explanation for the coded DNA language. The author asserts:

> Stereochemical **theory is unnatural** because it is based on **artificial** and not simple mechanisms **as required for a good theory**...because the evolution of the **mRNA** molecule, which would really **define the genetic code**, is still **necessary** for the **complete origin** of the genetic **code**.[320] (Emphasis added)

In other words, as Dr. Steven Hayes explained in a previous chapter, "You need a working system from the get-go."[321] It seems that the *stereochemical* explanation is a scientifically weak one at best!

COEVOLUTION

Coevolution is said to occur when one species' evolutionary journey affects the supposed evolution of another species, which, in turn, influences the evolution of the *original* species. The only problem is this assertion has never been categorically proven.[322]

The *coevolution theory* falls apart just as easily as the stereochemical theory. Simply put, *coevolution theory* was first proposed in 1877 by... wait for it...Charles Darwin!

That's right, almost 150 years after Darwin's earliest theory, even with the advent of our most recent digital microscopic and 3D rendering video technologies that prove otherwise, the explanation is still being proposed that *coevolution* is the answer. It appears a number of evolution "scientists" are desperately grasping at straws.[323]

It's becoming apparent that what we can now "see with our own eyes" is getting almost impossible to explain, especially when an intelligent design of the Creator is purposely left out of the rationale.

ERROR MINIMIZATION

The *error minimization theory* also speaks directly to an obscure intelligence that has somehow been coded into the biological process of DNA transcription and replication processes.

From another NIH paper, *A neutral origin for error minimization in the genetic code* (2009), we get the following explanation that screams, "*Outside intelligence is necessary!*"

> The genetic **code** has the **remarkable property** of **error minimization**, whereby **the arrangement** of amino acids to codons is **highly efficient at reducing** the **deleterious effects** of random point mutations and transcriptional and **translational errors.**[324] (Emphasis added)

A "remarkable property" indeed.

Imagine, a completely random and unintelligent explosion in the universe, which supposedly happened 13.8 billion years ago, then somehow "created" intelligent processes that could eventually "learn" how to avoid errors within the most complex biological code in the universe. Also, these processes, all these billions of years later, can actually "remember" what they've learned so they don't make additional mistakes in the future. Wow! The "accidental randomness" of evolution sure is intelligent, isn't it? Keep in mind, according to that NIH paper, these are the *three main theories* that attempt to describe the "highly nonrandom" nature of DNA coded instructions!

The fact is, because the secular scientists have left out the necessary element of an Intelligent Creator, they simply have no genuinely intelligent answers. This is what Dr. Hayes repeatedly emphasized, proving his assertion within the context of that broadcast interview.

Let's have a little more fun in the next chapter.

If you thought the foregoing explanations were painfully perplexing, wait until you see the following proposals for the intelligent design in 3D imaging now before the eyes of the entire planet.

53

OUT OF THIS WORLD

It's almost as though our Creator, Yeshua, is gently asking today's evolutionists, "Do you have eyes to see yet?"

P anic and indignation are often the reactions of a person who doesn't have the "eyes to see" obvious truth.

In the earthly days of Yeshua and His disciples, those emotions were often displayed in the expressions, attitudes, and actions of the Pharisees. As you'll remember, the interactions boiled down to this…the Creator of the universe and long awaited Messiah was standing right in the midst of the ruling religious elite. Yeshua was performing miracles, often in their immediate presence, that only God Himself could carry out. Yet, instead of acknowledging what they saw with their own eyes, they ignored the obvious truth. His actions upset their power, wealth, and influence. So…they hated Him for what He did.

Sadly, that same pattern is also painfully common in the world of evolutionary science. In that world, it appears the scientific Pharisees still live!

UNIVERSAL GENETIC CODE—2017

By 2017 the NIH papers were still struggling to explain the admitted nonrandom and highly complex language of DNA that is now before their eyes like never before in history. Almost identical to the Pharisees of old, they too appear to be in a concerted panic over the dilemma they are facing, and have an indignant refusal to even consider an outside source of intelligent input. Yet somehow they have no problem accepting that our own, comparably simple, computer languages

226

were designed and coded by intelligent human beings. We would be considered foolish for even insinuating that computer codes which we currently use simply happened by random co-evolution processes over billions of years.

Observe the same old repeated explanations in the 2017 NIH scientific paper, *Origin and Evolution of the Universal Genetic Code*.

> The standard **genetic code** (SGC) is virtually **universal** among extant [currently observable] life forms…The structure of the standard genetic code (SGC) is **nonrandom** and **ensures high robustness** of the **code** to mutational and **translational errors**.[325] (Emphasis and brackets added)

THE HEAD BANGER—2022

In 2022 the panic appeared to be intensifying, at least according to the following NIH piece, which was given the somewhat convoluted title, "The genetic code is very close to a global optimum in a model of its origin taking into account both the partition energy of amino acids and their biosynthetic relationships."

That paper attempted to bring finality to the *most likely* theory for why the DNA code is so robust, nonrandom, and virtually unexplainable, particularly concerning the source of its indispensable information input.

The exposé follows a similar pattern of many of its predecessors. It's basically a shopping cart list full of theories attempting to understand how, with no outside intelligent design, the information process of DNA *could have* arrived in its present condition. The authors go about systematically unfolding, and eventually dismantling, several different evolutionary theories. Then they ultimately land on the following, the one they claim to like the best.

> Therefore, we will discuss our observations within the **theories** proposed **to explain the origin** of the organization of the **genetic**

code, reaching the **conclusion** that the **coevolution theory** is **the most strongly corroborated** theory.[326] (Emphasis added)

If "coevolution" (the theory in which we've already exposed enormous scientific fallacies) is the most "strongly corroborated theory," then these authors are basically admitting: "This is the best we've got! We will not admit even the *possibility* of an outside intelligent programmer that invented the 'code'. So let us revert back to Charles Darwin, who, in the 1800s, had zero access to the technological observations and discoveries of our modern times."

Panic and *indignation* are the two words that spring to mind. They are Pharisees who claim they can "see," but in actuality they are almost stone blind!

THIS CHANGES EVERYTHING—2023

This is my last example of the *panic* and what I consider *obstinate indignation* of evolutionary DNA biologists. But I've saved the best for last! You'll see.

This piece, published in July 2023, entitled, *The Evolution of Life Is a Road Paved with the DNA Quadruplet Symmetry and the Supersymmetry Genetic Code*, is really reaching at straws.

> **We also show** that single-stranded **RNA had the complete code of life** in the form of the Supersymmetry Genetic Code table[327] simultaneously with **instructions of codons' relationship** as to **how to develop the DNA molecule** on the principle of Watson-Crick[328] pairing.
>
> Our hypothesis that **all twenty amino acids are necessary** for the origin of life on the Earth, which **entirely changes our view on evolution,** confirms **evidence of organic** natural amino acids from the **extra-terrestrial asteroid** Ryugu, which is nearly as old as our solar system.[329] (Emphasis added)

Yes, you read that correctly. These authors suggest since we now understand that RNA had the "complete code of life" *from the beginning,* and that "all twenty amino acids are necessary for the origin of life" (as Dr. Stephen Hayes previously asserted), then there must have been an outside source. I'm right there with them…up until now.

Then their other shoe drops!

BEHOLD YOUR CREATOR

It appears the authors of that 2023 paper have discovered the *intelligent designer* they have been ardently seeking! According to them, this "intelligence" is the result of an asteroid ironically named *Ryugu* (Japanese for "The Dragon Palace"),[330] which collided with primordial earth. This explanation seems to make sense to the authors because it's "nearly as old as our solar system," even though this actually *proves* nothing.

But what is this latest *intelligent designer,* "Ryugu"? A CNN article from March 2023 gives us our answer. Let's examine evolution's *grand designer* of DNA information systems and biological machine processes. Remember that the NIH-endorsed author made the bold statement that *this* "entirely changes our view on evolution."

> In June 2018, the Japanese spacecraft left Ryugu for Earth in November 2019 and returned the sample capsule to Earth on 5 December 2020. The samples showed the **presence of organic compounds,** such as **uracil** (one of the four components in RNA) and **vitamin B3…**
>
> In March 2023, scientists announced that **uracil and vitamin B3** were detected in samples retrieved from Ryugu. Unlike previous instances when **nucleobases and vitamins were found in certain carbon-rich meteorites.**[331] (Emphasis added)

Yes. That proves it! Or maybe not. Actually, it doesn't even come close to explaining it! The presence of these incomplete ingredients of life existing on random asteroids only observes—but in no way explains—the basics of the existence of life. For example, it doesn't explain how all the ingredients came about in the first place.

This also doesn't explain how all the ingredients *knew* to come together in order for the nine million known species of life to form. Nor does it clarify how those ingredients understand how to *communicate* in intricately inexplicable *codes,* in order to create those millions of species.

It's almost as though our Creator, Yeshua, is prodding today's evolutionists and asking them, "Do you have eyes to see yet?"

SETTLED SCIENCE

So, the next time someone tells you that "evolution is settled science," remember what you've just read over these last few chapters. Keep in mind what biological scientists are now seeing in these 3D videos of digital microscopic reality, with their own eyes, and how they are scratching their heads in wonderment, desperately attempting to explain what they are seeing. It's like the Pharisees seeing the man who was born blind—standing right before them, yet they refused to believe what they were in fact physically witnessing!

From now on, when the fallacious argument of evolution is made, you will know what the issues are truly about, and that it's *not* "settled science." No matter how loudly they scream and insist that it is.

It's actually a matter of not having the "eyes to see."

54

THE BELIEVER

I could never again say atheism is the only logical choice
for a scientifically trained person. —Dr. Francis Collins

Dr. Francis Sellers Collins, born April 14, 1950, is an American physician-geneticist. He discovered the genes associated with a number of diseases and also led the Human Genome Project (HGP) that we explored in chapter 46. He also served as director of the National Institutes of Health (NIH) in Bethesda, Maryland, under three different presidential administrations, from August 2009 through December 2021.[332]

Prior to being appointed director of the NIH, though, Collins led the HGP and other genomics research initiatives as director of the National Human Genome Research Institute (NHGRI), one of the 27 institutes and centers at NIH. By the time he joined NHGRI, Dr. Collins had already earned a reputation as a *gene hunter* at the University of Michigan.[333]

THE CONVERSION OF AN AGNOSTIC

By graduate school, Collins considered himself to be an agnostic. A conversation with a hospital patient, however, led him to question his lack of religious views, and he began to investigate various faiths. He familiarized himself with the evidence *for* and *against* God in cosmology, and on the recommendation of a Methodist minister, used *Mere Christianity* by C. S. Lewis as a foundation to develop his own religious views.[334]

Dr. Collins continues to maintain that the basic evolutionary process is the vehicle through which the biblical creator God chose to

231

"create." Of course, I do not subscribe to that belief system, mainly because the contextual Word of God categorically does not support it, and neither does the truest and most recent science—as you have already seen in the last several chapters.

Still, Dr. Collins is adamant that he is no longer an agnostic and believes that salvation is only available to humanity through Jesus Christ alone. For this admission, I praise the Lord of Glory. I can only imagine how his faith must have been astronomically strengthened as a result of his work on the HGP, as well as, very recently, being able to observe the latest 3D imaging of what occurs within the DNA replication process.

SCHOOLBOY ARGUMENTS

Following is a brief excerpt of a much lengthier interview with Dr. Collins in 2006, conducted by Salon.com—in my opinion, one of the most liberal websites in the cyber world. Dr. Collins' testimony is quite telling, especially considering he came to faith in Jesus Christ in 1977, when he was 27-years old, a little over twenty years before he was the director of the Human Genome Project.[335]

> [Dr. Collins said]: **I met this Methodist minister** in this little town in North Carolina and asked him a number of blasphemous questions. And he smiled and answered a few them but said, "You know, I think you'd learn a lot if you'd **read this book** on my shelf. It was written by somebody who has traveled the same path—a scholar who was an atheist at Oxford and tried to figure out whether there was truth or not to religion."
>
> The book was "Mere Christianity" by C.S. Lewis. And within the first three pages, I realized that my arguments against faith **were those of a schoolboy.**
>
> Ultimately, I realized I couldn't go back to where I was. **I could never again say atheism is the only logical choice** for a scientifically trained person...After I had struggled for a

couple of years...I fell on my knees and accepted this truth—
that **God is God, that Christ is his son and that I am giving
my life to that belief.**

I think [it's] an enormous act of hubris, to say [believing in
God is a great "cop out"]—because we're now so wise about
evolution and how life forms are related to each other—that
we have no more need of God. Science investigates the natural
world. If God has any meaning at all, **God is outside of the
natural world...**

So for a scientist to say, "I know for sure there is no God,"
seems to commit a very serious logical fallacy...**I can't imagine** how nature, in this case **the universe, could have created
itself.** And the very fact that **the universe had a beginning
implies** that **someone was able to begin it.** And it seems to me
that had to be **outside of nature.** And **that sounds like God.**[336]
(Emphasis and brackets added)

In an earlier 2002 PBS interview with Bob Abernethy, Dr. Collins
described his faith in the following biblical manner. The entire transcript of the PBS article, called *The Believer*, can be read at the quoted
reference.

BOB ABERNETHY: Are you a mainline **Protestant?** An
Evangelical Protestant? **What are you?**
DR. FRANCIS COLLINS: I guess I'd call myself **a seri-
ous Christian.** That is someone who **believes** in **the reality** of
Christ's death and resurrection, and who tries to integrate that
into **daily life** and not just relegate it to something you talk
about on Sunday morning.[337] (Emphasis added)

Thankfully, there are those instances when even the most ardent
atheists, agnostics, and hard-core evolutionists have had their eyes
opened by the Holy Spirit of God.

In these prophetic days, my prayer is that many more will gain the spiritual *sight* only our Creator can offer. That's why this book was written.

Next, we'll go back to the literal beginning, to once again experience some of the most thrilling revelations you might have ever laid your eyes upon!

PART EIGHT

FIRST THINGS

In the beginning was the Word, and the Word was with God, and the Word was God. He was in the beginning with God. All things were made through him, and without him was not anything made that was made. In him was life, and the life was the light of men. The light shines in the darkness, and the darkness has not overcome it. (John 1:1–5)

55

THE HEBREW
CONNECTION

*Every letter representation in the most ancient Proto-Sinaitic
alphabet also had a meaning or idea associated with it.*

I n my previous book, *Yeshua Protocol*, I included a section titled
"The Beginning." In that particular portion of the book, I disclosed
several revelations emanating from the first verse of the Bible, "In the
beginning, God created the heavens and the earth."

Through several embedded illustrations, I then went on to connect
those disclosures to a number of Old and New Testament passages
demonstrating the numerous contextual links that are absolute human
impossibilities. Yet there they are! Right before our eyes. Those revelations, along with their corresponding illustrations, proved to be
jaw-dropping for a great number of readers.

In this, and the next two brief chapters, I have reproduced abbreviated and edited introductory material from *Yeshua Protocol*. This
material will greatly assist in the presentation of the new material
that follows. Naturally, if you've already read *Yeshua Protocol*, you can
skip these chapters and go right to the chapter titled "The Magnified
Word." If you aren't familiar with that material, though, it is critical
that you read on.

PROTO-SINAITIC

The most ancient precursor to what we know as the Modern Hebrew
alphabet is the *Proto-Sinaitic* alphabet, consisting of letters drawn as
stick figures, or *pictograms*. Those letters were usually rudimentary

portrayals of animals, tools, human body parts, and other generally recognizable objects of everyday life.[338]

Each picture was meant to represent the predominant sound of a specific letter of that alphabet. For example, if this same phenomenon were true in today's English alphabet then a depiction of a fish would indicate the "f" sound, a figure of a man would represent the sound "m," a figure of a hand would indicate the "h" sound, and so forth.

Most language experts agree that the Proto-Sinaitic script was the precursor to what would evolve into a number of modern alphabets of the world, including the biblical alphabet of the Old Testament that is academically known as *Paleo Hebrew,*[339] the alphabet used to write the original manuscripts of the Old Testament documents.[340]

HEBREW IDEOGRAMS

Every letter representation in the most ancient Proto-Sinaitic alphabet also had a *meaning* or *idea* associated with it. Those letter meanings are referred to as *ideograms.* For example, the sound made by the letter *Ayin* was represented by a pictogram of an "eye." However, the Ayin also held the ideographic meaning of the eye itself, as in *the eye of God, to see,* or even the idea of *seeing God's salvation.*[341]

The ideogram meanings of the Proto-Sinaitic alphabet transferred over to the Paleo Hebrew of the Old Testament writings, and even into the Modern Hebrew letters. Even today, many Hebrew people around the world attempt to decipher the potential meanings associated with particular Hebrew words by combining the Proto-Sinaitic/Paleo *meanings* of each Hebrew letter into a single message.[342]

IDEOGRAM CARRY-OVER

Those ancient pictograms are rarely depicted in the Modern Hebrew alphabet schematics, and seldom referenced in academic circles. Despite this, a large number of Hebrew-speaking individuals, as well as a smaller assortment of Hebrew scholars, continue to be ardent researchers of the ancient letter meanings, or *ideograms.*[343]

In 2013, an article titled *In the Beginning: The Origins of the Hebrew Alphabet*, from *Haaretz*,[344] Israel's premiere Orthodox-leaning news publication, verified the existence of the modern recognition of the Hebrew ideograms.

Four elements distinguish the Hebrew alphabet from others.... Third, **the names of the Hebrew letters have meaning** [ideas] in the Hebrew language. That **doesn't actually matter when writing or reading,** but it is **nice to know.**[345] (Emphasis added)

Hebrewtoday.com, often used by teachers and academic publications, is an Israeli institution that describes itself as a professional Hebrew language learning establishment. It is also in line with *Haaretz's* assessment concerning the alphabet ideograms.[346]

Hebrew Today attests:

Each letter in the Hebrew alphabet has both **a literal and mystical meaning.** This means that **each name** has a **mystical** significance, **based on the letters** which form the name.[347] (Emphasis added)

THE MEZUZAH

Affixed on the doorpost of almost every modern Jewish household and business around the world is the Hebrew *Mezuzah*—a slender "box" that contains important scriptures.[348] The ideographic element of the Hebrew alphabet is also demonstrated by the fact that, on practically every one of those Mezuzahs is emblazoned the singular Hebrew letter "Shin," pronounced *sheen*.[349]

The *Shin* is placed on the Mezuzah precisely because of its spiritually symbolic meaning. Since the earliest days of the The Shin Hebrew language, the Shin has represented one of the most majestic names *of God*. The Shin stands for *El Shaddai...God Almighty.*[350]

When used in this way, the Shin is a glaring example of the ancient Hebrew alphabet ideogram still in use today. Its message attests to the desired blessings of God upon the home or business to which it is attached.

Next, we'll examine the ideographic "message" of combining the first and last letters of the Hebrew alphabet, the *Aleph and the Tav*. In so doing, the Hebrew language begins to unveil one of its most striking mysteries, the meaning of which goes directly to who we are in Yeshua.

56

THE ALEPH
AND THE TAV

I am the first and the last, the beginning and the end.

In Isaiah 44:6 Yahweh declares He is the *first and the last*. The first letter of the 22-letter Hebrew alphabet is *Aleph*, and the last letter is *Tav*. This verse declares Him to be the *Aleph* and the *Tav*, and is a symbol of our all-encompassing, Omnipotent God.

> Thus says the LORD, the King of Israel and his Redeemer, the LORD of hosts: "I am the first and I am the last; besides me there is no god." (Isaiah 44:6, emphasis added. Also see Isaiah 41:4, 48:12)

THE ALEPH

Proto-Sinaitic | Paleo-Hebrew | Modern

The ancient *Proto-Sinaitic* Aleph, the first letter of the Hebrew alphabet, was originally represented by the pictographic form of an ox head. In the illustration above you can observe the evolution of how that letter has been written down through the millennium.

The symbol of the Aleph carried with it the "meaning" of the *leader*, or the One who is *most powerful*. Thus, this first letter was often used to ideographically represent El, or Elohim—God Himself. The Harvard Theological Review confirms this in a publication titled *Yahweh and the God of the Patriarchs*, which explains that, since ancient times, the Hebrew letter Aleph represented the one true Creator God[351] and was pronounced *El*.[352]

THE TAV

Proto-Sinaitic | Paleo-Hebrew | Modern

The last letter of the Hebrew alphabet, the *Tav*, conveys the most startling revelation of all. In ancient pictographic representations, the Tav was represented by a symbol that looks like the *crucifixion cross* of Yeshua. It retained that appearance, even in the Paleo-Hebrew, the original script of the Hebrew Scriptures, and remained in use until nearly the 2nd century BC.[353] And, of all things, the ideographic *meaning* of the letter Tav is the *mark*, the *sign*, or the *covenant*.

So, by declaring that He is both the *Aleph* and the *Tav*, Yeshua affirms that He is *God with us*, completely *one* with the Father, as well as being the Word that became flesh in order to become our Savior through the cross. Therefore, He truly is the *Aleph* and the *Tav*, God's "sign" to the world. He is the God who went to the cross to make His ultimate covenant of salvation with us![354]

Next, you'll observe a picture of the ancient Paleo-Hebrew script, called the *Siloam Inscription*. It is the world's oldest verified archeological example, recognized by archeologists the world over.

The *Siloam Inscription* was discovered in 1880 when exploring the Siloam tunnel, also known as *Hezekiah's tunnel*, in Jerusalem[355]

From the ancient Paleo-Hebrew writing of the Siloam Inscription we observe that the *Aleph* and *Tav* letters of the Old Testament Hebrew script were in fact depicted in the manner I have described. Especially noteworthy is the distinctive shape of the *Tav* (again, the last letter of the Hebrew alphabet) in the form of a crucifixion cross. Below is the

Siloam Inscription, from the website of David Graves, PhD, renowned archeologist and former archeology professor at Oxford University, England.[356]

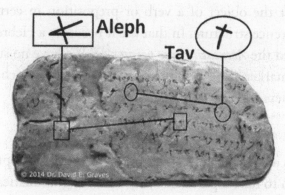

This is also precisely what Yeshua (Yahweh in the flesh) meant when He describes Himself in the book of Revelation as the *Alpha* and *Omega*, as is written in the Greek language of the New Testament.

> I am the **Alpha and the Omega [Hebrew- Aleph and the Tav]**, the first and the last, the beginning and the end." (Revelation 22:13, emphasis and brackets added; also see Revelation 1:8, 21:6.)

GRAMMAR MARKER

When the *Aleph* and the *Tav* are joined together as one Hebrew word, it is called the *eth*, phonetically pronounced *et*.

את
The Aleph/Tav

The English language has no equivalent of the meaning of the Hebrew *eth,* and therefore remains unwritten and unpronounced in English translations of the Old Testament scriptures.[357]

However, this unique two-letter Hebrew word is found over *eleven thousand times* in the Old Testament Hebrew texts. It is found on practically every single page of the Tanakh, either free-standing, or in

conjunction with other words and letters.[358] So what is this monumental and grammatical mystery behind the *eth*?

Strong's Exhaustive Concordance defines the *eth* as generally used
to point out the object of a verb or preposition in certain cases of
Hebrew sentence structure. In that use it becomes a Hebrew grammar
marker called the *Accusative case pointer*.[359] We have no such need for
a grammar marker like this in the English language, which is why most
English readers consider this marker to be a bit odd.[360]

THE SPIRITUAL MEANING

However, in a large number of its appearances in the scriptures, the *eth*
doesn't seem to have a particularly discernable grammatical purpose at
all. In these strange cases its proper linguistic significance holds varying opinions of interpretation.[361]

Because of this surprising phenomenon, certain "mystical" interpretations of the *eth* are often suspected. According to orthodox Rabbi
Eli Brackman the spiritual way of looking at the occasional non-gram-
mar-marker presence of the *Aleph-Tav (eth)* is "ultimately…the most
satisfactory explanation."[362]

Since Hebrew language scholars and Jewish rabbis admit there certainly are deeply spiritual meanings sometimes attached to the *eth*, this
fact brings up an important consideration…the *eth* (Aleph-Tav) is also
the name that Yahweh/Yeshua uses for Himself when referring to His
eternal nature. He is the Alpha and the Omega, the Aleph and the Tav,
the First and the Last, the Beginning and the End.

But how is the Aleph-Tav in Hebrew Scriptures relevant to our
walk with Yeshua? To find that out, let's go back to the beginning, in
the first seven words of the Word of God. This is where our study of
"having eyes to see" gets really exciting.

57

THE ONE
IN THE MIDDLE

One can make of this image whatever they wish,
but there is no disputing the truth of its presence.

Let's observe Genesis 1:1 in both the English and the Hebrew. Unbelievably, the first verse of the Bible uses the word "eth," but the *way* in which it is used is the most revealing.

In English, the first verse of the Bible is expressed in *ten words*.

In the beginning God created the heavens and the earth. (Genesis 1:1).

The grammatical use of *eth* in this verse is pointing the verb "created" to the objects of "what" was created...the heavens and the earth.

In the Hebrew text, however, something much more profound can be seen in the eth, other than a mere grammar marker. In Hebrew, Genesis 1:1 is made up of only seven words, and from that number, as many know, comes the biblical connotation of completeness, and perfection. This numerical meaning is the very essence of the entire message of Genesis 1:1.[363]

hā·'ā·reṣ	wə·' êṯ	haš·šā·ma·yim	' ēṯ	'ĕ·lō·hîm;	bā·rā	bə·rê·šîṯ
הָאָרֶץ	וְאֵת	הַשָּׁמַיִם	אֵת	אֱלֹהִים	בָּרָא	בְּרֵאשִׁית
the earth	(and)	the heavens	(eth)	Elohim	created	In the beginning

245

THE ETH IN THE MIDDLE

As noted, most experts in Hebrew grammar would point out that the only function of Aleph-Tav (*eth*) in Genesis 1:1 is as the accusative case pointer, indicating the object of the verb *created,* is Elohim. In this case, I would agree with the Hebrew grammar experts, except for the word "only."

Since Aleph-Tav is the very same term employed by Yeshua as His divine title, it also means that this two-letter, uninterpreted Hebrew word is pointing to Yeshua as the Creator. This is true because Yeshua says it does!

The New Testament declaration of Yeshua confirms this. Observe how the Apostle Paul describes it in his letter to the church at Colossi.[364]

For in [Yeshua] all things were created: things in heaven and on earth, visible and invisible, whether thrones or powers or rulers or authorities; all things have been created through him and for him. **He is before all things,** and **in him all things hold together.** (Colossians 1:16–17, NIV; emphasis added)

The Apostle John mirrors the same understanding of the *eth* in Genesis 1:1.

In the beginning was the Word, and the Word was with God, and the Word was God. He **was in the beginning** with God. All things were **made through him**, and without him was not anything made that was made....And **the Word became flesh** and dwelt among us, and we have seen his glory, glory as of the only Son from the Father, full of grace and truth. (John 1:1–3, 14, emphasis added)

The message of Colossians 1 and John 1 is the same as that which appears to be "coded" in the first verse of the Bible! Everything about Genesis 1:1 points directly to Yeshua, the Alpha and the Omega—the Aleph and the Tav.

THE GOLGOTHA POINTER/PREDICTION— FROM THE BEGINNING

The Gospels tell us there were three crucifixions carried out on Gol-gotha's hill on the day of Yeshua's execution.[365] Jesus hung on the cross in the middle, and the two thieves were on either side of Him. Remarkably, there are also three depictions of those "Golgotha crosses" in Genesis 1:1.

Remember from the illustration in the last chapter that the Pro-to-Sinaitic and the Paleo Hebrew pictographic form of the *Tav*, the last Hebrew letter of the alphabet, was in the shape of a cross, a symbol that was identical to the sign of the crucifixion cross.

We also saw that the *Tav* carried with it the ideographic meaning of the *sign of the covenant*. Indeed, the cross of Yeshua is the globally recognized *sign* of Christianity to this day, and this cross sign is found squarely in the middle of Genesis 1:1, along with two other crosses.

Looking at the seven Hebrew words that comprise Genesis 1:1, we find the *Tav* is used exactly three times. They appear in that verse in a strikingly symmetrical manner, with the *eth* (the Aleph/Tav of Yeshua) being that verse's center word. The cross symbols of the *Tav* are only visible in the Paleo Hebrew, the alphabet in which Genesis 1:1 was originally written.

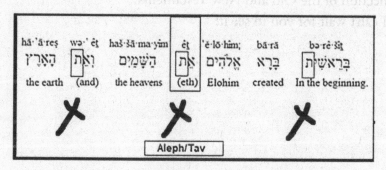

The Aleph/Tav is the name Yeshua/Yahweh ascribes for Himself.

Imagine that! Through the presence of the three *Tav*'s used in that verse, Genesis 1:1 paints a profound picture of Golgotha's hill, as it was on the day of Jesus' crucifixion. The visual of those three "crosses" places Yeshua on that hill exactly as the New Testament describes, as the one in the middle, between two others. One can make of this image whatever they wish, but there is no disputing the truth of its presence.

What we've uncovered reveals the deeply relevant biblical message connecting the Old Testament to the New Testament. Genesis 1:1 is genuinely portraying the eternal truth that Yeshua, the *Aleph/Tav*, created everything. He is God the Creator, in the flesh. He was the Lamb slain before the foundation of the world, and the One in the middle on Golgotha's hill, securing our covenant-salvation in the person of *Yeshua HaMashiach*.

◆◆◆

Again, if you've not read *Yeshua Protocol*, I want to encourage you to do so. If the information you've just seen is thrilling to you, then you'll be absolutely *exhilarated* by the other revelations embedded in Genesis 1:1. The imagery found in the book connects other passages of the Old and New Testaments, which will truly amaze you.

However, what you will see in the next few chapters should prove to be yet another stunning revelation of the humanly impossible interconnection of the Old and New Testaments.

I can't wait for you to see it!

58

THE MAGNIFIED WORD

He gives wisdom to the wise and knowledge to the discerning.
He reveals deep and hidden things. (Daniel 2:21–22, NIV)

The very first Hebrew word in Genesis 1:1 is *Bereshith*, pronounced *beh-rah-sheet.* That one Hebrew word comprises the three English words "in the beginning."

Bereshith is spelled with six Hebrew letters. Hebrew reads from right to left, so the six letters comprising the first Hebrew word in the Bible are *Bet, Resh, Aleph, Shin, Yud, Tav.*

Tav Yud Shin Aleph Resh Bet

One oddity that you might have already noticed is that the *Bet,* the first letter of the word, is much larger than the letters that follow. The Hebrew script has no capital letters, so it's not larger because it is capitalized, as it would be in English. Rather, the Bet is "magnified"—a Hebrew term for letters that are occasionally scripted as larger than normal.

There are only seventeen places in the first five books of the Old Testament (the Torah) wherein a letter is magnified. Most Hebrew scholars agree that this magnification of specific letters is meant to signal the reader to look deeper at that letter, and/or the words associated with it, as there is often a hidden mystery or a deeper meaning to be discovered. As you'll see, this is dramatically true of the *first* letter of the *first* verse, on the *first* page of scripture![366]

The Hebrew word *Bereshith* comes from the word *reshith*, which simply means "the beginning." In *Bereshith*, the *Bet* serves as the preposition "in." Thus, *Bereshith* is a compound Hebrew word meaning "in the beginning."

Also, since the *Bet* of *Bereshith* in Genesis 1:1 is magnified, and the ideogram of the letter means "house or dwelling," then the magnification of *Bet*, in this case, means the "House of God."[367] It doesn't mean just "any" house; it is magnified, so this emphasis is pointing to God's House!

THE IDEOGRAM MESSAGE OF BERESHITH

Now comes the first major revelation of the first word in the Word of God. When we take each individual Hebrew letter of Bereshith and assign those letters their ancient ideographic meanings, here's what we discover:

Bet—(magnified) The House of God[368]
Resh—The Head[369]
Aleph—The First—the Creator, God Himself[370]
Shin—God Almighty[371]
Yod—The Hand of God[372]
Tav—The Covenant, the Sign[373] (The letter is in the shape of a cross)

From the Hebrew letter ideogram meanings of *Bereshith* (with the magnified *Bet*) we clearly see the following message.

From the **House of God**…the **Head**, who is the **Creator** Himself, **God Almighty**, stretches out His **own Hands** to make His **Covenant** with us…the **Sign** of that covenant is the **Cross**! (Emphasis added)

If you think that revelation is amazing, and perhaps even humanly impossible, wait until you see the next chapter!

It seems the intricate mysteries of God's Word simply never end.

How precious to me are your thoughts, O God! How vast is the sum of them! If I would count them, they are more than the sand. I awake, and I am still with you. (Psalm 139:17–18)

59

ELEVEN
SUPERNATURAL
WORDS

Behold, the former things have come to pass,
and new things I now declare; before they spring forth
I tell you of them. (Isaiah 42:9)

In addition to the *ideographic meaning* of the first word in the Bible, we also discover something else about this magnified Hebrew word.

From the Hebrew word *Bereshith* there are at least *eleven* full Hebrew words—including the original word *Bereshith*—that can be seen within it! As we learned from the last chapter, there are actually twelve words in this one, since the word *Reshith* (the beginning) is also there. Of course, *twelve* is a significant number, which is another point of "magnification".[374]

Please understand, I'm not playing a "letter scramble" game, taking a random selection of the letters from a word, and then rearranging them to create new words. Rather, the other separate words, found within that first word of the Bible, exist in consecutive and/or symmetrically connecting patterns of letters, forming eleven full Hebrew words out of the midst of that one word...*Bereshith*.

With each of those eleven words, I've also given an example of its use, so you can see it is an actual word used in the Hebrew Scriptures. I highlighted those eleven Hebrew words by underlining the corresponding letters within the entire word *Bereshith*.

252

1. בְּרֵאשִׁית (Bet-resh-aleph-shin-yod-tav) (Bereshith) – In the Beginning (Genesis 1:1)

2. בְּרֵאשִׁית (Bet-resh-yod-tav) (Brit) – Covenant (Genesis 6:18)

3. בְּרֵאשִׁית (Bet-yod-tav) (Beit) – House (Genesis 12:1)

4. בְּרֵאשִׁית (Bet-resh) (Bar-Aramaic) – Son (Psalm 2, Daniel 7)

5. בְּרֵאשִׁית (Bet-resh-aleph) (Bara) – Created (Genesis 1:1)

6. בְּרֵאשִׁית (Bet-resh-aleph-shin) (Barash) – Presides (Exodus 24:17)

7. בְּרֵאשִׁית (Resh-aleph-shin) (Rosh) – Head (Genesis 49:26)

8. בְּרֵאשִׁית (Aleph-shin-yod-tav) (Ashu-yet) – Pillar/Foundation (Jeremiah 50:15)

9. בְּרֵאשִׁית (Aleph-shin) (Resh) – Fire, or the fire of sacrifice (Genesis 22:6)

10. בְּרֵאשִׁית (Shin-tav) (Shot) – Appointed (Genesis 4:25)

11. בְּרֵאשִׁית (Shin-yod) (Shy) – Gift (Psalm 68:29)

THE MESSAGE

Following is a sample of how the message of that entire first Hebrew word *Bereshith* can be laid out in context.

From the Beginning, and from the **Covenant House** of God, the **Son Created** it all. And He **Presides** as the **Head** of everything. He is the **Pillar and Foundation** of every single thing. He also became the **Fire of Sacrifice** [an image of the "Burnt Offering" in the Old Testament]—securing the **Covenant** with humanity that emanated from the **House of God.** Therefore, He alone is the **Appointed Gift** of Heaven. (Emphasis and brackets added)

To build on this exciting fact, in writing the book of Colossians, the Apostle Paul included the *Bereshith*, using all eleven words, or at least the undeniable *concepts* of them. Read the following Scripture to find the connection with the first word in the Bible:

He is the image of the invisible God, the firstborn of all creation. For by him all things were created, in heaven and on earth, visible and invisible, whether thrones or dominions or rulers or authorities—all things were created through him and for him.

And he is before all things, and in him all things hold together. And he is the head of the body, the church. He is the beginning, the firstborn from the dead, that in everything he might be preeminent.

For in him all the fullness of God was pleased to dwell, and through him to reconcile to himself all things, whether on earth or in heaven, making peace by the blood of his cross. (Colossians 1:15–20, emphasis added)

Notice, the *Aleph* and the *Tav* are also found in *Bereshith*. In the middle of those two letters is a Hebrew word that we've already noted, which is the word that spells *The Gift*.

בְּרֵאשִׁית - The Aleph and the Tav

בְּרֵאשִׁית - The Gift!

The message of this connectivity is majestic! At the heart of the *Aleph-Tav* is the greatest gift ever given to humankind—The Word that became flesh, and went to the cross for us, in our place, so that we could forever be with Him in His soon-coming Kingdom. This is "the gift," appointed from the beginning.

What are the chances?

Think of it! What six letter English word could also contain at least eleven other English words in it, without playing a mere letter-scramble with it? *None,* I dare say.

More astoundingly, even if we did find a six letter English word that contained 11-12 other English words, if we put them together, in order, how could they possibly tell the synopsis of the story of our life? This is impossible in the English language, but not for Yahweh/Yeshua; He is the *Living Word!*

These seemingly impossible revelations are found in the first letter of the first word of a book containing sixty-six other books, written by more than forty authors over a period of at least 1500 years, and hand copied and distributed for over 1,000 years. Yet, each book is congruent with the whole story, telling of humanity's redemption through Yeshua HaMashiach!

The immutable fact is, no other book in the history of humanity is like the Word of God. It is supernatural, from the first letter of the first word, in the very first sentence, to the first sentence of the last book of the Bible, Revelation. This sentence beautifully sums up the message of *Bereshith*!

Then the angel showed me the river of the water of life, bright as crystal, flowing from the throne of God and of the Lamb (Revelation 22:1)

By the way, the last word of the Bible, in Revelation 22:21, is "Amen," which means "so let it be." Therefore, the messages of the *first* word and the *last* word of the Word of God, *Beresthith* and *Amen*, come together to convey the message: "I am the Beginning and the Amen."

Thus says the LORD, the King of Israel and his Redeemer, the LORD of hosts: "**I am the first and I am the last**; besides me there is no god." (Isaiah 44:6)

"I am the Alpha and the Omega, the first and the last, **the beginning and the end.**" (Revelation 22:13, emphasis added)

The next several chapters will relay the mind-bending, but *true*, account of an unexpected encounter I had with the Lord that changed my perspective forever. This supernatural experience truly gave me "eyes to see."

It is my prayer that through this account, the Lord of Glory might give you a deeper understanding of what's actually going on around us—in the unseen realms...and give you peace and strength.

PART
NINE

THE DECISION

Son of man, you are living among a rebellious people. They have eyes to see but do not see and ears to hear but do not hear, for they are a rebellious people. (Ezekiel 12:2)

Then turning to the disciples he said privately, "Blessed are the eyes that see what you see! For I tell you that many prophets and kings desired to see what you see, and did not see it, and to hear what you hear, and did not hear it." (Luke 10:23–24)

I counsel you to buy from me gold refined by fire, so that you may be rich, and white garments so that you may clothe yourself and the shame of your nakedness may not be seen, and salve to anoint your eyes, so that you may see. (Revelation 3:18)

60

THE DAY
MY EYES WERE OPENED

Do not forget to show hospitality to strangers,
for by so doing some people have shown hospitality
to angels without knowing it. (Hebrews 13:2)

I'm going to share with you the true account of when I had an encounter with an angel.

It happened in my first five years as pastor of what was then a small church in the rural Florida panhandle. That glorious rendezvous with the "other side" shook my world, the aftershocks of which are still rippling through my life and ministry today.

I never asked the Lord to do such a thing before that day, and I never will. It was a gift, and as of this writing, I have not had another "visitation" like it. If I understand Scripture correctly, we can open ourselves up to great spiritual vulnerability, even the dark kind, in actively seeking such appearances from the unseen realm.[375]

I am convinced this particular angelic appearance was genuine, and I believe you will be as well, especially when you read the context and circumstances that were the foundation for that experience.

It took me a couple of days to understand the significance of that encounter. To this day I still draw tremendous strength from the experience, mainly because it occurred at such a crucial point in my life and ministry.

This is how the story unfolded...

HANGING IN THE BALANCE

Through no fault of their own, our church family was forced to endure an extremely difficult season of spiritual warfare during the early 1990s. The eventual disclosure of that situation exploded throughout the local community, with every imaginable twist and version of the story springing forth like a blooming field of daisies on an early spring morning.

Because of everything that transpired, I faced the difficult task of having to remove several people from our church membership. If that had been the only matter we had to deal with, the ordeal would have been much simpler, but, as it turned out, that was just the beginning of a much larger scenario. I will not unfurl all the sordid details here, but suffice it to say, this entire affair eventually escalated into a gut-wrenching experience, touching the lives of many innocent people along the way.

Through the next several weeks, the specifics of the saga became clearer to me. I realized the future of my fledgling ministry hung in the balance. It could all be gone in a flash. I was determined, though, to do the right thing—the *biblical* thing—regardless. I would not "sweep this under the carpet," as I literally had been *ordered* to do by a key church leader who, it turned out, was behind the fueling of the disruption. When the issue was finally brought before the church membership, one man was voted out of the church and another one had already left in shocking disgrace, of his own accord. A number of others left the church in the next few weeks.

In those days, the community where our church was located was still very small. We were living in one of those areas with a small town feel, where everyone knew everyone else's business, or at least *thought* they did. Gossipy untruths about our harrowing situation were recounted by some as fact, even though most of the tales were not even close to the truth of the matter.

Idle chatter only grew worse as the saga took on its own grotesque life. My desire to give up the ministry was heating up with each passing day, and the time of decision was rapidly approaching. Only my wife and I knew of my near decision to walk away from our ministry altogether.

In the meantime, the wave of public defamation began to build like a great tsunami headed straight for us. It seemed our community had never before seen a local congregation actually remove someone from membership because of abject and unrepented sin.[376]

It was while we were still wading through the immediate aftermath of that hellish scenario when I was given "eyes to see."

THE LIFTED VEIL

A week or two after handling the upheaval, I was standing in front of the elevators on the first floor of our local hospital. The patient I planned to visit that morning was on the fourth floor, and I had just pushed the "Up" button. My mind was still reeling from the monumental mess we had been through as I found myself constantly questioning every detail of the matter. Satan relentlessly tormented me through this self-critical thought process.

"Had I handled everything exactly as I should have?" I wondered.

Just then the elevator stopped and the door clunked open. As I entered, I noticed only one other person onboard—an elderly gentleman with a pleasant countenance. I nodded at him and smiled, expecting him to exit, knowing he had just come from one of the upper floors, but he didn't move. Instead, he simply returned the smile and asked, "What floor?"

The man had an unusually inviting quality about him, and a dignified presence. He was dressed in a nice suit, along with his perfectly styled, full head of wavy, gray hair. I had never seen this man before, but I felt as though there was an instant connection between us. It was a puzzling sensation—yet he exuded a comforting presence. The elevator door closed, and we lurched upward. I found it odd that he had remained on the elevator with me.

I started to introduce myself. However, instead of me leading the way in the typical "elevator chat," he spoke up first.

"You're Pastor Carl Gallups, aren't you?"

I was startled by the matter-of-fact nature of his greeting. "Yes, I am," I replied. "Do we know each other?" I asked.

I reached out to shake his hand, wondering how he knew me. I quickly flipped through the pages of my memory, but had no recollection of him at all.

As he shook my hand he replied, "No, Pastor Gallups. You wouldn't know me. We've never met." He paused for a few seconds then added, "But I know all about you." He smiled again, and looked straight ahead, staring at nothing.

I remember thinking, "What an odd thing to say to someone you've just met. What did he mean that he knew *all about me*? How was that even possible?" Remember, this happened in the days when we didn't have global Internet services, with in-depth "people search" capabilities. In fact social media was virtually nonexistent, or still in its earliest stages of development.[377]

Before I could inquire how the man had come to know so much about me, he spoke again. It was as though he was staying one step ahead of my brainwaves.

"The truth is," he said, "I'm a *fellow minister* with you in this community."[378]

Ah! That was it…

The community was still small, so I assumed he was a pastor whom I had not yet come across. I was fairly certain I was at least familiar with almost all the pastors in our county, but thought he might be new to the area. I was opening my mouth to ask the gentleman exactly what he "knew" about me when, again, as though he knew my intentions, he spoke first.

"That horrible matter that you recently had to handle at your church…"

I smiled as I thought to myself, "Well, goodness! Everyone in our county knows about *that*! There's no secret there! So basically, he just thinks he knows everything about me!"

"You need to know something, Pastor Gallups," he continued. "The Father has sent me to tell you this."

I froze in my tracks. I could barely speak. Who was this guy? The next words he spoke absolutely floored me.

61

THE UNKNOWABLE
DETAIL

*My eyes had seen and my ears had heard, but my mind
had trouble accepting.*

The elevator arrived at the fourth floor in front of the nurses' station. When the door opened, I hit the "Hold" button, then looked at the two on-duty nurses and smiled. They smiled back, acknowledging my presence in the holding elevator.

But I was mesmerized by this man. The questions swirled around in my mind: What was it he supposedly knew? How could he presume to be speaking to me for "the Father," when, before this day, we had never even crossed paths?

The "minister" on the elevator spoke up, revealing a very specific piece of information about the nightmare my wife and I had been enduring. It was an extremely private detail of what we were *still* enduring, an intimate detail that only my wife and I were privy to. It was practically impossible for anyone else outside the two of us to have known.

Today, only a handful of my most trusted church leaders know about the specifics to which I'm referring. If you were to ask them about it, they would assure you there was no possibility this stranger could have possessed that knowledge at the time. In fact, to this day, decades later, not a soul has ever indicated they knew anything about what only my wife and I knew. So the gentleman's disclosure of that bit of intel should have been my first clue.

I was flabbergasted. How could this stranger be familiar with the

264

intimate facts about something we had so carefully kept private? Yet this mysterious person, claiming to be a fellow minister, stood right there before me and in just a few short sentences had dropped the substance of the matter right into my lap. Again, as if he instantly knew my thoughts, and the fact that I was literally stunned silent, he continued.

> The Father sent me to comfort you, Pastor Gallups, and to tell you that you have handled the situation correctly. He wanted me to tell you to get on with your ministry. *Don't quit.* He is *pleased* with you.

I just stood there nodding my head, like a baboon in a zoo waiting for another peanut to be tossed into my cage. The conversation had become increasingly surreal, and I honestly didn't know how to respond. I remember thinking, "How does he know I am seriously considering leaving the ministry?" Again, no one knew that detail either, only my wife and I.

But he still wasn't finished. "That horrible thing that I told you I know about," he said, "it was actually an unclean spirit." He then named the spirit, further proving he knew exactly what he was talking about regarding this "unknown" detail.

Then he continued, "That spirit was sent to you as a ploy. It was meant to ensnare you—to *destroy* you. Its entire purpose was to gain power over you, and thus, the church as a whole. It was a demonic 'leverage' that would have been humanly impossible for you to overcome. But you walked right through the trap that had been laid for you. The Father is pleased; *greatly* pleased!"

THE EXIT

I still have so many questions I wish I would have asked the man on the elevator. I certainly should have pressed for more details. After all, it was *he* who had invaded *my* life—and privacy—not the other way around.

I should have asked where his church was located and how long he had been in the community. I should have inquired as to how he came to possess such intimate and humanly unknowable information about the situation, about my wife and me. At the time, though, my mind was a swirl of inexpressible thoughts, as though I had become mute.

As if he were still keenly aware of my inner turmoil, my deeply private thoughts, he simply smiled, stretched out his hand to shake mine, and exited the elevator. He turned toward the hall on our right and entered the big double doors of the hospital's rehab unit. I watched him until the doors flapped shut behind him. His last words to me were, "Please excuse me, I've got someone else to see."

I then turned to the left and stopped at the nearby nurses' station to get the room number of my congregant. Armed with that information, I started down the hall to visit the one I had come to pray with, but I was still in a fog. *Who was that guy?*

The greatest shock was yet to come.

The Vanishing

My *eyes* had seen and my *ears* had heard, but my *mind* had trouble accepting.

After briefly visiting with our hospitalized church member, I went straight back to the nurses' station, located right across from the elevator bank from where I had recently exited. The same two nurses who had seen us get off the elevator were still there.

"Excuse me," I said. "Who was that pastor on the elevator, the one who was with me when we got off? I saw him go into the rehab unit. Has he come out yet? I really need to speak to him. Can you help me?"

They both looked at me as though they thought I might be confused.

"There was no one on the elevator with you, Pastor Gallups," one of the women said. "You were the only one who came out."

I couldn't believe what I had just heard. "We were right here when you got off the elevator...we saw you on it, and we saw you exit it," she insisted. "We didn't see anyone else, and we didn't see you *talking* to anyone." she continued.

The other nurse asserted, "And no one has come through here from the rehab unit since then, either."

"I certainly don't remember anyone who fits the description you just gave us, as having been here today—*at all*," the first nurse agreed.

I was mortified, and for a brief moment, began to doubt my own sanity. To this day, I don't recall how I explained myself to those poor nurses. All I know is that I turned and went straight through the doors to the rehab unit, and inquired at that unit's nurses' station at the end of the long hall. I described my "friend" to them, hoping they had seen him. I was told the same thing: "No such person has come into this unit."

I left the hospital in a daze. I had shaken the man's hand, for goodness sake! He was real—flesh and blood! Could it be that I had peered behind a cosmic veil—if only for a brief moment? As biblically legitimate as I knew that possibility was, I simply couldn't believe it might have happened to me. I was in a deep fog, shaken to the core of my being. It had been many years since I had experienced that level of emotionally spiritual upheaval.

I went home and told my wife what happened. She responded in a matter-of-fact manner. "That's amazing! It sounds to me like you were visited by an angel." Was it all so obvious? Why was I fighting it?

ACCOUNTABILITY

A few days later I related what had happened to me, by calling a meeting with a select group of spiritual confidants. I sat down with my associate pastors and our deacon ministry team, several of whom had lived in our area their entire lives. They knew of no such pastor in our community fitting the description I was able to give them. They promised to help me search out this mysterious "minister." Although, one of them, at the conclusion of the story of my encounter, offered up the same explanation as my wife: "Pastor, you've had an angelic encounter. That's all there is to it." Another confirmation to my spirit.

LIFE-CHANGING

I have since shared the story on several occasions with my congregation, when it felt appropriate. I have even written about it in my 2016 book, *Gods of the Final Kingdom*, and since its release, the story has been shared all over the world. It took years, however, before I was willing to write about it, or broadcast it in any way. I had to be certain the man I had spoken to on the elevator was not a pastor or a member of a congregation anywhere in our area.

Decades later, there has been no revelation in the matter. I've never again seen or heard from this man who "knew everything" about me. It was as though he had simply vanished. Yet, he was *there*, on that elevator—and he *knew* what no one else knew.

As you might guess, I am convinced I was visited by one of heaven's *sons of God*.[379] Even these many years later, it would be difficult to persuade me otherwise.

In reality, none of this should have surprised me. I know the Word of God, and what it says about these matters. But actually living through the experience of it can be another thing entirely! I have since come to grips with the biblical reality that angels, disguised as humans, truly move and minister among us at times. Sometimes they are sent for the distinct purpose of undergirding our spiritual strength, especially in times of great trouble.[380]

That angelic visitation occurred at a critical point in my ministry, and the message was even more significant: *The Father is pleased. You did the right thing. Now, press on. Don't give up. But the final decision is yours.*

Looking back, I now realize the "Word from our Father" spoken by this mysterious visitor, which lined up with Scripture, was validated with the disclosure of that shocking but crucial bit of private evidence that he had revealed. Most importantly, the man/angel never even came close to exalting himself; his only concern was to do the will of the "Father" who, he claimed, had sent him—*to me*. The conversation held no benefit to him, at all; the benefit was specifically for me, it gave me the courage I needed to keep on the right track.

All praise to Yeshua, who helps us to have eyes to see—just when we need them the most!

Are not all angels spirits in the divine service, sent to serve for the sake of those who are to inherit salvation? (Hebrews 1:14, NRSV)

62

ON THE BRINK

The world at large still basks in its own blindness,
thinking they can see.

Thank you for taking this journey with me! I pray you have gained at least a certain degree of spiritual sight you've never before experienced.

The deepest mysteries of God's Word are being unfurled in our day: from the encoded message of the first word in the Bible, to the *stranger than fiction* world of AI, to the depths of our own DNA's unfathomable intercommunication systems, and into the unprecedented explosion of the multitudes of mind-bending technologies...

We can also add to that list the prophetically foretold resurrection of Israel and the biblically corresponding nations presently aligning against that returned nation, along with the world's obsession with a soon expected "alien visitation" [381]...all the signs are here. It's happening now. This, and so much more is now occurring in the sight of all humanity for the first time in history. The long-ago foretold, last days events of the Word of God are rushing in like a flood. History records those fulfilled events. Our calendars mark many of them. Today's headlines from mainstream media sources herald them, without even seeming to realize their happenings were all presciently spoken of in only one singular source on the planet—the Word of God...the Holy Bible.

Sadly, most of the world simply doesn't recognize the prophetic nature of these phenomena. It appears our world has entered into the days of Noah and the days of Lot, both of which Yeshua prophesied.

Just as it was in the days of Noah, so **also will it be** in the days of the Son of Man. People were eating, drinking, marrying and being given in marriage up to the day Noah entered the ark. Then the flood came and destroyed them all. **It was the same** in the days of Lot. People were eating and drinking, buying and selling, planting and building. But the day Lot left Sodom, fire and sulfur rained down from heaven and destroyed them all. **It will be just like this** on the day the Son of Man is revealed. (Luke 17:26–30, NIV; emphasis added)

THE GENUINE VISITATION

Today, our planet is on the precipice of yet another unprecedented prophetic explosion…the promised return of Yeshua HaMashiach. We are the generation now living in the most prophetic times the world has ever seen since the first coming of Yeshua. We are the ones that have been "raised up for such a time as this!" (Esther 4:14)

Of course, when Yeshua returns He is not coming back as Heaven's Sacrificial Lamb. This time He is returning as the victorious King, the Judge of the Universe, the Lion of the Tribe of Judah! This is the coming visitation that Satan dreads. This is the genuine coming visitation that will change everything…forever, to the glory of Yeshua HaMashiach!

…then **they will look on Me whom they pierced.** Yes, they will mourn for Him as one **mourns for his only son,** and grieve for Him as one grieves for a firstborn. (Zechariah 12:10, NKJ; emphasis added)

Behold, he is coming with the clouds, and **every eye will see him,** even **those who pierced him,** and all tribes of **the earth will wail** on account of him. Even so. Amen. (Revelation 1:7, emphasis added)

Then **will appear** in heaven the sign of the Son of Man, and then **all the tribes of the earth** will mourn, **and they will see the Son of Man** coming on the clouds of heaven with power and great glory. (Matthew 24:30, emphasis added)

Then **the kings of the earth** and the great ones and the generals and the rich and the powerful, and everyone, slave and free, **hid themselves in the caves** and among the rocks of the mountains, calling to the mountains and rocks, "Fall on us and **hide us from the face of him who is seated on the throne**, and from the wrath of the Lamb, for the great **day of their wrath** has come, and **who can stand?**" (Revelation 6:15–17, emphasis added)

Every single prophecy of Yeshua's first coming: His signs and wonders, His crucifixion, resurrection, and ascension—and even the birth of the church,[382] were all foretold many centuries before they occurred...and yet they were all fulfilled to a tee, only in Yeshua HaMashiach.

Think of the gravity of it all. While the religious elders of the first century continually demanded a "sign from Heaven" in order to "believe"...the *Sign* they were longing for was standing right before them, in their midst! They were looking at Him with their own eyes— but in their arrogance, pretentiousness, and pride...they could not see Him for who He really was.

The world at large still basks in its own blindness, thinking they can *see*. Like the Jewish sages of old—they go on believing in their own ridiculous fables and myths, even when there is startling evidence right before their eyes that their comical fairytales of a cosmic sludge pond and accidental beginnings to all of life and matter are disastrously incorrect.

The bottom line is that we have our work cut out for us! We cannot force people to open their spiritual eyes. Even Yeshua, who *could* have forced such a thing, didn't do it. Neither should we attempt to do so. But we must tell them, show them, pray for them, befriend them, and love them…if they will let us. And through the Holy Spirit, who can soften their hearts, perhaps they will be able to see with new eyes, *eternal* eyes. *Spiritual* eyes. This is the way Yeshua did it.

Charles Haddon Spurgeon[383] said it like this:

> We ought not to suffer any person to perish for lack of knowing the gospel. We cannot give men eyes, but we can give them light.[384]

I am honored to be a fellow servant with you in that great Mystery of the Universe, the preaching of the Gospel to the glory of the Name of Yeshua HaMashiach! We are ambassadors of the rapidly approaching Kingdom. The Genuine Kingdom. The First Kingdom. The Eternal Kingdom. The Final Kingdom!

Let us then endeavor to faithfully serve as Yeshua's ambassadors. Satan's vile reign on this earth will soon come to an end, and one day in the not so distant future, we will meet around Heaven's Throne. On that day the redeemed people of Yahweh will join our voices with countless angelic beings proclaiming *Baruch Ha'shem Yeshua HaMashiach, Adonai, Melech Ha'olam! Nehalelcha!*

Blessed be the Name of Yeshua—our Messiah and Lord, King of the Universe! We worship You!

I certainly look forward to that day, our blessed Hope…I pray that you will be there!

ACKNOWLEDGMENTS

I could not accomplish any of my ministry endeavors without the Spirit-led insights of my wife, my childhood sweetheart, and my best friend…Pam. She is my proofreader, assistant researcher, pre-editor, honest critic, and the one I lean on when, sometimes, I'm about to give up.

I also want to thank my son, Pastor Brandon Gallups, and my grandson Parker Gallups. They are well educated in theological foundations, and they have likewise assisted me in the research efforts for a number of my books. This book was no exception.

Thank you Marlene, Joanne, Hannah, and Shelby—you round out the indispensable and precious "girl factor" in all our lives! I love you dearly.

A huge thanks to the Defender Publishing associates who see that my books eventually land in your hands. They are Donna Howell (Defender Publishing CEO), Angie Peters (Editor), Rob Weddle (Editor), Jeffery Mardis (Cover Designer), and Joe Horn (CEO of Skywatch TV).

A SPECIAL TRIBUTE

I wish to give a very special tribute to the family of my dear friend, mentor, brother in the Lord Jesus Christ, and my longtime publisher—Dr. Thomas Horn, Founder and CEO of Skywatch TV and Defender Publishing…to the entire Horn family, *I love you*. More than you'll ever know. Thank you for taking me in as one of your own for all these years.

I don't have the words to adequately describe the impact that your incredible Tom Horn has had on my life. His insights into the Word of

God, and their applications to life itself, were almost inexhaustible. Yet now, in the presence of the Creator of the Universe, my dear brother Tom "sees" everything as it *really* is, in all its glorious entirety!

> For now we see in a mirror dimly, but then face to face. Now I know in part; then I shall know fully, even as I have been fully known. (1 Corinthians 13:12)

ABOUT THE AUTHOR

Carl Gallups has been the senior pastor of Hickory Hammock Church in Milton, Florida, since 1987.

He is a graduate of the Florida Law Enforcement Officer Academy. He is also a graduate of Florida State University (BSC in Criminology) and New Orleans Baptist Theological Seminary (MDiv in Theology) and has served on the board of regents at the University of Mobile in Mobile, Alabama, since 2000.

He is a former decorated Florida law enforcement officer, having served under three sheriffs with two county sheriff's offices, and has also worked in an administrative capacity in the Central Office of the Florida Department of Corrections in Tallahassee.

Pastor Gallups is also a critically acclaimed Amazon Top 60 best-selling author. His book *Final Warning* was in the Top 60 of all of Amazon's books for several weeks. A number of his other popular books have made it into the Top 300s on Amazon's bestseller's charts.

Carl was also an internationally known talk-radio host of *Freedom Friday With Carl Gallups*, 2002–2022, heard by audiences around the globe on three live streamed Gulf Coast radio stations (AM and FM), and several other online radio station sites and popular podcast platforms. He continues to be a regular guest on numerous television and radio programs around the world.

In addition to being a frequent guest speaker at national prophecy and Bible conferences, Carl has preached the gospel of Jesus Christ on three continents and in four nations, including Peru and Israel, and from the West Coast to East Coast of the United States—including Hawaii and Alaska. He has also preached, on several occasions, in the Canadian provinces of British Columbia, Alberta, and Ontario.

Pastor Gallups lives in Milton, Florida, with his beloved wife, Pam. You can find more information about Carl at www.carlgallups.com. Carl's life promise Scripture is Romans 8:28, 31:

And we know that in all things God works for the good of those who love him, who have been called according to his purpose…What, then, shall we say in response to these things? If God is for us, who can be against us?

ENDNOTES

1   Piper, Kirstie. "I thought I was pro-life until I saw an ultrasound," Focus on the Family, 9-30-21, https://www.focusonthefamily.com/pro-life/abortion/i-thought-i-was-pro-life-until-i-saw-an-ultrasound.

2   "In antiquity, crucifixion was considered one of the most brutal and shameful modes of death. Probably originating with the Assyrians and Babylonians, it was used systematically by the Persians in the 6th century BC. Alexander the Great brought it from there to the eastern Mediterranean countries in the 4th century BC, and the Phoenicians introduced it to Rome in the 3rd century BC. It was virtually never used in pre-Hellenic Greece. The Romans perfected crucifixion for 500 years until it was abolished by Constantine I in the 4th century AD."

   Retief, L Cilliers. "The history and pathology of crucifixion," PubMed, NIH, 12-9-03, https://pubmed.ncbi.nlm.nih.gov/14750495.

3   The immersive narrative section is told from the mouth of the apostle John – as an eyewitness to the events of John 7-9, as well as to the crucifixion scene itself.

   Some narrative-styled liberties have been taken – but none of them do violence to the scriptural context and/or doctrinal solidarity. I pray that you would simply enjoy the immersive narrative and, along the way, take a look at the attached endnotes embedded throughout. Those notes give invaluable scholarly backing to much of the narrative that has been created for this section, as well as that which has not been "created" but is right there in the scriptures – yet sometimes overlooked in our routine studies of God's Word.

4   While The day of evil can include the general evils of life that cause us to engage in continual spiritual warfare, the prophecy given in Ephesians contextually refers (in its greatest fulfilled sense) to Satan's final stand…in the very last days.
   (1) Expositor's Greek Testament
   Regard must be had to the definiteness given to the word [day] by the [Greek] article, which marks it out as in some sense or other a single day, a critical day, a time of peculiar peril and trial. Hence the choice must be between the time immediately preceding the Parousia, the searching day of the future in which the powers of evil will make their last and greatest effort. (Emphasis added) https://biblehub.com/commentaries/ephesians/6-13.htm.
   (2) Myer's New Testament Commentary
   The evil day here manifestly appears as a peculiar and still future day, for the conflict of which the readers were to arm themselves. Hence also not: every day, on which the devil has special power; but the emphatic designation could suggest to the reader only a single, morally evil, day well known to him, and that is the day in which the Satanic power puts forth its last and greatest outbreak, which last outbreak of the

anti-Christian kingdom Paul expected shortly before the Parousia.(Emphasis added). https://biblehub.com/commentaries/ephesians/6-13.htm.

5 This quote is edited a bit, in full context, by the author. The entire original quote can be seen at the following link: John 9:3. "Ellicott's Commentary for English readers," https://biblehub.com/commentaries/john/9-3.htm.

6 According to John 9. Whether or not this was a "special sabbath" as a part of the Feast of Tabernacles, or the regular sabbath that followed, almost a week after the Feast – is largely unknown. Scholars hold differing views. The matter of exactly "which" sabbath, however, is largely of no consequence to the larger narrative and teaching of this section.

   See several of the differing commentary entries here: https://biblehub.com /commentaries/john/9-14.htm.

7 See John 7:1-3. The Feast of Tabernacles – or "Booths." It commemorates the period when the Israelites lived in the wilderness. It is the last of the Seven Feasts of the Lord (Deuteronomy 23). The next Feast would be Passover, in March/April of the next year – about 5 months away. Passover is the first of the Seven Feasts of the Lord; and is the Feast during which Yeshua was crucified and resurrected.

8 Based on the events recorded in John 8 and 9.

9 According to John 9. Whether or not this was a "special sabbath" as a part of the Feast of Tabernacles, or the regular sabbath that followed, almost a week after the Feast – is largely unknown. Scholars hold differing views. The matter of exactly "which" sabbath, however, is largely of no consequence to the larger narrative and teaching of this section.

   See several of the differing commentary entries here: https://biblehub.com/com-mentaries/john/9-14.htm.

10 Ellicott's Commentary for English Readers. There is a chain connecting the sin of humanity and its woe, but the links are not traceable by the human eye. In the Providence of God vicarious suffering is often the noble lot of the noblest members of our race... Permitted by God, it is yet overruled by Him. It has borne its fearful fruit in the death and curse of humanity, but its works have led to the manifestation of the works of God in the divine plan of redemption. It is so in this instance. The blindness of this beggar will have its result, and therefore in the divine counsel had its purpose, in the light which will dawn upon the spiritual as well as upon the physical blindness, and from him will dawn upon the world. https://biblehub.com/commentaries/john/9-3.htm.

11 "Shriveled Useless Eyes" – This distinct possibility is heavily suggested by the entire narrative of John 9. Jesus' use of mud/clay, and the fashioning of eyes that now worked, is reminiscent of the Genesis creation account of humanity! He may have had "eyes" – but they were useless and no doubt hideously deformed. It could be that the man had little to no "eye-organs" at all. Regardless of which it was – the text itself is clear...after the healing, people had a hard time recognizing the formerly blind man. His eyes were restored, changing the appearance of his face. See the below commentaries and CDC medical information.

   (1) Anophthalmia – (Center for Disease Control) CDC
   "Anophthalmia is a birth defect where a baby is born without one or both eyes." https://www.cdc.gov/ncbddd/birthdefects/anophthalmia-microphthalmia.html#:~:text=Anophthalmia%20is%20a%20birth%20defect,fully%2C%20so%20they%20are%20small.

Also See: https://hermeneutics.stackexchange.com/questions/15747/are-there-any
-clues-as-to-the-nature-of-the-mans-blindness-in-john-9

(2) Ellicott's Commentary on John 9:1

The **use of clay** - a symbolism, which is to be **traced to the first Creation**, when man
was **formed from the dust** of the earth. We find this as early as Irenaeus, and it may
well, therefore, represent an oral explanation, going back to the days of the Evangelist
himself. The thought would be **that our Lord will here exercise the same creative
power as that which made man**, and will complete, by the gift of sight, this man, who
had hitherto been maimed and **without the chief organ of sense [eyeballs]**. (Emphasis
and brackets added). https://biblehub.com/commentaries/john/9-6.htm.

(3) Aquinas' Catena Aurea on John 9:1-41

"Theophylact. Some think that the clay was not laid upon the eyes, but **made into eyes**."
(Emphasis added). https://thedivinelamp.wordpress.com/2017/02/26/aquinas-catena
-aurea-on-john-91-41.

(4) GotQuestions.org on John 9

Jesus' use of mud in John 9 was meant to parallel God's original creation of man: "The
LORD God formed the man from the dust of the ground" (Genesis 2:7). In other
words, Jesus showed His power as the Creator by imitating the original creation of man.
The creative power of Jesus' miracle was not lost on the man who was healed: "Since the
world began it has been unheard of that anyone opened the eyes of one who was born
blind. If this Man were not from God, He could do nothing" (John 9:32-33, NKJV).
https://www.gotquestions.org/Jesus-spit.html.

12 Got Questions? "What happened at the Pool of Siloam?" Accessed July 22, 2023,
    https://www.gotquestions.org/Pool-of-Siloam.html.

13 The Pool of Siloam. Recent Excavation in Jerusalem.
    Herlihy, Brianna. "Steps where Jesus walked and healed a blind man unearthed for first
    time in 2,000 years: New archeological discovery unearths steps into the Pool of Si-
    loam," Fox News, 9-7-23, https://www.foxnews.com/world/steps-where-jesus-walked-
    and-healed-a-blind-man-unearthed-for-first-time-in-2000-years.

14 Ellicott's Commentary for English Readers
    The interval, then, from Passover to Tabernacles is one of about five months. The feast
    continued for seven days, during which all true Israelites dwelt in booths, in remem-
    brance of their dwelling in tabernacles when they came out of the land of Egypt. Like
    the Feast of Unleavened Bread (Passover) and the Feast of Harvest (Pentecost), this
    Feast of In-gathering was one of the "three times in the year" when every male Jew was
    required to appear before the Lord God (Exodus 23:14). Josephus speaks of it as the
    holiest and greatest of the feasts. It was at once a thankful memorial of the national de-
    liverance, and a yearly rejoicing at the close of each succeeding harvest (Deuteronomy
    16:13-16).

15 After this **Jesus went about in Galilee**. He would not go about in Judea, because the
    Jews were seeking to kill him. Now the Jews' Feast of Booths was at hand. (John 7:1-2,
    emphasis added)
    Cambridge Bible For Schools and Colleges
    "To this ministry in Galilee, of which S. John tells us nothing, most of the incidents

narrated Matthew 14:34 to Matthew 18:35 belong. The tenses here are all imperfects, implying continued action." https://biblehub.com/commentaries/john/7-1.htm. The major biblical locations in the Roman district of Galilee are Nazareth, Capernaum, Cana, Nain, Tiberius, Magdala, Gennesaret, and Chorazin. See: https://bible-history. com/biblemaps/galilee-in-the-time-of-jesus.

16   "The route from Galilee to Jerusalem via Samaria remained the shortest and easiest route, a journey that took only three days." See: Christian History Institute – Issue 59. "On the Road," Accessed June 24, 2023, https://christianhistoryinstitute.org/magazine/ article/on-the-road.

17   "Along their way, travelers risked dangers and hardships. Attacks by wild beasts remained a threat until the end of the nineteenth century, particularly along the Jordan Valley. Worse than the lions, which were eradicated from Palestine during the 1800s, were the unpredictable Syrian bears in the hills. Far more likely were attacks by bandits along lonely stretches, as described in the parable of the Good Samaritan. These attacks were often politically motivated..." See: Christian History Institute – Issue 59. "On the Road," Accessed June 24, 2023, https://christianhistoryinstitute.org/magazine/article /on-the-road.

18   "The route from Galilee to Jerusalem via Samaria remained the shortest and easiest route, a journey that took only three days." See: Christian History Institute – Issue 59. "On the Road," Accessed June 24, 2023, https://christianhistoryinstitute.org/magazine /article/on-the-road.

19   The "brothers."
     My Note: The term "brothers" is disputed among the scholars. Some believe it means his "relatives" – both half-brothers and/or cousins, etc. Others think it applies only to Jesus' literal brothers and half/brothers (through Joseph). For this narrative, I have simply chosen to make it about His relatives in general...as the earliest Hebrews were also inclined to use the word "brother" in that context throughout the Old Testament, starting in Genesis (See Genesis 31:32; Genesis 31:46 for examples). This fact is without dispute. Whichever the case, this one fact is not necessarily detrimental to the interpretation that I give the bigger picture here, in this part of the narrative.
     Gill's Exposition of the Entire Bible
        They [Jesus' "brothers"] therefore are to be understood of **some distant relations of Mary or Joseph, that dwelt at Nazareth, or Capernaum**, or in some of those parts; and the feast of tabernacles being at hand, they put him upon going up to it...(Emphasis added). https://biblehub.com/commentaries/john/7-3.htm.
     (2) Matthew Henry's Concise Commentary
     Christ's discourse **with his brethren**, some of his kindred, **whether by his mother or his supposed father is not certain** but they were such as pretended to have an interest in him, and therefore interposed to advise him in his conduct. https://www.studylight. org/commentary/john/7-3.html.
     (3) Clarke's Commentary
     It is certain that the Hebrews gave the name of brethren **to all the relatives of a particular family**. See Genesis 31:32; Genesis 31:46. https://www.studylight.org/commentary /john/7-3.html.

(4) Dummelow's Commentary on the Bible (Compiled by 40 scholars)
The unbelief of the brethren was removed after the resurrection by the appearance to
James (1 Corinthians 15:7; Acts 1:14). Being unbelievers, they **were evidently not of
the number of the Twelve.** For an account of them see on Matthew 12:50. https://
www.studylight.org/commentaries/eng/dcb/john-7.html

20 Expositor's Greek Testament
John 7:5. "For not even did His brothers believe in Him"; but this does not mean that
they did not believe He wrought miracles, but that they had not submitted to His
claim to be Messiah. They required to see Him publicly acknowledged before they
could believe. Therefore this clause is introduced to explain why they urged Him to go
to Jerusalem. https://biblehub.com/commentaries/john/7-5.htm.

21 Expositor's Greek Testament
"Go ye up to the feast. I go not up yet to this Feast, for my time is not yet fulfilled."
His time for manifesting Himself publicly was not yet come, and therefore He did not
wish to go up to the feast with His brothers, who were eager for some public display.
Had He gone in their company He would have been proclaimed, and would have
appeared to be the nominee of His own family. It was impossible He should go on any
such terms.

22 The Feast of Booths (Succoth) was the last of the seven Feasts of the Lord listed in
Leviticus 23. However, the Jews had added the Feast of Dedication, as a commemora-
tion/celebration of their victory over their time of Greek oppression under Antiochus
Epiphanes. It was also known among the Jews as the Festival of Light. (John 10)

23 "Are you mad? Do you have a demon?"
(1) Cambridge Bible for Schools and Colleges
[Thou hast a devil] The multitude who have come up from the provinces know nothing
of the designs of the hierarchy, although dwellers in Jerusalem (John 7:25) are better
informed. These provincials think He must be possessed to have such an idea. Comp.
John 10:20, and also Matthew 11:18, where the same is quoted as said of the Baptist. In
both cases extraordinary conduct is supposed to be evidence of insanity, and the insanity
is attributed to demoniacal possession. In John 8:48 the same remark is made, but in
a much more hostile spirit (see note there); and there Christ answers the charge. Here,
where it is the mere ignorant rejoinder of a perplexed multitude, He takes no notice of
the interruption. https://biblehub.com/commentaries/john/7-20.htm.
(2) Bengel's Gnomen
(Thou hast a demon) The foulest formula of reviling. Possessed, mad. They think that
the hidden design to murder Him could not have become known to Jesus Himself
except through an evil spirit. https://biblehub.com/commentaries/john/7-20.htm.

24 Myer's New Testament Commentary
The healing on the Sabbath, John 5:2 ff., the only miraculous work which He had
done in Jerusalem, see John 2:23, comp. also John 10:32, but the only one during the
last visit, for the remembrance of which the fact of its being so striking an instance of
Sabbath-breaking would suffice. https://biblehub.com/commentaries/john/7-21.htm.

25 In reference to John 7:27 see: Adam Clarke's Commentary on the Bible
No man knoweth whence he is—The generality of the people knew very well that the

Messiah was to be born in Bethlehem, in the city, and of the family, of David; see John 7:42. But, from Isaiah 53:8, Who shall declare his generation? They probably thought that there should be something so peculiarly mysterious in his birth, or in the manner of his appearing, that no person could fully understand. Had they considered his miraculous conception, they would have felt their minds relieved on this point. The Jews thought that the Messiah, after his birth, would hide himself for some considerable time; and that when he began to preach no man should know where he had been hidden, and whence he had come.

It was probably in reference to the above that the people said, No man knoweth whence he is. However, they might have spoken this of his parents. We know that the Messiah is to be born in Bethlehem, of the family of David; but no man can know his parents: therefore they rejected him: John 6:42, Is not this Jesus, the son of Joseph, whose father and mother we know?

Clarke's Commentary. "John 7:27:, https://www.studylight.org/commentary/john /7-27.html.

26 Ellicott's Commentary for English Readers
The words commanding the observance in Deuteronomy 16:13, and Numbers 29:12, mention only seven days; but this latter passage is followed in John 7:35 by a reference to the solemn assembly on the eighth day. With this agree the words in Leviticus 23:35-36; Leviticus 23:39, and Nehemiah 8:18. Later the eight days of the festival are certainly spoken of as in the Talmud, in 2 Maccabees 10:6, and Jos. Ant. iii. 10, § 4. The best modern authorities are for the most part agreed that it was the eighth day, i.e., the 22nd of Tishri, that is here referred to. It was the "great day" as the octave of the feast, and the day of holy convocation. https://biblehub.com/commentaries/john/7-37.htm.

27 See John 6:22-59.
28 See Exodus 17.
29 See Isaiah 12:3-6 for the quote.
Ellicott's Commentary for English Readers
If any man thirst, let him come unto me, and drink.—These words were almost certainly suggested by part of the ritual of the festival, which consisted in a solemn procession with music, and headed by a priest, which went on each morning from the Temple to the pool of Siloam, where the priest filled a golden vase with water and carried it to the Temple amid the joyful cries of the people. He then poured it out on the western side of the altar of burnt-offering; while another priest poured a drink-offering of wine, at the same time, on the eastern side of the altar, and the people during this act chanted the words of "the Hallel," Psalms 113-118.

The current Rabbinical interpretation of the symbolism connected it with the gift of the latter rain, which was at this season; and also with the gift of the Holy Spirit. The Talmud says expressly, "Therefore is its name called the house of drawing, because from thence is drawn the Holy Spirit," as it is said, "with joy shall ye draw water out of the wells of salvation" [Isaiah 12:3-6] (Jer. Succa, v. 1). Thoughts like these would be connected with this ritual by the Jews and by Jesus Himself, and the exact form which his own thought takes is marked by the words, "If any man thirst."

He stands there on the great day of the feast, and around Him are men who for seven successive mornings have witnessed acts and uttered words telling, though they know it not, of the true satisfaction of spiritual thirst, and thinking of the descent of showers on the thirsty ground, and in some vague way of the Holy Spirit's presence. They are as the woman of Samaria was by the side of the true well. For everyone who really knew his need, the source of living water was at hand.

That very Feast of Tabernacles, with its dwelling in tents, moreover, brought vividly to their minds the wilderness-life; and as in the past chapter the manna has formed the basis of His teaching about the Bread of Life, so here the striking of the rock and the streams gushing forth in the desert would be present to their minds. In the interpretation of one who was himself a Pharisee, [the apostle Paul] and was taught in the schools of Jerusalem, "that rock was Christ" (1Corinthians 10:4, emphasis and brackets added). https://biblehub.com/commentaries/john/7-37.htm.

See also: MacLaren's Expositions. Also at https://biblehub.com/commentaries/john/7-37.htm.

30 The entirety of the Hallel is the combined Psalms 113-118. The verses quoted in the narrative section are Psalms 113:1-3 and Psalm 114:7-8.

31 Ibid. Ellicott's Commentary for English Readers
"In the interpretation of one who was himself a Pharisee, [the apostle Paul] and was taught in the schools of Jerusalem, "that rock was Christ" (1Corinthians 10:4, emphasis and brackets added). https://biblehub.com/commentaries/john/7-37.htm.
See also: MacLaren's Expositions. Also at https://biblehub.com/commentaries/john/7-37.htm.

32 See John 6.

33 Ibid. Ellicott's Commentary for English Readers
If any man thirst, let him come unto me, and drink.—These words were almost certainly suggested by part of the ritual of the festival. https://biblehub.com/commentaries/john/7-37.htm.
See also: MacLaren's Expositions. Also at https://biblehub.com/commentaries/john/7-37.htm.

34 Jamieson-Fausset-Brown Bible Commentary
Had those who gave it made the inquiry which the case demanded, they would have found that Jesus "came out of Galilee" (Joh 7:41) and "out of Bethlehem" both, alike in fulfilment of prophecy as in point of fact. (Mt 2:23; 4:13-16). https://biblehub.com/commentaries/john/7-42.htm.

35 Pulpit Commentary
But some said, Both the Christ come out of Galilee? Here criticism was at once at work upon obvious appearances, but misunderstood facts. Was he not called "Jesus of Nazareth"? His life had been spent there, his ministry in the main restricted to the northern province. These questions give a vivid scene and portray a great emotion. The people are resting on the letter of prophecy (Micah 5:2), where the Messiah, as understood by their own teachers (see Matthew 2:5), was to proceed from Bethlehem; but they overlook the remarkable prediction in Isaiah 9:1, where Galilee is spoken of as the scene of extraordinary illumination. John 7:41.https://biblehub.com/commentaries/john/7-41.htm.

36 What Did Jesus Write in the Dirt?

(1) Gill's Exposition of the Entire Bible

Jesus stooped down, and with his finger wrote on the ground;...**he wrote in legible characters the sins of the woman's accusers**; and the learned **Wagenseil** makes mention of an **ancient Greek manuscript** he had seen, in which were the following words, "**the sins of every one of them...** (Emphasis added). https://biblehub.com/commentaries/john /8-6.htm

Notes on the biography of the aforementioned Wagenseil in Gill's Commentary entry: Johann Christoph Wagenseil, professor of Oriental languages at the University of Altdorf from 1674 to 1697, is particularly known for his Tela ignea Satanae, which he published in 1681. The work contains a noteworthy and positive section on Mishnah and Talmud. His esteem for the Mishnah had already in 1674 materialized in an annotated Latin translation of tractate Sotah, which in 1700 was included in Surenhusius's complete Latin Mishnah edition. https://academic.oup.com/book/43094/chapter -abstract/361564003?redirectedFrom=fulltext.

(2) Henry's Complete Commentary on the Bible

Some Greek copies here read, **He wrote on the ground**, enos hekastou auton tas hamartias--**the sins of every one of them**; this he could do, for he sets our iniquities before him; and this he will do, for he will set them in order before us too. (Emphasis added) https://www.studylight.org/commentary/john/8-6.html.

(3) Clarke's Commentary

With his finger wrote—Several MSS. add **their sins who accused her**, and the sins of all men. (Emphasis added). We never find that Christ wrote anything before or after this. https://www.studylight.org/commentary/john/8-6.html.

(4) Barclay's Daily Study Bible

The Armenian translates the passage this way: "He himself, bowing his head, was writing with his finger on the earth to declare their sins; and they were seeing their several sins on the stones." The suggestion is that **Jesus was writing in the dust the sins of the very men who were accusing the woman.** The normal Greek word for to write is graphein (G1125) ; but here the word used is katagraphein, which can mean **to write down a record against someone**...Jesus was confronting those self-confident sadists with the record of their own sins. (Emphasis added). https://www.studylight.org/commentary /john/8-6.html.

(5) Kelly Commentary on Books of the Bible

He simply stoops down, and **with His finger writes on the ground**. He allowed them to think of the circumstances, of themselves, and of Him. When they continued to ask, and He lifted Himself up and spoke to them those memorable words, He again stoops, that they might weigh them in their consciences. **It was the light of God cast on their thoughts, words, and life.** The words were few, simple, and self-evidencing. He that is without sin among you, let him first cast the stone at her." **The effect was immediate and complete.** His words penetrated to the heart. (Emphasis added). https://www. studylight.org/commentary/john/8-6.html.

(6) Smith's Bible Commentary (Chuck Smith - Calvary Chapel)

...starting with the oldest of those Pharisees in the crowd, who were really pushing Him and challenging...**Jesus begins to write their names and write the things they**

have been doing. (Emphasis added). https://www.studylight.org/commentary/john/8-6.html.

(7) Enduring Word Commentary - David Guzik

"The normal Greek word for to write is graphein; but here the word used is katagrapheini, which can mean **to write down a record against someone.**" (Emphasis added). https://enduringword.com/bible-commentary/john-8.

37 Jeremiah 17:10, 13 (ESV). I have inserted the Hebrew word Yahweh where the English text says LORD. In the Hebrew text, the actual word is Yahweh.

38 From Isaiah 12:2-3 (ESV). Where I have inserted the words "Yeshua" – the text in English actually says **salvation.** However, the word for salvation in Hebrew is **Yeshua!** The English text also has "God" in verse 2. The Word in the Hebrew text is **El or Elohim.** The same with **Yahweh** in verse 3. The English text in most versions translates it as the **Lord God.** The Hebrew word in the text is **Yah or Yahweh.**

39 Jesus was fulfilling Jeremiah 17: 10, 13.

(1) Fuente: A Popular Commentary on the New Testament:
Thereby Jesus takes the position of a divine judge both of the woman who is brought to Him and of the very persons themselves who present her to Him. A sentence is not only pronounced: it is written. This act has a meaning **analogous to that of the saying of Jeremiah** (Jeremiah 17:13): Those who turn aside from Me shall be written in the earth. https://www.biblia.work/bible-commentary/exegetical-and-hermeneutical-commentary -of-john-86.

(2) Jamieson, Fausset and Brown's Commentary Critical and Explanatory on the Whole Bible

(See Jeremiah 17:13, "they that depart from me shall be written in the earth". It could be that Christ was writing their names in the earth, thus **fulfilling this prophecy in Jeremiah.** They knew the Old Testament and this passage, and were convicted in their hearts.) https://www.biblia.work/bible-commentary/exegetical-and-hermeneutical-commentary-of-john-86.

(3) Bengel's Gnomen

Scribes, write judgments against others; I also can write against you, John 8:26, "I have many things to say and to judge of you." Your sins have been written in your heart; and your names in the earth: **Jeremiah 17:1; Jeremiah 17:13,** "The sin of Judah is written with a pen of iron, and with the point of a diamond; it is graven upon the table of their heart;—they that depart from Me, shall be written in the earth, because they have forsaken the Lord." **(What suppose that He wrote the names of the accusers?)** (Parenthesis in the original, Emphasis added). https://biblehub.com/commentaries/john/8-6.htm.

40 Jamieson-Fausset-Brown Bible Commentary
In saying, "Go and sin no more," which had been before said to one who undoubtedly believed (Joh 5:14), more is probably implied than expressed. If brought suddenly to conviction of sin, admiration of her Deliverer, and a willingness to be admonished and guided by Him, this call to begin a new life may have carried with it what would ensure and naturally bring about a permanent change. (This whole narrative is wanting in some of the earliest and most valuable manuscripts, and those which have it vary to some extent. The internal evidence in its favor is almost overpowering. It is easy

to account for its omission, though genuine; but if not so, it is next to impossible to account for its insertion). https://biblehub.com/commentaries/john/8-11.htm.

41 (1) Ellicott's Commentary for English Readers
On the eve of the Lesser Festival (the middle of the eight day feast), and on each of the five nights which followed, there was an illumination in the court of the Temple to celebrate the "Rejoicing of the Water-Drawing."…Since the teaching of the last chapter, there had been an interval of, it may be, several hours. We may naturally think that the shades of evening were now drawing on. He is standing in the Treasury near to the court of the women (Note on John 8:20), where for the six nights last past there had been a great light, reminding those who could read its meaning of the greater light which illumined the footsteps of their fathers. https://biblehub.com/commentaries /john/8-12.htm.
(2) For an opposing view on the day and timing of this event see:
Myer's NT Commentary
This renewed coming forward to address them is not, however, to be placed on the last day of the feast, but is so definitely marked off by John 8:20 as a special act, and so clearly distinguished from the preceding, that it must be assigned to one of the following days; just as in John 8:21 the similar transition and the recurring πάλιν introduce again a new discourse spoken on another day. https://biblehub.com/commentaries/ john/8-12.htm.

42 John 8:20. Ellicott's Commentary for English Readers. He [Yeshua] is standing in the Treasury near to the court of the women…https://biblehub.com/commentaries/ john/8-12.htm.

43 Ibid. Ellicott's Commentary for English Readers. On the eve of the Lesser Festival (the middle of the eight day feast), and on each of the five nights which followed, there was an illumination in the court of the Temple…

44 "Where is your Father?"
(1) Enduring Word Commentary - David Guzik. Where is Your father? The Pharisees probably intended this as a deeply cutting insult to Jesus. They referred to the controversy around His virgin birth, and to the rumors that it was not a miraculous conception, but an impure one. "In the East, to question a man's paternity is a definite slur on his legitimacy." (Tenney) In referring to Jesus' parentage, the Pharisees thought they had some damaging or scandalous information on Him. They must have thought, "Watch how He reacts when we reveal what we know about Him." So they insulted the parentage of Jesus, calling Him an illegitimate child. The implication was, "We were not born of fornication, but we don't know about you, Jesus." (Emphasis added). https://enduringword.com/bible-commentary/john-8.
(2) Lange's Commentary on the Holy Scriptures: Critical, Doctrinal and Homiletical John 8:19. Where is thy Father?— An intentional misapprehension and malicious mockery. Therefore no doubt also a feint, as if they were inquiring after a human father of Jesus (Augustine, and others); the use of [the specific Greek language in this text] is not against this….the irony might possibly have gone even to this wicked extent. (Emphasis added). https://www.studylight.org/commentaries/eng/lcc/john-8. html.

(3) Dr. Constable's Expository Notes

Their request [Where is your father?] was **probably an intentional insult** (cf. John 8:41). "In the East, **to question a man's paternity is a definite slur on his legitimacy.**" [Note: Tenney, "John," p. 93.] (Emphasis added). https://www.studylight.org/commentaries/eng/dcc/john-8.html.

45 They didn't know He meant "the Father – God."

(1) My Note: The Greek language of this text in the Gospel of John is clear, and emphatic. Therefore, according to John, this particular listening audience of religious elites flatly did not understand that Yeshua literally meant the Father of all Creation, Yahweh, was His Father. This shocking admission was so memorable that John records it here not only as fact, but to also build up his Gospel account concerning that entire week, to finally bring forth the grand crescendo of John 8 into view. This is the view I will disclose in the following chapters. In fact, verses 43-45 of this same chapter make it very clear that Yeshua also knew that they didn't understand that Yahweh was His Father.

Why do you not understand what I say? It is because you cannot bear to hear my word. You are of your father the devil, and your will is to do your father's desires. He was a murderer from the beginning, and does not stand in the truth, because there is no truth in him. When he lies, he speaks out of his own character, for he is a liar and the father of lies. But because I tell the truth, you do not believe me. (John 8:43-45)

(2) Pulpit Commentary

"That they had not perceived that Jesus was throughout in these references speaking of the Father of all - the supreme Source of all power, the Lord of hosts. Even when he had said, "Ye have not known me, nor my Father," they had not risen to such a conception of the Lord's meaning as to suppose that the supreme Father himself was being suggested to them and cited as the corroborative Witness, as the supernatural Aid and Divine Presence which was giving validity to all that Christ has said about himself. Their ignorance and lack of perception need not astonish us when we reflect upon the obscurity and non-receptivity of the apostles themselves, and the like obtuseness of theologians and cultivated men of the world in every age from that day to this." https://biblehub.com/commentaries/john/8-27.htm.

(3) Gill's Exposition of the Entire Bible

That they did not know that he meant God the Father by him that sent him, so deriving his mission and doctrine from him; their hearts were hardened, and **their eyes were blinded.** The Vulgate Latin version reads, "they did not know that he said, God was his Father".

(4) Ellicott's Commentary for English Speakers

Of these men St. John tells us now that they did not know that the Sender and the Father are one. The statement of their want of perception, which strikes us as so marvelous, is made just because it was marvelous. St. John remembers it many years afterwards, and remembers that on account of it Jesus proceeded to declare more fully that every act He did was done in the Father, and that every word He spoke was taught by the Father, and that in every event of His life the Father was present. https://biblehub.com/commentaries/john/8-27.htm.

(5) Matthew Poole's Commentary

The Jews (as we are told) used to call God The Father, in a way of eminency: they understood that he spake to them of his Father; but they would not understand when he
spake to them of his Father, or the Father, he meant God the Father of all; their minds
were blinded, that they could not see, and their hearts hardened, that they could not
understand. https://biblehub.com/commentaries/john/8-27.htm.

46 Ellicott's Commentary for English Readers
When ye have lifted up the Son of man.—Better, When ye shall have lifted up . . .
(Comp. Notes on John 3:14; John 6:62; John 12:32; John 12:34.) Both the Crucifixion
and Ascension are implied here. Now. For the first time, they are marked out as the
instruments of the Crucifixion (comp. Acts 3:15), and therefore the means by which He
will return to His Father's throne. https://biblehub.com/commentaries/john/8-28.htm.

47 Enduring Word Commentary - David Guzik
The Pharisees thought they had some damaging or scandalous information on Him.
They must have thought, "Watch how He reacts when we reveal what we know about
Him." So they insulted the parentage of Jesus, calling Him an illegitimate child. The
implication was, "We were not born of fornication, but we don't know about you,
Jesus." (Emphasis added). https://enduringword.com/bible-commentary/john-8.

48 See John 8:19 and John 8:41.

49 **My Note:** Actually, they had intimated this accusation twice in just a few moments…
Where is your father? (John 8:19, ESV) and: We are not the illegitimate ones! (John
8:41, ESV). See the following five commentary attestations of what I have presented in
the narrative.
Enduring Word Commentary - David Guzik
Where is Your father? The Pharisees probably intended this as a deeply cutting insult
to Jesus. They referred to the controversy around His virgin birth, and to the rumors
that it was not a miraculous conception, but an impure one. "In the East, to question a
man's paternity is a definite slur on his legitimacy." (Tenney) In referring to Jesus' parentage, the Pharisees thought they had some damaging or scandalous information on
Him. They must have thought, "Watch how He reacts when we reveal what we know
about Him." So they insulted the parentage of Jesus, calling Him an illegitimate child.
The implication was, "We were not born of fornication, but we don't know about you,
Jesus." (Emphasis added). https://enduringword.com/bible-commentary/john-8.
(2) Smith's Bible Commentary
This could be a reference to the virgin birth. They could be here declaring your mother
bore you out of wedlock. "We're not born of fornication." And it could be that the story of Mary had gotten around. That Joseph wasn't really the father of Jesus. And they
did not believe that He was conceived of the Holy Spirit, and so they are accusing Him
of being born out of wedlock .... Here it seems to be a low blow at Jesus, challenging
the virgin birth....All the way through, the accounts where Mary is brought into the
picture it's always in a very admirable way. Except here. "We're not born of fornication." You know your mother bore you out of wedlock. (Emphasis added). https://
www.studylight.org/commentary/john/8-19.html.
(3) Barclay's Daily Study Bible
When the Jews spoke like this, there may have been something **much more personal in**

it. It is certainly true in later times that **the Jews spread abroad a most malicious slander against Jesus.** The Christians very early preached the miraculous birth of Jesus. **The Jews put it about that Mary had been unfaithful to Joseph; that her paramour had been a Roman soldier called Panthers; and that Jesus was the child of that adulterous union.** [See this site for more info: https://www.erudit.org/en/journals/ltp/1900-v1-n1-ltp0550/1015256ar] It is just possible that **the Jews were flinging at Jesus even then an insult over his birth,** as if to say: "What right have you to speak to the like of us as you do?" (Emphasis added). https://www.studylight.org/commentary/john/8-3.html.

(4) Lange's Commentary on the Holy Scriptures: Critical, Doctrinal and Homiletical John 8:19. Where is thy Father?— **An intentional misapprehension and malicious mockery.** Therefore no doubt also a feint, **as if they were inquiring after a human father** of Jesus (Augustine, and others); the use of [the specific Greek language in this text] is not against this….the irony **might possibly have gone even to this wicked extent.** (Emphasis added). https://www.studylight.org/commentaries/eng/lcc/john-8.html.

50 (5) Dr. Constable's Expository Notes

Their request [who is your father?] was **probably an intentional insult** (cf. John 8:41). "In the East, **to question a man's paternity is a definite slur on his legitimacy.**" [Note: Tenney, "John," p. 93.] (Emphasis added). https://www.studylight.org/commentaries/eng/dcc/john-8.html. They had investigated his background, and His birth claims…

(1) Matthew 13:53-57 (Very early in Yeshua's ministry)

And when Jesus had finished these parables, he went away from there, and coming to his hometown he taught them in their synagogue, so that they were astonished, and said, "Where did this man get this wisdom and these mighty works? Is not this the carpenter's son? Is not his mother called Mary? And are not his brothers James and Joseph and Simon and Judas? And are not all his sisters with us? Where then did this man get all these things?" And they took offense at him. (ESV)

(2) Coffman's Commentaries on the Bible

From John 7:27, it is clear that the leaders claimed to know "whence" Jesus came; and both Matthew (Matthew 13:55 - is he not the carpenter's son?) and Luke (Luke 3:23 - being supposedly Joseph's son) mention the supposition that Joseph was Jesus' father. In this light, Jesus' declaration here that they did not know the Father is eloquent testimony of his virgin birth. https://www.studylight.org/commentaries/eng/bcc/john-8.html.

51 Regarding a potential connection to Yeshua's mother – Mary and Joseph, and the woman "caught" in adultery, see:

(1) Benson Commentary

It seems the expression, παραδειγματισαι, here rendered to make her [Mary – Yeshua's mother] a public example, "may perhaps refer to **that exemplary punishment which the law inflicted on those who had violated the faith of their espousals** before the marriage was completed. See Deuteronomy 22:23-24, where it is expressly ordered that a betrothed virgin, **if she lay with another man, should be stoned.** Emphasis added). https://biblehub.com/commentaries/matthew/1-19.htm.

(2) Barnes' Notes on the Bible

Adultery has always been considered a crime of a very heinous nature….In this case, therefore, the regular punishment would have been death in this painful and ignomin-ious manner [stoning]...Both to Joseph and Mary this must have been a great trial. Joseph was ardently attached to her, but her character was likely to be ruined, and he deemed it proper to separate her from him. Mary was innocent, but Joseph was not yet satisfied of her innocence...Mary was in danger of being exposed to shame. Had she been connected with a cruel, passionate, and violent man, she would have died in disgrace. (Emphasis added). https://biblehub.com/commentaries/matthew/1-19.htm.

(3) Gill's Exposition of the Entire Bible

The Greek word signifies to punish by way of example to others, to deter them from sinning; and with the ancients it denoted **the greatest and severest punishment.** Here it means either bringing her before the civil magistrate, **in order to her being punished according to the law in Deuteronomy 22:23 which requires the person to be brought out to the gate of the city and stoned with stones, which was making a public example indeed; or divorcing her in a very public manner, and thereby expose her to open shame** and disgrace. (Emphasis added). https://biblehub.com/commentaries/mat-thew/1-19.htm.

(4) Ellicott's Commentary for English Readers

To be taxed.—Literally, to register himself. She went up with him, not necessarily because she too had to be registered at Bethlehem, but because her state, as "being great with child," made her, in a special sense, dependent on Joseph's presence and protec-tion. (Emphasis added) https://biblehub.com/commentaries/luke/2-5.htm.

(5) Cambridge Bible for Schools and Colleges

It is uncertain whether her presence was obligatory (Dion. Hal. iv. 5; Lact. De Mort. Persec. 23) or voluntary; but it is obvious that at so trying a time, **and after what she had suffered** [the accusations of adultery and almost stoned to death] (Matthew 1:19), she would **cling to the presence and protection of her husband.** https://biblehub.com/commentaries/luke/2-5.htm. (Emphasis added)

(6) The Expositor's Greek Testament

If Bethlehem was Joseph's home, he would have gone to Bethlehem sooner or later in any case. Because of the census he went just then (Hahn). σὺν Μαριάμ , coming after ἀπογράψ., naturally suggests that she had to be enrolled too. Was this necessary? **Even if not, reasons might be suggested for her going with her husband:** her condition, **the intention to settle there as their real home,** preparing for what follows. (Emphasis added). https://www.studylight.org/commentaries/eng/egt/luke-2.html.

(7) **My Notes:** All of the foregoing mentioned circumstances and facts could have been easily discerned by the Pharisees of Yeshua's day as they did a background check on Him and His public ministry. This was their duty. They would have done their job thorough-ly. They had three years to investigate. It was only to their ultimate benefit to do so.

Besides this, there was a synagogue in the Nazareth area. This is where Yeshua read from the scroll of Isaiah to begin His ministry. It is also where the rabbi of that synagogue and the accompanying religious elite, as well as some simple members of His own community, attempted to kill him for blasphemy by shoving Him off a hill top (Luke 4:16-30). We can be certain the Pharisees of Yeshua's ministry days would have known of this affair.

Even earlier though, before Yeshua's birth, the rabbi in Mary's state of pregnancy would have most likely had a part in dealing with that most foreboding matter in Mary and Joseph's life...this "out of wedlock pregnancy." This too, the Pharisees of Yeshua's ministry days, could have easily found out – and attempted to capitalize upon it. Therefore, it is not far-fetched to imagine that the incident in John 8 of the woman caught in adultery was not concocted by the Pharisees with Yeshua's beginnings in mind.

The angst of Mary and Joseph about leaving Nazareth in those early days were, more than likely, born out when they left together for Bethlehem to "register for the taxation." And remember this biblical testimony, that the Pharisees had conducted this investigation, and spoke of it very early in Yeshua's public ministry:

"And when Jesus had finished these parables, he went away from there, and coming to his hometown he taught them in their synagogue, so that they were astonished, and said, "Where did this man get this wisdom and these mighty works? Is not this the carpenter's son? Is not his mother called Mary? And are not his brothers James and Joseph and Simon and Judas? And are not all his sisters with us? Where then did this man get all these things?" And they took offense at him." (Matthew 13:53-57, ESV).

(8) For an interesting and biblically connected musing upon the possibility of a connection to the woman caught in adultery and Yeshua's origins through Mary and Joseph, see the following article: Easter, Ashley. "Did Joseph's Protection of Mary Influence Jesus' Reaction To The Woman Caught In Adultery?" AshleyEaster.com, 12-22-16, https://www.ashleyeaster.com/blog/joseph-and-the-woman-caught-in-adultery.

52 Myer's New Testament Commentary
This day was a Sabbath (John 9:14); not, however, the one mentioned in John 7:37 (Olshausen), but a later one, see on John 8:12. https://biblehub.com/commentaries/john/9-1.htm.

53 Jesus replied, "If I glorify myself, my glory means nothing. My Father, whom you claim as your God, is the one who glorifies me. (John 8:54, NIV). Jesus answered, "If I glorify myself, my glory is nothing. It is my Father who glorifies me, of whom you say, 'He is our God.' (John 8:54, ESV).

Jesus answered, If I honour myself, my honour is nothing: it is my Father that honoureth me; of whom ye say, that he is your God. (John 8:54, KJV).
Expositor's Greek Testament
John 8:54. To their question Jesus, as usual, gives no categorical answer, but replies first by repelling the insinuation contained in their question and then by showing that He was greater than Abraham. He cannot get them to understand that it is not self-assertion on His part which prompts His claims, but fulfilment of His Father's commission. This "Father" of whom He speaks and who thus glorifies Him is the same..."of whom you say that He is your God". His witness therefore you ought to receive; and the reason why you do not is this, "you have not learned to know Him, but I know Him". The former verb denotes knowledge acquired, by teaching or by observation; in contrast to the latter, which denotes direct and essential knowledge. https://biblehub.com/commentaries/john/8-54.htm.

54 Before Abraham was, I am.

(1) Ellicott's Commentary for English Readers
(58) Before Abraham was, I am.—Better, Before Abraham was born, I am. Here they ask in wonder, not unmixed with scorn, if He was coeval with Abraham. The answer is that Abraham, like all men, came into being. There was a time when he was not. But **there was never a time when the Son of God was not.** In the time before Abraham, in the eternity before time (John 1:1), He still was. No word which expresses becoming can be used of His existence. **He is the I AM,** present equally in the human "was," and "is," and "is to come." (Emphasis added) https://biblehub.com/commentaries/john /8-58.htm.

(2) Jamieson-Fausset-Brown Bible Commentary
Before Abraham was, I am—**The words rendered "was" and "am" are quite different.** The one clause means, "Abraham was brought into being"; the other, "I exist." The statement therefore is not that Christ came into existence before Abraham did (as Arians affirm is the meaning), but that He never came into being at all, **but existed before Abraham had a being; in other words, existed before creation, or eternally (as Joh 1:1).** In that sense the Jews plainly understood Him, since "then took they up stones to cast at Him," just as they had before done **when they saw that He made Himself equal with God** (Joh 5:18). (Emphasis added) https://biblehub.com/commentaries/john /8-58.htm.

(3) Bengel's Gnomen
Thus the particle before and the present I am, elegantly cohere; comp. also Colossians 1:17, He Himself is before all things. https://biblehub.com/commentaries/john/8-58. htm.

55 Pulpit Commentary
It was the current idea and popular doctrine, not only that all suffering in this life had its origin in sin, and was a witness to the damage done to our nature by sin, by the disruption of our normal relations with the living God, but furthermore that every peculiar disaster pointed to some special or particular sin. Doubtless the Book of Job was a formal discussion of the question. The writer of that work repudiates the right of any onlooker to infer special sins from peculiar punishments. Jesus, moreover (Luke 13:1-3); had repeatedly discouraged the tendency to judge, but he did this by the still more solemn assurance that all men deserved the special fate of some. Still, the calamity of congenital blindness, with all its hopelessness, provided a very apt occasion for raising the question, "Who did sin, this man, or his parents?"

It is and always will be difficult to say whether the disciples thought that they had exhausted the alternatives, or believed that they had plausible reasons for thinking either alternative was possible. Some have argued that they had Scripture ground for the second of the suppositions, that the sin of the parents of the blind man was the real cause of the blindness of their son. Thus (Exodus 20:5) the idea is embedded in the Decalogue, and it is repeated in Exodus 34:7 and Numbers 14:18, that the iniquities of fathers are visited upon their children. https://biblehub.com/commentaries/john/9-2.htm.

56 Expositor's Greek Testament
The pool of Siloam, supplied from the Virgin's fountain (Isaiah 8:6), lay at the southeast corner of Jerusalem in the Kidron Valley. On the opposite side of the valley lies

a village Silwan representing the old name. The name is here interpreted as meaning "Sent" The word is so frequently used by Jesus of Himself that…we naturally apply it here also to [Jesus] , as if the noiseless stream which their fathers had despised (Isaiah 7:6) and which they could trace to its source, was a fit type of Him whom the Jews rejected because they knew His origin and because he had no external force. https://biblehub.com/commentaries/john/9-7.htm.

57 Ellicott's Commentary for English Readers (John 9:7)
The pool of Siloam was bound up with all the religious feelings of the Feast of Tabernacles. A solemn procession went each morning to it, and carried water from it to the Temple. That water had already led to the teaching of the gift of the Spirit to every man who should receive the Messiah (see Notes on John 7:37 et seq.), uttered, perhaps, on this very day (comp. John 9:1). There would be attached, then, to the pool of Siloam a sacred significance that would be in itself a help to faith. https://biblehub.com/commentaries/john/9-7.htm.

58 One suffering from temporary blindness, or even a presumably permanent blindness that had been caused later in life, might be explained away by the Pharisees, if the reasoning were stretched enough. But to heal one who was blind from birth, and one known to be so by his peers, was unexplainably extraordinary. See Ellicott's commentary entry:
Ellicott's Commentary
"Congenital blindness had always been regarded as incurable, and no instance to the contrary had ever been heard of (John 9:32)."
See: https://biblehub.com/commentaries/john/9-6.htm.

59 Cambridge Bible For Schools and Colleges
"Spittle was believed to be a remedy for diseased eyes (comp. Vespasian's reputed miracle, Tac. Hist. iv. 81, and other instances); clay also, though less commonly. So that Christ selects an ordinary remedy and gives it success in a case confessedly beyond its supposed powers (John 9:32)." https://biblehub.com/commentaries/john/9-6.htm.

60 Jesus had healed a blind man before this instance…see Matthew 9:29, and recounted in Mark 8:22. This man was also healed with spittle, but not with a mud mixture. Nor was there a command to "go wash."

Also, He would heal another blind man after this one here in John 9. That healing is mentioned in Luke 18:35, Mark 10:46, and Matthew 20:34. **But none of these instances are recorded as having been blind from birth**, a fact that surely would have been included in the description had it been a fact. See the **following commentaries on these other instances of healing the blind.** (Emphasis added)
Meyer's NT Commentary (Mark 8:22)
"The blind man [here] was not born blind. See Mark 8:24. [And he looked up and said, 'I see people, but they look like trees, walking.']" (Brackets added) See: https://biblehub.com/commentaries/mark/8-22.htm.
Pulpit Commentary (Luke 18:35)
An apparent discrepancy exists in the three accounts given of this act of our Lord. Luke speaks of one blind man who was healed as our Lord was entering the town. Matthew and Mark mention that the miracle took place as our Lord was leaving the place, and

Matthew mentions that two blind men (and not just one) received their sight at the bidding of Jesus…. In the words of Dr. Morrison, "The case seems to have begun as he entered into the city, but it culminated in all likelihood as he departed…."The fact of Mark and Luke only mentioning one blind man is easily explained. There was one evidently, a well-known character in Christian story - Bartimaeus. Two of the evangelists recorded his cure, as being of special interest to the Church, leaving the second among the numberless unrecorded miracles of healing of Jesus. It may be inferred that, as Mark specially names him, this man was well known in early Christian story. We know that after the cure he joined the company as one of the followers of Jesus." See: https://biblehub.com/commentaries/luke/18-35.htm.

61 No one born blind had ever had their sight restored…
(1) Ellicott's Commentary on the Bible
Of the six miracles connected with blindness which are recorded in the Gospels, this is the only case described as blindness from birth. In this lies its special characteristic, for "since the world began, was it not heard that any man opened the eyes of one that was born blind" (John 9:32). https://biblehub.com/commentaries/john/9-1.htm.
(2) Pulpit Commentary
There is no record of any cure of blindness in the Old Testament. The miracle stands forth with grand distinctness on the page of history. https://biblehub.com/commentaries/john/9-32.htm.
(3) Gill's Exposition of the Entire Bible
Since the world began…. "from eternity. [Never] was it heard that any man opened the eyes of one that was born blind; as not any physician by any natural means, or art, so not any prophet in a miraculous way, no not Moses himself; among all the miracles he wrought, which the Jews say were seventy six, and which were two more than were wrought by all the prophets put together, this is not to be found in the list of them, nor in the catalogue of miracles done by others….Wherefore it must follow, that Jesus, the author of this miracle, must be greater than any of the prophets, even than Moses himself, and has a greater confirmation of his mission from God, than either he or they had. https://biblehub.com/commentaries/john/9-32.htm.

62 Rabbi Moshe ben Maimon ("Maimonides"); translated by Eliyahu. "Shabbat – "Chapter Twenty One," Accessed August 2, 2023, https://www.chabad.org/library/article_cdo/aid/935242/jewish/Shabbat-Chapter-Twenty-One.htm.

63 Mark 7:9-13 and Matthew 23 (the entire chapter), but the verse quoted here is Matthew 23:28; NIV.

64 The Use of Spittle on the Sabbath, and rabbinical regulations concerning spittle in general.
Jerusalem Talmud, Shabbat 14:4 V98 - - - Spittle Forbidden For The Eye On The Sabbath, Guggenheimer, Heinrich W., 1999-2015, accessed August 3, 2023, https://www.sefaria.org/Jerusalem_Talmud_Shabbat.14.4.5?lang=bi&with=all&lang2=en
"Rav said, wine for exterior treatment of the eye is permitted, inside the eye it is forbidden. Samuel said, tasteless spittle is forbidden for the eye on the Sabbath."
Pulpit Commentary
The making of clay with the spittle and the sand was an infringement of the rule

('Shabbath,' 24:3). It was curiously laid down in one of the vexatious interpretations (preserved in Jerusalem Gemara on 'Shabbath,' 14) that while "wine could by way of remedy be applied to the eyelid, on the ground that this might be treated as washing, it was sinful to apply it to the inside of the eye" (Edersheim). And it was positively forbidden (in the same Gemara) to apply saliva to the eyelid, because this would be the application of a remedy. All medicinal appliances, unless in cases of danger to life or limb, were likewise forbidden. Consequently, the Lord had broken with the traditional glosses on the Law in more ways than one (see Winer, 'Bibl. Realw.,' 2:346; Lightfoot, ' Ad Joan. 9; 'Wetstein on Matthew 12:9; Wunsche, in loc.). John 9:14. https://biblehub .com/commentaries/john/9-14.htm.

Gill's Exposition Of The Entire Bible

Because he keepeth not the sabbath day: this they concluded from his making clay of spittle, and spreading it on the blind man's eyes, which was contrary to the traditions of their elders: one of whose rules and canons is (n), that "it is forbidden to put fasting spittle even on the eyelid on a sabbath day." An eye salve, or a plaster for the eye, if it was put on for pleasure, was lawful, but not for healing (o): but if it was put on, on the evening of the sabbath, it might continue on the sabbath day (p). (n) T. Hieros. Sabbat, fol. 14. 4. & Avoda Zara, fol. 40. 4. & T. Bab. Sabbat, fol 108. 2. & Maimon. Hilchot Sabbat, c. 21. sect. 25. (o) Piske Tosephot Sabbat, art. 67. (p) T. Hieros. Sabbat, fol. 3, 4. Maimon. ib. https://biblehub.com/commentaries/john/9-16.htm.

(4) Ellicott's Commentary for English Readers

The anointing the eyes with spittle on the Sabbath was specially forbidden by the decrees of the Rabbis. They held that no work of healing might be performed on the Sabbath except in cases of immediate danger. https://biblehub.com/commentaries /john/9-14.htm.

(5) Sefaria.org "Spittle" accessed on September 2, 2023, https://www.sefaria.org /search?q=spittle&tab=text&tvar=1&tsort=relevance&svar=1&ssort=relevance.

65 The rabbis basically formulate their rules, laws, and traditions about the Sabbath and the forbiddance of certain types of "work" (which they alone specifically defined), from Exodus 20:10.

Shabbat. Section: Zachor:

"In Exodus 20,10, after the Fourth Commandment is first instituted, God explains, "because for six days, the LORD made the heavens and the earth, the sea and all that is in them, and on the seventh day, he rested; therefore, the LORD blessed the Sabbath day and sanctified it".

"By resting on the seventh day and sanctifying it, we remember and acknowledge that God is the creator of heaven and earth and all living things. We also emulate the divine example, by refraining from work on the seventh day, as God did. If God's work can be set aside for a day of rest, how can we believe that our own work is too important to set aside temporarily?" Mechon-mamre.org. "Shabbat. Section: Zachor: To Remember," Accessed August 3, 2023, https://mechon-mamre.org/jewfaq/shabbat.htm.

66 **Sabbath Regulations against "kneading"** (This is just one example). "Although bran does not produce a mixture resembling a dough, it is forbidden to be mixed with water, lest one mix earth and the like. One may pour water over bran and stir it with a spoon

in all directions. **One may not mix it with one's hands,** so that it will not appear that one is kneading.

The accompanying footnote addendum #160, to this rabbinical law reads as follows: "But **not in circular movement, lest it appear that one is kneading** (Shulchan Aruch, Orach Chayim 324:3). This ruling relates to another difference of opinion among the Sages which was not resolved and was, therefore, perpetuated by the later Rabbis. Rabbi Yosse bar Yehudah (Shabbat 155b) mentions that **kneading involves actually mixing the dough with one's hands.** Rabbi Yehudah HaNasi differs and maintains that one is liable for kneading as soon as one pours water into flour." (Emphasis added). Chabad.org. "Shabbat, Chapter Twenty-One," Section 34, accessed August 3, 2023,https://www.chabad.org/library/article_cdo/aid/935242/jewish/Shabbat-Chapter-Twenty-One.htm#footnoteRef160a935242.

67 For example, see the commentary below among numerous others like it that I have previously referenced:
Enduring Word Commentary - David Guzik (John 8)
Where is Your father? The Pharisees probably intended this as a deeply cutting insult to Jesus. They referred to the controversy around His virgin birth, and to the rumors that it was not a miraculous conception, but an impure one. "In the East, to question a man's paternity is a definite slur on his legitimacy." (Tenney) In referring to Jesus' parentage, the Pharisees thought they had some damaging or scandalous information on Him. They must have thought, "Watch how He reacts when we reveal what we know about Him." So they insulted the parentage of Jesus, calling Him an illegitimate child. The implication was, "We were not born of fornication, but we don't know about you, Jesus." (Emphasis added). https://enduringword.com/bible-commentary/john-8.

68 To support the scholarly potentiality of the narrative that I'm laying out in this chapter, see the following three references:
(1) Smith's Bible Commentary (John 8:19)
This could be a reference to the virgin birth. They could be here declaring your mother bore you out of wedlock. "We're not born of fornication." And it could be that the story of Mary had gotten around. That Joseph wasn't really the father of Jesus. And they did not believe that He was conceived of the Holy Spirit, and so they are accusing Him of being born out of wedlock .... Here it seems to be a low blow at Jesus, challenging the virgin birth....All the way through, the accounts where Mary is brought into the picture it's always in a very admirable way. Except here. "We're not born of fornication." You know your mother bore you out of wedlock. (Emphasis added). https://www.studylight.org/commentary/john/8-19.html.
(2) Barclay's Daily Study Bible (John 8:3)
When the Jews spoke like this, there may have been something **much more personal in it.** It is certainly true in later times that **the Jews spread abroad a most malicious slander against Jesus.** The Christians very early preached the miraculous birth of Jesus. **The Jews put it about that Mary had been unfaithful to Joseph; that her paramour had been a Roman soldier called Panthers; and that Jesus was the child of that adulterous union.** It is just possible that **the Jews were flinging at Jesus even then an insult over his birth,** as if to say: "What right have you to speak to the like of us as you do?"

(Emphasis added). https://www.studylight.org/commentary/john/8-3.html.

(3) **See this site for more info** on the Jewish teaching about the Roman Soldier narrative mentioned above: https://www.erudit.org/en/journals/ltp/1900-v1-n1-ltp0550/1015256ar.

69 (1) Healing Power of the Spittle of the Firstborn & The Messiah's Spittle

"In the days of the Master, Jewish folk-medicine believed that human spittle remedied eye trouble and other ailments, sometimes in combination with a charm or invocation. For example, the Talmud tells an amusing story about how Rabbi Meir asked a woman to spit in his eyes to relieve eye irritation. **In addition, some of the sages considered the spittle of a firstborn son to possess medicinal qualities.** In the following quote from the Talmud, the rabbis submit the healing quality of a man's spittle as evidence in a rabbinic court to establish the man's firstborn right of inheritance:

A man once came before Rabbi Chaninah and testified to him, "I am sure that this man is the firstborn." Chaninah asked, "How is it that you are certain of this?" The man said, "Because when sick people came to his father he would tell them, **'Go to my son Shikchat. He is firstborn and his spittle heals.'"**...there is a tradition that **the spittle of the firstborn of a father heals.** (b.Bava Batra 126b)." (Emphasis added)

(2) See the next footnote for the direct quote from the Bava Batra 126b passage.

First Fruits of Zion. "The Messiah's Spittle," Torah Portions, accessed August 2, 2023, https://torahportions.ffoz.org/disciples/mark/the-messiahs-spittle.html.

70 From the Bava Batra 126b - The William Davidson Talmud (Koren - Steinsaltz). The teaching that follows would eventually make it's way into the Talmud many decades after the Christ event. These general teachings were in effect through the oral traditions in the time of Yeshua, and before. The Talmud legend regarding the spittle of the first born was meant to solidify the folklore and oral traditions that had been handed down through the ages past.

"The Gemara relates: There was a certain man who came before Rabbi Ḥanina and said to him: I know that this man is a firstborn. Rabbi Ḥanina said to him: From where do you know? He said to Rabbi Ḥanina: Because when people would come before his father to obtain a cure for their ailing eyes, he would say to them: Go to my son Shikhḥat, as he is a firstborn and his saliva heals this ailment.

"The Gemara asks: But perhaps he is his mother's firstborn? The Gemara answers: It is learned as a tradition that the saliva of a father's firstborn heals this ailment but the saliva of a mother's firstborn does not heal this ailment." Bava Batra 126b (Sections 11-12) - The William Davidson Talmud (Koren - Steinsaltz), Sefaria.org, Accessed August 4, 2023, https://www.sefaria.org/Bava_Batra.126b.12?lang=bi.

71 (1) As an interesting historical and archeological sidenote to this portion of the narrative, you might want to see:

1QS Column 11 - lines 21-22 (Of the Dead Sea Scrolls – "Community Rules.")

What shall one who is born of a woman be accounted before you - oh lord, for we are simply kneaded from the dust.

He spat saliva - molded clay and for dust is the longing of man.

What shall hand molded clay reply to the maker -

What council shall that hand molded clay understand? (Emphasis added) See:

http://www.ericlevy.com/Revel/DeadSeaScrolls/Vermes%20-%20CDDSE%20p97
-117%20Community%20Rule.PDF (Accessed July 12, 2023).

Also see: Pulpit Commentary (Genesis 2:7)

Whereas in this his creation is exhibited as a painful process of elaboration **from the
clay by the hand of God, who works it like a potter** (asah; LXX., πλάσσω), and, after
having first constructed man, by a subsequent operation forms woman. (Emphasis
added). https://biblehub.com/commentaries/genesis/2-7.htm.

But **we have this treasure in jars of clay,** to show that the surpassing power belongs to
God and not to us. (2 Corinthians 4:7, ESV.)

72 Psalm 146:8 "The LORD gives sight to the blind, the LORD lifts up those who are
bowed down, the LORD loves the righteous."

Isaiah 29:18 "In that day the deaf shall hear the words of a book, and out of their
gloom and darkness the eyes of the blind shall see." (Also see Isaiah 35:5 and 42:7)

73 Taking the formerly blind man to the Pharisees.

(1) Meyer's NT Commentary

John 9:13. These belong still to the persons designated in John 9:8. They act thus
because the healing had taken place on the Sabbath (John 9:14), the violation of which
they, in their servile dependence, believed it to be their duty not to conceal from the
guardians of the law who ruled over the people.... The Pharisees as a corporate body
are meant, and a number of them might easily have come together at one of their houses to form a kind of sitting. https://biblehub.com/commentaries/john/9-13.htm.

(2) Pulpit Commentary

The authorities before whom the discussion and examination were taken appear to possess the power of excommunication from the synagogue. It appears that, in Jerusalem,
there existed two minor councils or synagogue-courts, of twenty-three assessors each,
corresponding with the similar courts in the Jewish cities, standing in relation to the Sanhedrim and possessing the faculty of delivering the minor degrees of excommunication
from the congregation of Israel. https://biblehub.com/commentaries/john/9-13.htm.

74 Gill's Commentary

He is of age; at man's estate, as, with the Jews, one was, **who was at the age of thirteen
years**, if he could produce the signs of puberty: and such an one was allowed a witness
in any case, but not under this age; nor if he was arrived to it, if the above signs could
not be produced (q). **This man very likely was much older**, as may be thought from
the whole of his conduct, his pertinent answers, and just reasoning: wherefore his
parents direct the Sanhedrin to him for an answer to their third question. (Emphasis
added). https://biblehub.com/commentaries/john/9-21.htm.

75 Put out of the synagogue.

Barnes' Notes on the Bible

This took place in the temple…**It refers to excommunication from the synagogue.**
Among the Jews there were two grades of excommunication; the one for lighter
offences, of which they mentioned 24 causes; the other for greater offences. The first
excluded a man for 30 days from the privilege of entering a synagogue, and from
coming nearer to his wife or friends than 4 cubits. **The other was a solemn exclusion
forever from the worship of the synagogue, attended with awful maledictions and**

curses, and an exclusion from all contact with the people. This was called the curse, and so thoroughly excluded the person from all communion whatever with his countrymen, that they were not allowed to sell to him anything, even the necessaries of life (Buxtorf). It is probable that this latter punishment was what they intended to inflict if **anyone should confess that Jesus was the Messiah: and it was the fear of this terrible punishment that deterred his parents from expressing their opinion.** (Emphasis added). https://biblehub.com/commentaries/john/9-21.htm.

76 Barnes' Notes on the Bible
Wast born in sins - **That is, thou wast born in a state of blindness a state which proved that either thou or thy parents had sinned,** and that this was the punishment for it. See John 9:2. Thou wast cursed by God with blindness for crime, and yet thou dost set up for a religious teacher!...And especially do they consider it great presumption that one of an inferior age or rank should presume to advance an argument in opposition to prevailing opinions.
They cast him out—Out of the synagogue. They excommunicated him. See the notes at John 9:22. (Emphasis added). https://biblehub.com/commentaries/john/9-34.htm.

77 He worshipped Yeshua.
(1) Expositor's Greek Testament
John 9:38. He promptly uttered his belief and "worshipped" Jesus. In this Gospel [the Greek word used] is **used of the worship of God**: the word is, however, susceptible of a somewhat lower degree of adoration (Matthew 18:26); but it **includes the acknowledgment of supremacy and a complete submission.** (Emphasis and brackets added). https://biblehub.com/commentaries/john/9-38.htm.
(2) Jamieson-Fausset-Brown Bible Commentary
38. He said, Lord, I believe: and he worshipped him—a faith and a worship, beyond doubt, meant to express far more than he would think proper to any human "prophet" (Joh 9:17)—the unstudied, resistless expression, **probably of SUPREME faith and adoration,** though without the full understanding of what that implied. (Emphasis added). https://biblehub.com/commentaries/john/9-38.htm.

78 Pulpit Commentary
There is a difference between "becoming blind," and being "the blind." They ask whether they are blind also, i.e. as blind as those who have, according to Christ's own dictum, become so. They seem to admit that some who have the power of sight have been blinded by the very light that shines upon them, but they are in doubt with reference to their own case. John 9:40. https://biblehub.com/commentaries/john/9-40.htm.

79 The scriptures do not contain these exact words. Only "Are we blind too?" But what I've done is to add the context of the entire last week or so of Yeshua's life, and everything else that you, the reader, have learned from the immersive narrative and the accompanying commentary attestations of those narrative particulars.

80 Ibid.

81 There is nothing "darker" than the domain of Satan. This verse includes the domain of lost humanity, as well as the halls of Satan's unseen realms of darkness. Satan knew, and knows, more than humanity does – to be sure. However, regarding the Christ event, he did not know every detail concerning His presence...the details that would ultimately crush his stolen kingdom reign.

The Biblical Illustrator (Matthew 4:3 – What Satan Knew of Christ)
There seems little reason to doubt that Satan knew Jesus to be the promised One,
whose advent the prophets had foretold.

But although Satan was thus far in possession of the truth respecting Christ, **it does
not follow that [Satan] "knew the whole truth** respecting Him. (Emphasis added).
https://biblehub.com/commentaries/illustrator/matthew/4.htm.

82   Commentary on Colossians 2:15
(1) Myer's New Testament Commentary
In this doing away of the law was involved the victory and **triumph of God over the
devilish powers,** since the strength of the latter, antagonistic to God, is in sin, and the
strength of sin is in the law (1 Corinthians 15:56); with the law, **therefore, the power
of the devil stands or falls.** (Emphasis added). https://biblehub.com/commentaries/
colossians/2-15.htm.

(2) Matthew Poole's Commentary
It is easy to discern the word is borrowed from conquering warriors having put to
flight and disarmed their enemies, (as the word may well signify disarming, in opposition to arming, Romans 13:12 Ephesians 6:11, 14), and **signifies here, that Christ
disarmed and despoiled the devil and his angels,** with all the **powers of darkness.** We
have seen that by principalities and **powers are meant angels,** Colossians 1:16, with
Romans 8:37 Ephesians 1:21; and here he means **evil ones,** in regard of that power
they exercise in this world under its present state of subjection to sin and vanity, Luke
4:6 John 12:31 2 Corinthians 4:4 Ephesians 2:2 6:12 2 Timothy 2:26; whom **Christ
came to destroy, and effectually did on his cross defeat,** Luke 11:22 John 16:11 1
Corinthians 15:55 Hebrews 2:14 1Jo 3:8; delivering his subjects **from the power of
darkness,** Colossians 1:13, according to the first promise, Genesis 3:15. https://bible-
hub.com/commentaries/colossians/2-15.htm.

(3) Gill's Exposition of the Entire Bible
And having spoiled principalities and powers…Principalities of hell, the infernal
powers of darkness, the devil that had the power of death, the accuser of the brethren,
who often objected their debts, with all his works and posse: these Christ has divested
of their armour, wherein they trusted to have ruined men, as sin, the law, and death; he
has ransomed his people from him that was stronger than they, and taken the prey out
of the hands of the mighty; he has bruised the serpent's head, demolished his works,
destroyed him himself, and all his powers, and defeated all their counsels and designs
against his elect…https://biblehub.com/commentaries/colossians/2-15.htm.

83   Ibid.
84   Some might object to this notion by asking, "If Yeshua won our victory of sin and
death, then why does sin and death continue?"
That's a fair question. The simple and succinct answer can best be demonstrated with a
sports analogy:
You and I are on a team playing in a championship football game. It is now the fourth
quarter with 1 minute left on the clock. We are ahead by 100 points. We are on the
opposing team's 10 yard line. We have a first down, with at least four more plays to
go 10 more yards for yet another touchdown. The opposing team is humiliated and

angry, because they understand that no matter what happens – they have been terribly defeated. The game is essentially over. Oh, there may be 60 more seconds of play. But the game is over. We have won. Soon the buzzer (trumpet) will blow, announcing to all in attendance that the victory is ours! It had been ours…for a long, grueling game. But now the end is near. Soon, the trumpet sounds, and then, we will celebrate!

85 Following are examples of this plainly missed truth.

(1) Gill's Exposition of the Entire Bible

Which none of the princes of this world knew…**Meaning not the devils, as some have thought**…(Emphasis added). https://biblehub.com/commentaries/1_corinthians/2-8.htm.

(2) Matthew Poole's Commentary

Which none of the princes of this world knew; which Divine wisdom neither **Caiaphas, nor Pontius Pilate, nor any considerable number of the rulers of this age,** whether amongst **the Jews or amongst the heathens,** understood, though they heard of it. (Emphasis added). https://biblehub.com/commentaries/1_corinthians/2-8.htm.

(3) Expositor's Greek

Caiaphas and the Sanhedrin, Pilate and the Roman court (cf. Acts 13:27 f., 1 Timothy 6:13) saw nothing of the splendor clothing the Lord Jesus as He stood before them; so knowing, they could not have crucified Him. (Emphasis added). https://biblehub.com/commentaries/1_corinthians/2-8.htm.

86 What Did Satan Fully Know Of Jesus?

(1) Revised English Version Commentary

"Which none of the rulers of this age knew." **The "rulers of this age" are the Devil and his demons.** Scholars and Bible teachers are divided over this point. Many of them say that the "rulers of this age" are earthly rulers such as Herod, Pilate, and the Jewish leaders, while many others assert they are demons, not people. **The reason for the division is that the context is misunderstood,** and the vocabulary is ambiguous because it is general in nature and in one form or another is used of both earthly rulers and demonic rulers.

Because words like "rulers" can be used of people or demons, the context is the great key to understanding who these "rulers" are. From the context, we learn that what the "rulers" did not know was the Sacred Secret (cp. 1 Cor 2:7, mustērion). Neither earthly rulers nor demonic powers could have known the Sacred Secret, because it was hidden in God, as **we have seen from many verses** (cp. Rom. 16:25; 1 Cor. 2:7; Eph. 3:5).

So the rulers in 1 Corinthians 2:8 cannot be the earthly rulers. In contrast, the Devil would not have crucified Jesus if he knew that if he did crucify him, then every believer would have the fullness of holy spirit and "Christ in them," and that God's chosen people would no longer be just the Jews, but anyone on earth who chose to believe. It is the Devil who, if he had known that every Christian would have many blessings and the power to cast out demons, would not have crucified Jesus. It is the Devil who would have rather dealt with one man, Jesus, than with an army of God on earth, multitudes of Christians, all secure in their salvation and empowered by holy spirit.

Only by understanding that **if Satan had known the Sacred Secret he would not have crucified the Lord** can we understand the true reason for God keeping the Sacred Secret a secret and **fully appreciate the enormity and power** of what we have been given

in Christ. (Emphasis added). https://www.revisedenglishversion.com/1-Corinthians
/chapter2/8.

(2) Clarke's Commentary (Matthew 4:3 – the Temptation of Jesus)

If thou be the Son of God....It is certain, whatever Satan might suspect, he did not
fully know that the person he tempted was the true Messiah. Perhaps one grand
object of [Satan'] temptation [of Yeshua] was to find this out. (Emphasis and brackets
added). https://www.studylight.org/commentaries/eng/acc/matthew-4.html.

(3) The Biblical Illustrator (Matthew 4:3 – What Satan Knew of Christ)

There seems little reason to doubt that Satan knew Jesus to be the promised One,
whose advent the prophets had foretold.

But although Satan was thus far in possession of the truth respecting Christ, it does
not follow that [Satan] "knew the whole truth respecting Him. If Satan had no just
view of the person of Christ, of His true divinity, he would necessarily have imperfect
views of His perfect holiness. (Emphasis and brackets added). https://biblehub.com/
commentaries/illustrator/matthew/4.htm.

(4) Clarke's Commentary

Then entered Satan into Judas - The devil filled the heart of Judas with avarice;
and that infamous passion led him to commit the crime here specified [Jesus' crucifixion!]...What Satan could not do by the envy and malice of the high priests and
Pharisees, he effects by Judas. (Emphasis and brackets added). https://biblehub.com/
commentaries/clarke/luke/22.htm.

(5) Utley's Bible Commentary

[Is] Paul is speaking purely of human logic or the demonic activity behind human
logic; both are present. Humans are influenced because of their fallenness (cf. Romans
12:2; Galatians 1:14; Ephesians 2:2), but they are also influenced by the presence of
supernatural evil (i.e., angelic and demonic, cf. 2 Corinthians 4:4; Daniel 10:0). (Emphasis added). https://www.studylight.org/commentaries/eng/ubc/1-corinthians-2.html.

(6) David Guzik's Enduring Word Commentary:

Are the rulers of this age men or demonic powers?

This debate goes all the way back to the time of Origen and Chrysostom. On the
surface, it seems clear that the rulers of this age must refer to human rulers, because
only they didn't know what they were doing when they incited the crucifixion of Jesus.

However, one could say that demonic powers were ignorant of what would result
from the crucifixion of Jesus – the disarming and defeat of demonic powers (Colossians
2:15) – and had they known they were sealing their own doom by inciting the crucifixion, they would not have done it.

No matter who exactly the rulers of this age are, their defeat is certain: who are
coming to nothing. Their day is over and the day of Jesus Christ is here.

Which none of the rulers of this age knew: Why did the rulers of this age fail to
recognize God's wisdom? Because it came in a mystery; a "sacred secret" that could
only be known by revelation. It is the hidden wisdom that is now revealed by the
Gospel of Jesus Christ, which Paul preaches. (Emphasis added). https://enduringword.
com/bible-commentary/1-corinthians-2.

87 Guzik, David. "1 Corinthians 2," Enduring Word Commentary, https://enduringword
.com/bible-commentary/1-corinthians-2.

88 "Age".
Thayer's Greek Lexicon
In hyperbolic and **popular usage**: ἀπό τοῦ αἰῶνος (פְלוּעַם Genesis 6:4, cf. Deuterono-
my 32:7) **from the most ancient time down** (within the memory of man), from of old,
Luke 1:70; Acts 3:21; Acts 15:18.

As the Jews distinguished פְלוּעָה הַזֶּה the time **before the Messiah, and** פְלוּעָה אָבָה,
the time after the advent of the Messiah (cf. Riehm, Lehrb. d. Hebraerbr., p. 204ff;
(Schürer, § 29, 9)), **so most of the N. T. writers** distinguish ὁ αἰών οὗτος **this age**
(also simply ὁ αἰών, Matthew 13:22; Mark 4:19; ὁ ἐνεστὼς αἰών, Galatians 1:4; ὁ νῦν
αἰών, 1 Timothy 6:17; (2 Timothy 4:10); Titus 2:12), **the time before the appointed
return** or truly **Messianic advent of Christ.** (Emphasis added) https://biblehub.com
/greek/165.htm.
89 Ellicott's Commentary For English Readers (Ephesians 2:2)
Now, the word "power" (see Note on Ephesians 1:21), both in the singular and the plural, is used in this Epistle, almost technically, of superhuman power. Here, therefore, the
Evil One is described as "the prince," or ruler, of such superhuman power—considered
here collectively as a single power, prevailing over the world, and working in the children
of disobedience—in the same sense in which he is called the "prince of the devils," the
individual spirits of wickedness (Matthew 9:34; Matthew 12:24). https://biblehub.com
/commentaries/ephesians/2-2.htm.
90 Eon and Aion.
(1) BYUJ – "eon"
"An eon is a period of time equal to one billion years or 1,000,000,000 years. The word
is of Greek origin and approximately translates to 'age.'" https://repository.iimb.ac.in/
handle/2074/19233.
Greek #165. "aión," Thayer's Greek Lexicon.
"**Universally**: in the phrases εἰς τόν αἰῶνα, פְלוּעַל (Genesis 6:3), **forever**, John 6:51, 58;
John 14:16; Hebrews 5:6; Hebrews 6:20, etc. (Emphasis added)

In hyperbolic and **popular usage**: ἀπό τοῦ αἰῶνος (פְלוּעַם Genesis 6:4, cf. Deuteronomy 32:7) **from the most ancient time down (within the memory of man)**, from
of old, Luke 1:70; Acts 3:21; Acts 15:18. (Emphasis added). https://biblehub.com/
greek/165.htm.
91 Following is just one example of an otherwise respected commentary that misses the
entire biblical context of the matter and assigns "rulers of this age" only to human
rulers – even though the scriptures clearly say otherwise.
Cambridge Bible for Schools and Colleges
"These words seem to be written for the instruction of the class of persons who attach
importance to the opinions of those high in position and influence—the princes, or rather rulers of this world, its statesmen." https://biblehub.com/commentaries/1_corinthians
/2-8.htm.
92 Another example of respected scholars that agree...
(1) Albert Barnes' Notes on the Bible (Colossians 2:15)
There can be **no doubt** that the apostle refers to **the ranks of fallen, evil spirits** which
had usurped a dominion over the world, John 12:31, note; Ephesians 2:2. **The Saviour,**

by his death, **wrested the dominion** from them, and seized upon what they had captured **as a conqueror seizes upon his prey.** Satan and his legions had invaded the earth and drawn its inhabitants into captivity, and subjected them to their evil reign. Christ, by his death. subdues the invaders and recaptures those whom they had subdued (Emphasis added). Colossians 2:15, "Barnes' Notes on the Bible," Biblehub.com, https://biblehub.com/commentaries/colossians/2-15.htm.

93 1 Corinthians 2:8. "Revised English Version Commentary," Accessed August 28, 2023, https://www.revisedenglishversion.com/1-Corinthians/chapter2/8.

94 There are several phrases in Hebrew that represent the concept of the literal Temple, or Tabernacle of God. Following are just a few of those examples:

Bet-Elaha (House of God), Bet-Yahweh (House of the Lord), Mishkan (Dwelling Place or Tabernacle), Bet-Hamikdash (House of the Holiest Place), and others. Various translations will sometimes render these phrases as "temple". But the purpose of this chapter is to focus on the two Hebrew words Heykal and Miqdash. These two specific words have direct synonyms in the Greek, and are therefore used within their context in the New Testament documents.

95 There are at least 80 uses of this word, starting in 1 Samuel 1:9. Most of the time it refers to the Temple of the Lord that is on the Temple mount. However Heykal can also refer to a palace in general, but is used in this manner much less frequently. Heykal. #1964, https://biblehub.com/hebrew/1964.htm.

96 "The Sanctuary - Miqdash
(1) Miqdash ("**Sanctuary**"; e.g., Ex. 25:8) and ha-Qodesh ("The Holy Place"; e.g., Ex. 28:29). The **innermost sanctuary** is known as the **Qodesh ha-Qodashim**, "The Most Holy Place" or "**The Holy of Holies.**" (Emphasis added). See; https://www.encyclopedia.com/philosophy-and-religion/bible/biblical-proper-names/tabernacle.
(2) Miqdash: NAS Exhaustive Concordance: holy, holy place, holy places, sacred part, sanctuaries, sanctuary. (Used over 80 times in the Old Testament). Hebrew 4720. "miqdash," Biblehub.com, https://biblehub.com/hebrew/4720.htm.

97 However, there was also another, completely separate, room inside the Temple (heykal) itself. That room was called the gasith, the room in which the Sanhedrin held its formal meetings. It would be similar to a designated room inside our modern church buildings – one that was set apart – away from the sanctuary—for the purpose of holding staff meetings, and/or deacon and elder meetings, etc.
Meyer's NT Commentary
"Matthew 27:5...the room, **Gasith**, in which the Sanhedrim held its sittings..." (Emphasis added). Matthew 27:5. "Myer's Greek Testament," Biblehub.com, https://biblehub.com/commentaries/matthew/27-5.htm.

98 Hebrew #1687. "Debir," Biblehub.com, https://biblehub.com/hebrew/1687.htm.

99 "Holy of Holies, Hebrew Qodesh Ha-qadashim, **also called Devir, the innermost** and **most sacred area** of the ancient Temple of Jerusalem, accessible only to the Israelite high priest...." (Emphasis added). Editors of Britannica. "Holy of Holies," Britannica.com, 7-6-23, https://www.britannica.com/topic/Temple-of-Jerusalem.

100 At the following web address, you can see the Hebrew word debir as it is translated to "sanctuary" in the English versions. https://biblehub.com/interlinear/psalms/28-2.htm.

101 Hebrew. 1687. "Debir," https://biblehub.com/hebrew/1687.htm.

102 (1) The **"Holy of Holies" parallels debir**, or "oracle," explaining what the oracle is. **The oracle of which God speaks here** is none other than the **Most Holy Place, the inner room** wherein the Ark of the Covenant resided. Other translators render debir as "Holy Place," "sanctuary," "inner house," "hinder room," "back room," "recess," "inner sanctuary." **Debir is special**....The translators never render debir as the regular word for "behind" or "back." The oracle of God is the room wherein He abode, the Holy of Holies, from which He at times spoke. In the Old Testament, the oracle is **God's speaking place.** (Emphasis added). Bible Tools. "What the Bible says about Debir," accessed 8-23-23, https://www.bibletools.org/index.cfm/fuseaction/Topical .show/RTD/CGG/ID/1295/Debir.htm.
(2) "The Holy of Holies may certainly have become known as **Place Of The Word.**" (Emphasis added). Abarim Publications. "The name Debir: Summary," Accessed August 3, 23, https://www.abarim-publications.com/Meaning/Debir.html.
(3) Strong's Concordance: "**A place of Speaking** – the Holy of Holies." (Emphasis added). Hebrew #1687, Debir. "Strong's Concordance," https://biblehub.com/hebrew /1687.htm.
(4) Hebrew Word Lessons: "The Devir/debir shared the root letters dalet-bet-resh (DBR) with the Hebrew word, dabar/davar (Strong's 1697), meaning "WORD". In other words, **the Inner Sanctuary** could **also be described** as the **Holy Word Space.** It was the space where the Word of God lived; it was **the space where the Presence of YHWH spoke**...a place of oracle." (Emphasis added)
Hebrew Word Lessons. "Devir: The INNER SANCTUARY / Place of the WORD," 7-24-22, https://hebrewwordlessons.com/2022/07/24/devir-the-inner-sanctuary-place -of-the-word%EF%BF%BC.

103 Eve is an English given name for a female, derived from the Latin name Eva, in turn originating with the Hebrew חַוָּה (Chavah/Havah – chavah, to breathe, and chayah, to live, or to give life). The traditional meaning of Eve is life or "living". It can also mean full of life and mother of life. See: https://en.wikipedia.org/wiki/Eve_(name).

104 Abarim Publications
Meaning: Place Of The Word
Etymology of the name Debir: **The word** רִיבד **is identical to a nickname of the Holy of Holies** in Solomon's temple, and is derived of the magnificent root רבד (**dabar**), generally meaning **word.**
Dabar as a Verb
The verb רבד (dabar) means to formalize: to deliberately establish and pronounce something's name or definition. This causes the thing to become "real" in the mind of whoever understands this word, name or definition, and this in turn explains why all of creation was spoken into being, and Man in turn "named" all the animals by their name and finally his Wife by hers (Genesis 2:19-23). This principle sits at the base of nominal reasoning and thus human awareness and ultimately Information Technology. (Emphasis added). See: Abarim Publications. "The name Debir: Summary," Accessed August 3, 23, https://www.abarim-publications.com/Meaning/Debir.html.
Also See: https://www.abarim-publications.com/Dictionary/d/d-b-r.html.

105 Abarim Publications
    Meaning: Place Of The Word
    Etymology of the name Debir: **The word** ריבד **is identical to a nickname of the Holy of Holies** in Solomon's temple, and is derived of the magnificent root רבד (**dabar**), generally meaning **word**.
    Dabar as a Noun:
    Noun רבד (dabar) means word. It also means "thing" since the naming of a thing causes the experienced reality of the thing. All thus created "things" together form the whole of experienceable reality, which in turn is called the Word of God. (Emphasis added). See: Abarim Publications. "The name Debir: Summary," Accessed August 3, 23, https://www.abarim-publications.com/Meaning/Debir.html.
    Also See: https://www.abarim-publications.com/Dictionary/d/d-b-r.html.
106 Abarim Publications: "Noun רבד (dabar) means word. It also means "thing" since the naming of a thing **causes the experienced reality of the thing**. All thus created "things" together **form the whole of experienceable reality**, which in turn is called **the Word of God**." (Emphasis added). See: https://www.abarim-publications.com/Meaning/Debir.html. Also See: https://www.abarim-publications.com/Dictionary/d/d-b-r.html.
107 "Religion Information Data Explorer | GRF", accessed Sept. 1, 2023, www.global religiousfutures.org.
108 According to Guinness World Records, the Bible is the bestselling book of all time with an estimated 5 billion copies sold and distributed.
    Walch, Tad. "12 things I learned about the church that I didn't know before general conference". Deseret News. 10-4-20, https://www.deseret.com/faith/2020/10/4/21500695/october-general-conference-mormon-lds-elder-matthew-holland-elder-jeffrey-holland-elder-gong-covid.
109 Dale Martin (2009), Introduction to New Testament History and Literature, lecture 14: "Paul as Missionary". Yale University. 14. "Paul as Missionary," https://www.youtube.com/watch?v=3V8NeoY2qB4&list=PL279CFA55C51E75E0&index=15.
110 The New Testament holds the final interpretation of the Old Testament.
111 (1) Dr. McCartney, Dan G (PhD). "Should we employ the hermeneutics of the New Testament writers?" (Presented as a paper at the annual meeting of the Evangelical Theological Society in 2003.)
    Dr. McCartney, Dan G. "Should we employ the hermeneutics of the New Testament writers?" BibleResearcher.com, accessed September 2, 2023, https://www.bible-researcher.com/mccartney1.html.
    (2) Dr. Tom Hicks (Ph.D.) Hermeneutics: New Testament Priority
    One important aspect of biblical [interpretation] is the **principle of "New Testament priority."**...Earlier texts provide the interpretive context for later texts, but earlier texts never cite later texts and explain them directly. Rather, what we find is that **later texts make explicit reference to earlier texts and provide explanations of them**...
    The hermeneutical principle of New Testament priority simply recognizes these facts. Following the Bible's own example, interpreters should allow later revelation in Bible to explain earlier revelation, rather than insisting on their own uninspired interpretations of earlier revelation without reference to the authoritative explanations of later revelation. (Emphasis added)

Dr. Hicks, Tom. "Hermeneutics: New Testament Priority," Founders Ministry, accessed Sept. 14, 2023, https://founders.org/articles/hermeneutics-new-testament-priority.
(3) Dr. Kieran Beville (D.Litt., Ph.D.) "How Are We to Understand the New Testament Use of the Old Testament?"
The New Testament employs the Old Testament in a variety of ways. It does so to demonstrate that, in Jesus, the biblical prophecies, types, and shadows have all found their divinely appointed fulfillment....[Examples] From 1 Corinthians, we find Paul using the desert wanderings as typological of the Christian life. The author of Hebrews is concerned to write explaining how the Old Testament points forward to Jesus. In so doing, he draws heavily on Moses the man, as well as the Mosaic Law, with its sacrifices and Temple rituals. (Emphasis added)
Dr. Beville, Kieran (D.Litt., Ph.D.). "How Are We to Understand the New Testament Use of the Old Testament?" https://christianpublishinghouse.co/2020/01/10/how-are-we-to-understand-the-new-testament-use-of-the-old-testament.
(4) Penner, Erwin (M.Div. Th.M.) "Interpreting Old Testament Prophecy"
The biblical concept of **progressive revelation** teaches us that **we must** read the OT (and its prophecies) in a forward direction, realizing that **the OT revelation is preparatory of the NT**. We must also read the OT backward **in the light of NT truth since it gives us the final and fulfilled revelation.** (Emphasis added). Accessed September 9, 2023. Direction Journal. July 1977 · Vol. 6 No. 3 · pp. 38–47, https://directionjournal.org/6/3/interpreting-old-testament-prophecy.html.
(5) Christian Research Institute - Practical Hermeneutics column of the Christian Research Journal
The New Testament is not a mere appendix added to the writings of the Old Testament prophets. It is a revelation of the new order in Jesus Christ, in whom all previous revelation finds its fulfillment, and through whom all previous revelation must be understood." (Emphasis added)
From: Making Sense of Ezekiel's Temple Vision, Christian Research Institute (This article first appeared in the Practical Hermeneutics column of the Christian Research Journal, volume 35, number 03 (2012).

Some English translations actually insert the word "temple" in Romans 9:4. Yet, the word "temple" is not even in the Greek text in that verse. It is merely an insert of "clarification" or "commentary." This happens quite frequently, even in the best of English versions. Following is an example of how "temple" shows up in that verse in one translation, but its more correct rendering, from the literal Greek, is found in another version.

Theirs is the adoption to sonship; theirs the divine glory, the covenants, the receiving of the law, the **temple** worship and the promises. (Romans 9:4, NIV, emphasis added)

They are Israelites, and to them belong the adoption, the glory, the covenants, the giving of the law, the worship, and the promises. (Romans 9:4, ESV, emphasis added)

112 I really like the following literal translation of that verse. The word used in this translation is not "temple." Instead, it is "sanctuary." And the word sanctuary (from the Hebrew miqdash, or the Greek naos), as we now understand from all our previous study on this subject, truly is the best English word to use in the most literal sense.

Jesus answered and said to them, 'Destroy this **sanctuary** [naos], and in three days I will raise it up.' (John 2:19; Young's Literal Translation, emphasis and brackets added)

113 John 2:19.

(1) "Ellicott's Commentary For English Readers,"Biblehub.com, https://biblehub.com/commentaries/john/2-19.htm. See also:

(2) Cambridge Bible For Schools and Colleges

The word used in these three verses for 'temple' means the central sacred building (naos), whereas that used in John 2:14 means the whole sacred enclosure (hieron). The latter is never used figuratively. https://biblehub.com/commentaries/john/2-19.htm.

(3) Bengel's Gnomen

The body of Jesus, about to be raised again, is the temple and dwelling-place of the Godhead. Therefore Jesus is the Lord of the temple at Jerusalem, which was the type of the body of Jesus. https://biblehub.com/commentaries/john/2-19.htm.

114 John 2:19. "Barnes' Notes on the Bible," Biblehub.com, https://biblehub.com/commentaries/john/2-19.htm.

115 The Body of Christ

1 Corinthians 12:27-28: Now you are the body of Christ, and each one of you is a part of it. (NIV)

Ephesians 4:11-12: It was He who gave some to be apostles, some to be prophets, some to be evangelists, and some to be pastors and teachers, to prepare God's people for works of service, so that the body of Christ may be built up... (NIV)

116 I know that a definitive statement such as this, especially one that goes against so much of the relatively modern teaching regarding a "third temple" in the last days, can be a bit off-putting to some readers. However, I assure you that I am biblically correct in this matter. Following is a demonstration of that fact. Look at Ephesians 2:19-22 again.

So then you are no longer strangers and aliens, but **you are** fellow citizens with the saints and **members of the household of God**, built on the foundation of the apostles and prophets, **Christ Jesus himself being the cornerstone**, in whom the whole structure, being **joined together**, grows into **a holy temple in the Lord**. In him you also are being **built together** into a **dwelling place for God** by the Spirit. (Ephesians 2:19-22, emphasis added)

That passage is the only definitive and contextual passage in the New Testament that speaks of a literal "rebuilt" temple in the last days. And that temple is conclusively defined as the Body of Christ, the ecclesia (Greek - the called out ones, or the "church"). If we say otherwise, we are saying that someone – Paul, Jesus, John, Peter, etc. – is not telling the truth. But we know they cannot contradict each other. And they do not do so.

For a thorough but easy to read investigation of this truth I urge the reader to get Messianic Rabbi Zev Porat's book titled, "Blood Alliance." (Defender Press – 2024). Zev asked me to contribute to several sections of that book (The Temple Frenzy, and Ezekiel's Temple Vision). Those two sections together comprise about a dozen (five-page) chapters on this matter. In that study, we examine every single relevant passage from both the Old and New Testaments, paying very close attention to the words of Daniel, Ezekiel, Jesus, John, and Paul. The passages from Daniel and Ezekiel are interpreted from the nuances of the Hebrew language (Zev Porat's mother tongue), their greater Old Testament contexts, and from the ultimate and final interpretations of those words and concepts given through the New Testament, and especially from Jesus himself. The scholarship you are now reading in this book, is the same genre you'll encounter in Zev's book. There you will exegetically discover the truth of this matter in much greater detail.

117 **For example** – the scriptures usually cited for a "rebuilt third temple in the last days" are represented by the following quote from a contemporary Christian commentary site, GotQuestions.org.
"The temple will be rebuilt in Jerusalem (Daniel 9:27; Matthew 24:15; 2 Thessalonians 2:3-4; Revelation 11:1)." (Parentheses in the original) See: https://www.gotquestions.org /end-times-Israel.html.

As you might have noticed, the matter is usually stated categorically, as if there were no room for other interpretations, even those that have been around much longer – and by renowned scholarship. But this is simply not the case. As you will soon discover in this book – the reference to 2 Thessalonians 2:4 is proof that it is categorically impossible that the naos used there means a "third temple on the Temple Mount." Each of the other scriptures listed by GotQuestions.org (representative of similar lists) are just as easily eliminated in a scholarly, contextual, exegetical manner, as having anything to do with a literal temple building on the Temple Mount in the last days.

I urge the reader to have a look at Messianic Rabbi Zev Porat's book "Blood Alliance" (Defender Publishing – January 2024). He includes about a dozen chapters on this topic. Those chapters are thoroughly researched and heavily referenced by renowned and trusted scholars, as well as the additional Hebrew and Greek word studies that many in today's "third temple" circle omit from their presentations. You will be absolutely shocked by what you will discover in Rabbi Zev's work.

118 Mooney, Brit. "Is the Third Temple in Jerusalem Literal or Symbolic?" Crosswalk.com, 5-17-21, https://www.crosswalk.com/special-coverage/end-times/what-is-the-third -temple.html.

119 I must also point out, not all English translations insert the word "temple" in these verses. Some translations (Holman Christian Standard, Legacy Standard Bible, International Standard Version, and Young's Literal Translation) contain the word "sanctuary" as the translation of naos that Paul used in that verse. The word sanctuary comes much closer to the exact meaning that Paul is conveying by using naos – rather than "temple".

120 This truth is often labeled as Contextual Hermeneutics in scholarly circles. The summation of contextual hermeneutics is nicely summed up by Dr. Keith A. Burton - associate professor of New Testament at Oakwood College, Huntsville, Alabama, in the following manner:
"Firstly, since we belong to a church that claims to be built on and directed by the leadings of the Holy Spirit and the Word of God contained in the 66 books of the Bible, we all need to approach the Bible in a context of faith. If we don't believe that **the Bible is** divinely—as opposed to merely ethically—**authoritative**, then it loses its ultimate thrust and usefulness among us. Secondly, **we need to understand the historical nature of the Bible** and skillfully discern between those biblical mandates that are

culturally and historically bound, and others that convey a universal relevance. Thirdly, we need to remember that the Bible is written in languages and literary genres that were once used in social intercourse. Consequently, the words therein are not from a cryptic lexicon, but can be understood after responsible exegesis. Finally, when applying our findings to the contemporary context, we need to be willing to accept the results of our search for meaning, even if they go against our most cherished personal opinions." (Emphasis added)

Dr. Burton, Keith, A. "Contextual Hermeneutics
A wholistic view of biblical interpretation," Ministry Magazine, March 2000 Edition, https://www.ministrymagazine.org/archive/2000/03/contextual-hermeneutics.

121 For a detailed exegetical study of this matter, I would urge you to read the revelatory book by Messianic Rabbi Zev Porat (Tel Aviv), Blood Alliance (Defender Publishing - 2024).

122 Most who hold to a "rebuilt temple" in the last days refer to 2 Thessalonians 2:4 as a prooftext of their position. However, after our study of what that verse actually means, in its grammatical and historical context, we see that this particular interpretation has been fundamentally mistaken for the last several hundred years.

123 Aramaic was the native language of Jesus and of Israel in the 1st century AD. The Aramaic Bible in Plain English is a modern English translation of the scriptures written in Aramaic.
The Peshitta Holy Bible Translated, Translated by Glenn David Bauscher, Lulu Publishing, Copyright © 2018 Lulu Publishing. 3rd edition Copyright © 2019.

124 Apostasy or Rebellion (the most often used English translation of the Greek – apostasia. (1.) Strong's Concordance: defection, apostasy, revolt. (2.) HELPS Word-studies: 646 apostasía (from 868 /aphístēmi, "leave, depart," which is derived from 575 /apó, "away from" and 2476 /histémi, "stand") – properly, departure (implying desertion); apostasy – literally, "a leaving, from a previous standing." (3.) NAS Exhaustive Concordance: defection, revolt, forsake
(4.) Thayer's Greek Lexicon: ἀποστασία, ἀποστασιας, ἡ (ἀφισταμαι), a falling away, defection, apostasy; in the Bible namely, from the true religion: Acts 21:21; 2 Thessalonians 2:3; ((Joshua 22:22; 2 Chronicles 29:19; 2 Chronicles 33:19); Jeremiah 2:19; Jeremiah 36: 29, 32.
See: Greek. 646. "Apostasia," Biblehub.com, https://biblehub.com/greek/646.htm.

Author's Note: I include these established Greek Lexicon interpretations of apostasia because there is a modern school of thought that somehow tries to torture that Greek word into meaning the "rapture of the church." As you can see, in no contextually correct grammatical manner can that be the proper interpretation. There is only one other use of this word in the entire New Testament and it's found in Acts 21:21, where it almost always interpreted "forsake," having nothing whatsoever to do with the rapture of the church.

125 See the following three (of numerous other) references that attest to this assertion.
(1) Apostasy In the Last Days Church.
Thayer's Greek Lexicon
STRONGS NT 646: ἀποστασία (Apostasy – GK #646. Apostasia)

ἀποστασία, ἀποστασιας, ἡ (ἀφισταμαι), a falling away, defection, apostasy; in the Bible **namely, from the true religion:** Acts 21:21; 2 Thessalonians 2:3; ((Joshua 22:22; 2 Chronicles 29:19; 2 Chronicles 33:19); Jeremiah 2:19; Jeremiah 36:29, 32. (Emphasis added). https://biblehub.com/greek/646.htm.

(2) Ellicott's Commentary For English Readers

"That falling away" must undoubtedly imply that **the persons so apostatizing had formerly held** (or, perhaps, still professed to hold) **the Christian faith:** men cannot fall from ground which they never occupied. This vast and dreadful Apostasy (see Luke 18:8), so clearly and prominently taught to the ancient **Church**...The **"Man of Sin,"** then, **will have at one time formed (or will still profess to form) part of the Christian Church, and the Apostasy will culminate in him.** (Emphasis added). https://biblehub.com /commentaries/2_thessalonians/2-3.htm.

(3) Cambridge Bible For Schools and Colleges

We must distinguish, then, between "the apostasy" and "the man of lawlessness," in that the former is the **corruption of the church**, while the latter is the **culmination of the evil** of the world...But **the two influences**, though not identical, **are in combination.** The former naturally contributes to the latter, **an apostate Church paving the way for the advent of an atheistic world-power.** (Emphasis added). https://biblehub.com /commentaries/2_thessalonians/2-3.htm.

126 Three (of many more) scholarly affirmations of my assertions.

(1) Coffman's Commentary On The Bible

There can be no way that this is a reference to the Jewish temple. Paul, who wrote the Corinthians that "Ye are the temple of God," would never have made that...the **"temple of God"** historically.

First, it means the church of Jesus Christ; but [secondly] **in context it means the apostate church** of Jesus Christ, a deduction that is mandatory from the fact of the **apostasy being Paul's subject in this paragraph.** Therefore, whenever and **wherever the "man of sin" appears it will be in the church apostate.** (Emphasis and brackets added)

2 Thessalonians 2:4. "Coffman's Commentary on the Bible," studylight.org, https:// www.studylight.org/commentary/2-thessalonians/2-4.html.

(2) Alford's Greek Testament Critical Exegetical Commentary

[This word naos was] **used metaphorically by Paul** in 1 Co 3:17: and why not here? [in 2 Thessalonians 2:4]. **See also** 1 Corinthians 6:16; Ephesians 2:21. **From these passages it is plain** that such **figurative sense** [applying to the Church, and not the Temple at Jerusalem] was **familiar** to the Apostle. (Emphasis and brackets added)

2 Thessalonians 2:4. "Alford's Greek Testament Critical Exegetical Commentary," Study light.org, https://www.studylight.org/commentaries/eng/hac/2-thessalonians-2.htm.

(3) The Pulpit Commentary

It appears more correct to refer the expression metaphorically to the Christian Church. It is a favorite metaphor of Paul to compare believers in particular, or the Church in general, to the temple of God. (Emphasis added)

2 Thessalonians 2:4. "Pulpit Commentary," Biblehub.com, https://biblehub.com/commentaries/2_thessalonians/2-4.htm.

127 Biblical Worldview from Pulpits in America

Among senior pastors 41% have a biblical worldview, while only 28% of associate pastors do. And only 13% of teaching pastors and 4% of executive pastors hold to a biblical worldview. Among children's and youth pastors, the number is 12%.

Munsil, Tracy. "New Study Shows Shocking Lack of Biblical Worldview Among American Pastors," May 12, 2022 | American Worldview Inventory, (Cultural Research Center (CRC), https://www.arizonachristian.edu/2022/05/12/shocking-lack-of-biblical -worldview-among-american-pastors.

128 The biblical examples of the prophecies concerning the literal return of Israel in the last days are numerous. Forty-six of those verses are listed at this website: https://bible .knowing-jesus.com/topics/Rebirth-Of-Israel.

129 This exponential explosion of info and communications technologies is an unprec- edented and indisputable reality. The documentation that confirms this assertion is ubiquitous. See:

(1) Prof. Eng. Ph.D. Greu, Victor. "The Exponential Development of the Information and Communications Technologies – A Complex Process Which is Generating Prog- ress Knowledge From People to People," Accessed Sept. 5, 2023, http://crd-aida.ro /RePEc/rdc/v4i2/3.pdf.

(2) Kurzweil, Ray. "The Singularity Is Near: When Humans Transcend Biology," Sep- tember 26, 2006, https://www.amazon.com/The-Singularity-Is-Near-Transcend/dp /0143037889/ref=sr_1_1?ie=UTF8&qid=1358884294&sr=8-1&keywords=singularity +is+near.

Bio of Ray Kurzweil - He is one of the world's leading inventors, thinkers, and futurists, with a twenty-year track record of accurate predictions. Called "the restless genius" by The Wall Street Journal and "the ultimate thinking machine" by Forbes magazine, Kurzweil was selected as one of the top entrepreneurs by Inc. magazine, which described him as the "rightful heir to Thomas Edison." PBS selected him as one of "sixteen revolutionaries who made America," along with other inventors of the past two centuries. An inductee into the National Inventors Hall of Fame and recipient of the National Medal of Technology, the Lemelson-MIT Prize (the world's largest award for innovation), thirteen honorary doctorates, and awards from three U.S. presidents.

(3) I would also encourage you to read my previous book Yeshua Protocol, (Defender Publishing – March 2023). In that book, I do an exegetical breakdown and in-depth study of the most important Old and New Testament prophecies that predict the unprecedented explosion of technology in which we are now living.

130 The unprecedented global apostasy of our times.

Decline of a Biblical Worldview

(1) "The groundbreaking worldview research conducted by the Cultural Research Center at Arizona Christian University in 2020 revealed that just 6% of U.S. adults have a biblical worldview." See: https://www.arizonachristian.edu/wp-content/up- loads/2021/05/CRC_AWVI2021_Release01_Digital_01_20210413.pdf.

(2) "Most Americans (68%) still consider themselves to be Christians. Among these self-identified Christians, though, only 6% have a biblical worldview. Less than half of the self-identified Christians can be classified as born-again, defined as believing that they will go to Heaven after they die but only because they have confessed their sins

and accepted Jesus Christ as their Savior. Within the born-again population (just 33% of the adult population), a shockingly small proportion (13%) hold a biblical worldview." https://www.arizonachristian.edu/2023/02/28/biblical-worldview-among-u-s-adults-drops-33-since-start-of-covid-19-pandemic.

Churches Denying the Prophetic Return of Israel (BDS)

"US churches including the Presbyterian Church USA, the United Church of Christ and the United Methodist Church (UMC) and several Quaker bodies have voted to divest from Israeli and international companies targeted by the BDS (Boycott, Divest, and Sanction) movement." See: https://bdsmovement.net/impact/major-churches-divest.

Churches affirming Gay Marriage

(4) "Overall, a solid majority of white mainline Protestants (62%) now favor allowing gays and lesbians to wed, with just 33% opposed, according to a 2015 Pew Research Center survey. A similar share (63%) say there is "no conflict" between their religious beliefs and homosexuality." https://www.pewresearch.org/short-reads/2015/12/21/where-christian-churches-stand-on-gay-marriage.

(5) Number of churches promoting LGBTQ agenda

See: This article at Wikipedia is heavily resources from denominational rulings and documentation. https://en.wikipedia.org/wiki/List_of_Christian_denominations_affirming_LGBT_people.

131 Matthew 24:14 "And this gospel of the kingdom will be proclaimed throughout the whole world as a testimony to all nations, and then the end will come."

This is a prophecy from the mouth of Yeshua Himself, declaring the unprecedented preaching of the Word of God as a definitive sign of the last days "generation." We are the first generation to be fulfilling this prophecy.

Myer's N T Commentary

This…should be taken [to mean] over the whole habitable globe, a sense which is alone in keeping with Jesus' consciousness of His Messianic mission, and with the whole world which follows. (Brackets added) https://biblehub.com/commentaries/matthew/24-14.htm.

(2) Expositor's Greek Testament

Matthew 24:14 asserts the preaching of the gospel of the kingdom: time for preaching it in the whole world, of all nations, before the end. https://biblehub.com/commentaries/matthew/24-14.htm.

(3) Vincent's Word Studies

World Lit., the inhabited. The whole habitable globe. https://biblehub.com/commentaries/matthew/24-14.htm.

(4) Pulpit Commentary

So in the present age we are not to expect more than that Christian missions shall reach the uttermost parts of the earth, and that all nations shall have the offer of salvation, before the final appearance of Christ. The success of these efforts at universal evangelization is a mournful problem. "When the Son of man cometh, shall he find the faith upon the earth? https://biblehub.com/commentaries/matthew/24-14.htm" (Luke 18:8). Matthew 24:14.

132 Barna. "Bible Engagement in a New World," 5-18-16, https://www.barna.com/research/bible-engagement-in-a-new-world.

133 Dastagir, Alia E. "Marsha Blackburn asked Ketanji Brown Jackson to define 'woman.' Science says there's no simple answer," USA Today, 3-24-22, https://www.usatoday .com/story/life/health-wellness/2022/03/24/marsha-blackburn-asked-ketanji-jackson -define-woman-science/7152439001.

134 Abortion – the world's number one cause of death – Epidemic
   (1) Global abortion deaths are estimated to be at least "73 million abortions per year." Guttmacher Institute. "Unintended Pregnancy and Abortion Worldwide," March 2022, https://www.guttmacher.org/fact-sheet/induced-abortion-worldwide.
   (2) SPUC. "Abortion leading cause of death around the world, killing more people than cancer and disease in 2022," Society for the Protection of Unborn Children, 1-5-23, https://www.spuc.org.uk/Article/385407/Abortion-leading-cause-of-death-around -the-world-killing-more-people-than-cancer-and-disease-in-2022.

135 "In 2019, the top 10 causes of death accounted for 55% of the 55.4 million deaths worldwide."
   W.H.O. "The top 10 causes of death," World Health Organization, 12-9-20, https:// www.who.int/news-room/fact-sheets/detail/the-top-10-causes-of-death.

136 "Research Starters: Worldwide Deaths in World War II," National WW2 Museum – New Orleans, accessed Sept. 23, 2023, https://www.nationalww2museum.org /students-teachers/student-resources/research-starters/research-starters-worldwide -deaths-world-war.

137 Global Mental Illness
   (1) National Library of Medicine. "The worldwide epidemic of mental illness, psychiatric and behavioral emergencies, and its impact on patients and providers," 2017 Jan-Mar; 10(1): 4–6., https://www.ncbi.nlm.nih.gov/pmc/articles/PMC5316796.
   (2) National Library of Medicine. "The epidemiology of depression across cultures," Annu Rev Public Health. 2013; 34: 119–138.
   "The World Health Organization (WHO) has ranked depression the 4th leading cause of disability worldwide (90) and **projects that by 2020, it will be the second leading cause.**" https://www.ncbi.nlm.nih.gov/pmc/articles/PMC4100461.
   Murray CJL, Lopez AD, editors. The Global Burden of Disease: A Comprehensive Assessment of Mortality and Disability from Diseases, Injuries, and Risk Factors in 1990 and Projected to 2020. Cambridge, MA: Harvard University Press; 1996. [Google Scholar] "Most comprehensive study of comparative disease burdens ever undertaken. Major depression estimated to be among the most burdensome disorders worldwide." https://scholar.google.com/scholar_lookup?title=The+Global+Burden+of+Disease:+A+-Comprehensive+Assessment+of+Mortality+and+Disability+from+Diseases,+Injuries, +and+Risk+Factors+in+1990+and+Projected+to+2020&publication_year=1996&.

138 The global opioid epidemic is now on par with global alcohol and cannabis abuse.
   (1) "Opioid use disorder and opioid addiction remain at epidemic levels in the U.S. and worldwide."
   Azadfard, Mohammadreza; Huecker, Martin R.; Leaming, James M. See: "Opioid Addiction," National Library of Medicine. Updated 7-21-23, https://www.ncbi.nlm .nih.gov/books/NBK448203.
   (2) "Globally, **alcohol use disorders were the most prevalent of all substance use**

disorders, with 100·4 million estimated cases in 2016 (age-standardized prevalence 1320·8 cases per 100 000 people, 95% uncertainty interval [95% UI] 1181·2–1468·0). The most common drug use disorders were **cannabis dependence** (22·1 million cases; age-standardized prevalence 289·7 cases per 100 000 people, 95% UI 248·9–339·1) and **opioid dependence** (26·8 million cases; age-standardized prevalence 353·0 cases per 100 000 people, 309·9–405·9).

> See: The Lancet. "The global burden of disease attributable to alcohol and drug use in 195 countries and territories, 1990–2016," Published: November 01, 2018. https://www.thelancet.com/journals/lanpsy/article/PIIS2215-0366(18)30337-7/fulltext.

139 1 John 4:3 "Every spirit that does not confess Jesus is not from God. This is the spirit of the antichrist, which you heard was coming and now is in the world already."

140 "The Chicago Health Department declaring Elim Romanian Pentecostal Church to be a "nuisance," and as such the city threatened "Summary Abatement" – a process whereby the city could immediately and without notice SEIZE AND DESTROY ALL CHURCH PROPERTY.

Think about that a moment – a group of peaceful Christians worshipping the Lord within the confines of their own perfectly sanitized and structurally sound building were deemed a nuisance -- for which the city was threatening to bulldoze their church!" Liberty Council. "Communist Christmas in Chicago," December 25, 2020, https://lc.org/newsroom/details/20201225communist-christmas-in-chicago.

141 Parks, Kristine. "Attacks against churches doubled in 2023, report warns: 'Growing disdain for Christianity': There were 436 hostile acts against Christians in US in 2023, per new report," Fox News, 2-25-24, https://www.foxnews.com/media/attacks-churches-doubled-2023-report-warns-growing-disdain-christianity.

142 "There is more persecution today than during any other time in Church history, and it only continues to escalate."
Bontrager, Emily. "Christian Persecution Increased to 360 Million in 2021, According to Open Doors' 2022 World Watch List," For The Martyrs, 1-27-22, https://forthemartyrs.com/christian-persecution-increased-2021-open-doors-2022-world-watch-list.

143 "The Woman" In this context is the "invisible church" – born again believers – the naos, the debir, the Holy Word Place. But the invisible church came forth from both the nation of Israel and the "spiritual Israel" (Ephesians 2).
(1) Jamieson-Fausset-Brown Bible Commentary
Satan's first effort was to root out the Christian Church, so that there should be no visible profession of Christianity. Foiled in this, he wars (Re 11:7; 13:7) against **the invisible Church**, namely, "those who keep the commandments of God, and have the testimony of Jesus." (Emphasis added). https://biblehub.com/commentaries/revelation/12-17.htm.
(2) Ellicott's Commentary For English Readers
Out of a thousand seeming defeats the Church of Christ has arisen; the banner of the Lord has been lifted up over every flood. But the foe will not give up his attacks. He can make war upon individual Christians; he may cease to assail the collective Church of Christ, but he can assail Christians by a thousand discomforts, by petty opposition, by undermining their morals, by making them unpopular, not as Christians, but **as**

"**very particular**" **Christians**. (Emphasis added). https://biblehub.com/commentaries
/revelation/12-17.htm.

(3) Barnes' Notes On The Bible

The "woman" represents the church, and the phrase "the remnant of her seed" must
refer to her scattered children, that is, to the scattered members of the church, wherever
they could be found. The reference here is to **persecutions against individuals, rather
than a general persecution against the church itself.** (Emphasis added). https://biblehub
.com/commentaries/revelation/12-17.htm.

(4) Expositor's Greek Testament (Israel and the Church)

[This is the] Hebrew application of the symbolism [found in] Genesis 37:9-10...The
original figure was that of **Israel personified** as a **pregnant goddess-mother**, but it
probably represented to the prophet the **true Israel or Zion of God** (Wernle, 276–288)
in which his **Christ had been born** (cf. John 16:21, with John 14:30, also En. xc.
37). The idealization was favored by the current conceptions of Zion as pre-existent
in heaven (cf. Revelation 19:8, Revelation 21:8, and Apoc. Bar. iv. = widow) and **as a
mother** (4 Esd. 9:38–10:59). The prophet views **the national history of Israel** as a long
preparation for the anguish and woe **out of which the messiah was to come.** (Emphasis added) https://biblehub.com/commentaries/revelation/12-1.htm.

(5) Cambridge Bible for Schools and Colleges (Israel)

Who then, or what, is the typical or mystical Mother of Christ?

The **ideal Israel, "the daughter of Zion."** See especially Micah 4:10; Micah 5:3 : where
it is **her travail** from which He is to be born Who is **born in Bethlehem**. This accounts
for the only features that support the other view, the appearance in her glory of the
Sun, Moon, and stars of Song of Solomon 6:10, and the mention of "the remnant of
her seed" in Revelation 12:17. (Emphasis added). https://biblehub.com/commentaries
/revelation/12-1.htm.

144 Ibid.

145 Clark, Jeffery. "Harvard physicist searching for UFO evidence says humanity will view
alien intelligence like 'God': 'A very advanced scientific civilization is a good approximation to God,' Prof. Loeb told Fox News Digital," Fox News, August 14, 2023,
https://www.foxnews.com/media/harvard
-physicist-searching-ufo-evidence-says-humanity-will-view-alien-intelligence-like-god.

146 In this and the following several chapters about the prophecies of Yeshua, Daniel, and
Revelation that speak to an explosion of technological advancements in the last days,
much of the material comes from my last book Yeshua Protocol (Defender Publishing,
2023). I have reduced that material to an edited version here, in these several chapters,
because the truths represented are absolutely vital to our continued journey in this
book. Therefore, if you desire an even deeper dive into these truths, I urge you to read
Yeshua Protocol as well.

147 The Tech Explosion of the early 1950s, just after the prophesied return of Israel to the
Middle East:

(1) Roser, Max and Ritchie, Hannah. "Technological Progress", Accessed Feb. 20,
2022, https://ourworldindata.org/technological-progress.

(2) Dyson, George. "1953: The Year That Revolutionized Life, Death, and the Digital

Bit," The Atlantic, 3-6-12, https://www.theatlantic.com/technology/archive/2012/03/1953-the-year-that-revolutionized-life-death-and-the-digital-bit/254013.

148 Whitwam, Ryan. "Clearview Plans Facial Recognition Database That Knows Every Person on Earth." Extreme Tech, 2-18-2022, https://www.extremetech.com/extreme/331819-clearview-plans-facial-recognition-database-that-knows-every-person-on-earth. Also See: https://www.washingtonpost.com/technology/2022/02/16/clearview-expansion-facial-recognition.

149 The Bible itself is clear in the matter in the asserted existence of multiple dimensions of physical reality. From Genesis to Revelation we read of the Garden Paradise that is currently cut off from our physical realm, but has been visited by humans (Paul and John for example). We also read about Heaven, hell, the angelic realm, the demonic realm, the coming dimension of eternal separation – the Lake of Fire, and so much more. Today's science may not call those dimensions by these biblical names, but they are keenly aware that many different dimensions of physical reality may very well be present, beyond our own universe. For examples of this much supported physics theory, see the following physics research sites.

(1) "The supermassive black hole M87*, which rose to fame in 2019 when it became the first void to be imaged and revealed a fuzzy orange donut (then later sharpened by AI into a skinny ring), is now **confirmed to be spinning.**" "…the spinning black hole is so massive that **it pulls the surrounding fabric of space and time inward in what's called frame-dragging.**"

Sharmila, Kuthunur. "1st black hole imaged by humanity is confirmed to be spinning, study finds," September 28,2023, https://www.space.com/historic-donut-black-hole-is-spinning-new-study-finds.

(2) "The existence of alternative histories with black holes suggests this might be possible", Prof Hawking said. "**The hole** would need to be large and **if it was rotating it might have a passage to another universe.**"

Griffin, Andrew. "Stephen Hawking: Black holes may offer a route to another universe," March 14, 2018, https://www.independent.co.uk/news/science/stephen-hawking-black-holes-space-physics-parallel-universes-science-theory-time-a8255036.html.

(3) "**Every Black Hole contains another universe?** All the black holes found so far in our universe—from the microscopic to the supermassive—may be **doorways into alternate realities.**" According to a mind-bending new theory, **a black hole is actually a tunnel between universes**—a type of wormhole.

Thanfor, Ker. National Geographic News. "Every Black Hole Contains Another Universe? And our universe may sit in another universe's black hole, equations predict," 4-12-10, https://www.nationalgeographic.com/science/article/100409-black-holes-alternate-universe-multiverse-einstein-wormholes.

(4) "[The String Theory of Physics supposes that] instead of living in a universe with three dimensions of space and one of time, **we live in one with either 9, 10 or 25 dimensions of space.** These extra dimensions are then curled up so tightly that we don't notice them – much like a silken thread appears one-dimensional until you get close enough to notice its width."

de Schwanberg/Alamy, Victor. "String theory," New Scientist, August 2019, https://www.newscientist.com/definition/string-theory.

(5) The CERN Hadron Collider.

"The Large Hadron Collider (LHC) is the world's largest and most powerful particle accelerator. It first started up on 10 September 2008, and remains the latest addition to CERN's accelerator complex. The LHC consists of a 27-kilometre ring of superconducting magnets with a number of accelerating structures to boost the energy of the particles along the way." Accessed 2-20-22, https://home.cern/science/accelerators/large-hadron-collider.

(6) CERN. "**Extra dimensions**, gravitons, and tiny black holes," Accessed 2-20-22, https://home.cern/science/physics/extra-dimensions-gravitons-and-tiny-black-holes.

(7) Irani, Ardeshir. "Dark Energy, Dark Matter, and **the Multiverse**," The Dark Energy Research Institute, Oct. 2021, https://www.scirp.org/journal/paperinformation.aspx?paperid=106493.

"CONCLUSION: [The New Physics – facilitated by the latest CERN discoveries] NP proves that **our 3-D Universe** is not at the center of the Multiverse, but rather it **is only one among hundreds of thousands of other 3-D Universes**. We hold no special privilege within the Multiverse creation and annihilation process." (Emphasis and brackets added)

150 As late as 1915, horse-drawn covered wagon travel was still in sporadic use in America. Consider the following attestation from a heavily resourced Wikipedia article:
John Stewart Williamson (April 29, 1908 – November 10, 2006), who wrote as Jack Williamson, was an American science fiction writer, one of several called the "Dean of Science Fiction. Williamson was born April 29, 1908, in Bisbee, Arizona Territory. According to his own account, the first three years of his life were spent on a ranch at the top of the Sierra Madre Mountains on the headwaters of the Yaqui River in Sonora, Mexico. He spent much of the rest of his early childhood in western Texas. **In search of better pastures, his family migrated to rural New Mexico in a horse-drawn covered wagon in 1915.** https://en.wikipedia.org/wiki/Jack_Williamson. Citing: Isaac Asimov's Science Fiction Magazine, November 1979, editorial "The Dean of Science Fiction" by Isaac Asimov, page 6. And, Williamson, Jack. Wonder's Child: My Life in Science Fiction (Benbella Books, 2005).

151 That number was 4.5 billion people in 2019.
ICAO. "ICAO / Annual Report 2019 / The World of Air Transport in 2019," accessed Feb. 24, 2022, https://www.icao.int/annual-report-2019/Pages/the-world-of-air-transport-in-2019.aspx.

152 Science Daily. "Big Data, for better or worse: 90% of world's data generated over last two years," 5-22-13, https://www.sciencedaily.com/releases/2013/05/130522085217.htm.

153 A zettabyte is a measure of digital storage capacity and is 2 to the 70th power bytes, also expressed as 1021 (1,000,000,000,000,000,000,000 bytes).
See also: Exabyte - An extraordinarily large unit of digital data, one Exabyte (EB) is equal to 1,000 Petabytes or one billion gigabytes (GB). Some technologists have estimated that all the words ever spoken by mankind would be equal to five Exabytes. https://www.teradata.com/Glossary/What-is-an-Exabyte#:~:text=An%20extraordinarily%20large%20unit%20of,be%20equal%20to%20five%20Exabytes.

154 Seed Scientific. "How Much Data Is Created Every Day?" October 28, 2021, https://seedscientific.com/how-much-data-is-created-every-day.

155 "Quantum computing is a rapidly-emerging technology that harnesses the laws of quantum mechanics to solve problems too complex for classical computers. Today, IBM Quantum makes real quantum hardware—a tool scientists only began to imagine three decades ago…"
IBM. "What is quantum computing?" IBM, Accessed Oct. 4, 2023, https://www.ibm.com/topics/quantum-computing.

156 60 Minutes – YouTube video. "Companies, countries battle to develop quantum computers," 60 Minutes, 12-4-23, https://www.youtube.com/watch?v=K4ssT6Dzmn-w&ab_channel=60Minutes.
Also See: IBM. "IBM Debuts Next-Generation Quantum Processor & IBM Quantum System Two, Extends Roadmap to Advance Era of Quantum Utility," IBM, 12-4-23, https://newsroom.ibm.com/2023-12-04-IBM-Debuts-Next-Generation-Quantum-Processor-IBM-Quantum-System-Two,-Extends-Roadmap-to-Advance-Era-of-Quantum-Utility.

157 Mueller, John Paul and Massaron, Luca
Updated: 05-26-2023 "What is AI Technology?" (From the book, What is Artificial Intelligence For Dummies – 12-24-21) accessed website on October 8, 2023, https://www.dummies.com/article/technology/information-technology/ai/general-ai/4-ways-define-artificial-intelligence-ai-254174.

158 Wong, Scott, Thorp V, Frank, Nobles, Ryan and Brown-Kaiser, Liz. "Elon Musk warns of 'civilizational risk' posed by AI in meeting with tech CEOs and senators," NBC News, 9-13-23, https://www.nbcnews.com/politics/congress/big-tech-ceos-ai-meeting-senators-musk-zuckerberg-rcna104738.

159 Elkind, Elizabeth. "Tech ethics expert warns AI race will 'end in tragedy' if Washington doesn't act: Tristan Harris said AI could end in 'tragedy'", Fox Business, 9-16-23, https://www.foxbusiness.com/politics/tech-ethics-expert-warns-ai-race-end-tragedy-washington-doesnt-act.

160 Grogan, Joe, Lopez, Naomi. "AI in health care: The perils of Biden's executive order: The potential of AI to transform the doctor's office is just the tip of the iceberg", Fox News, 12-5-23, https://www.foxnews.com/opinion/ai-health-care-perils-bidens-executive-order.

161 Panic from AI inventors over the future use of AI.
(1) Darcy, Oliver. "Experts are warning AI could lead to human extinction. Are we taking it seriously enough?" CNN Business, 5-31-23, https://www.cnn.com/2023/05/30/media/artificial-intelligence-warning-reliable-sources/index.html.
(2) Piper, Kelsey. "AI experts are increasingly afraid of what they're creating: AI gets smarter, more capable, and more world-transforming every day. Here's why that might not be a good thing." Vox.com, 11-8-22, https://www.vox.com/the-highlight/23447596/artificial-intelligence-agi-openai-gpt3-existential-risk-human-extinction.
(3) Yudkowsk, Eliezer. "Pausing AI Developments Isn't Enough. We Need to Shut it All Down," TIME.com, 3-29-23, https://time.com/6266923/ai-eliezer-yudkowsky-open-letter-not-enough.

162 Eberhart, Chris. "Congressman has grim take after access to UFO footage: 'We can't

handle it'" Fox News, 7-12-23, https://www.foxnews.com/us/congressman-has-grim
-take-after-access-to-ufo-footage-we-cant-handle-it.

163 Thomas, Jim. "UFO Official: Alarming Activity 'in Our Backyard'," Newsmax.com,
10-10-23, https://www.newsmax.com/newsfront/ufo-alien-activity-kirkpatrick/2023
/11/10/id/1141867.

164 Bunker, Theodore (Newsmax). "Report: CIA Office Recovered UFO Crashes for Decades," Newsmax.com, Nov. 28, 2023, https://www.newsmax.com/newsfront/ufo-cia
-daily-mail/2023/11/28/id/1143952.

165 The Galileo Project and Dr. Avi Loeb's Bio
(1) Harvard University. "The Galileo Project for the Systematic Scientific Search for
Evidence of Extraterrestrial Technological Artifacts," Accessed October 24, 2023,
https://projects.iq.harvard.edu/galileo/home.
(2) Bio: Avi Loeb is the head of the Galileo Project, founding director of Harvard University's Black Hole Initiative, director of the Institute for Theory and Computation
at the Harvard-Smithsonian Center for Astrophysics, and the former chair of the astronomy department at Harvard University (2011-2020). He chairs the advisory board
for the Breakthrough Starshot project, is a former member of the President's Council
of Advisors on Science and Technology, and previously served as chair of the Board on
Physics and Astronomy of the National Academies. https://projects.iq.harvard.edu
/galileo/news/spherule-analysis-finds-evidence-extrasolar-composition.

166 Clark, Jeffery. "Harvard physicist searching for UFO evidence says humanity will view
alien intelligence like 'God'," Fox News, 8-14-23, https://www.foxnews.com/media
/harvard-physicist-searching-ufo-evidence-says-humanity-will-view-alien-intelligence
-like-god.

167 (1) Military Forces (YouTube Channel). "US Unveils an Invisible UFO Breakthrough! TR-
3B Anti-Gravity Aircraft," Military Forces, Posted August 2023, https://www.youtube
.com/watch?v=cUW0wQduCrY.
(2) Hollings, Alex. "TR-3B: Does America have a reverse engineered UFO? Sandbox.
us. 8-13-23, https://www.sandboxx.us/news/airpower/tr-3b-does-america-have-a
-reverse-engineered-ufo.

168 Vander Plaats, Robert Lee (born April 12, 1963) is an American politician and political
activist. Since 2010, he has been the president and CEO of The Family Leader, a socially
conservative organization in Iowa. https://en.wikipedia.org/wiki/Bob_Vander_Plaats.

169 You can read the full article and see the video footage here:
Mettler, Zachary. "Tucker Carlson Starts Reading Scripture and Discovers These Two
Truths," The Daily Citizen, 7-17-23, https://dailycitizen.focusonthefamily.com/tucker-
carlson-starts-reading-scripture-and-discovers-these-two-truths.

170 Ibid.

171 Ibid.

172 Lee, Michael. "China, US race to unleash killer AI robot soldiers as military power
hangs in balance: experts," Fox News, 10-17-23, https://www.foxnews.com/us/china-
us-race-unleash-killer-ai-robot-soldiers-military-power-hangs-balance-experts.

173 Aitken, Peter. "FBI chief warns that terrorists can unleash AI in terrifying new ways,"
Fox News, 10-20-23, https://www.foxnews.com/us/fbi-chief-warns-terrorists-can
-unleash-ai-terrifying-new-ways.

174 Nolan, Lucas. "Former Google Boss Eric Schmidt Raises Alarm on AI Development, Compares to Nuclear Weapons," Breitbart, 11-29-23, https://www.breitbart.com /politics/2023/11/29/former-google-boss-eric-schmidt-raises-alarm-on-ai-development -compares-to-nuclear-weapons.

175 Elkind, Elizabeth. "Nancy Mace previews House hearing on AI deepfakes," Fox News, 11-4-23, https://www.foxnews.com/politics/nancy-mace-to-hold-house-hearing-on-ai -deepfakes.

176 Lukey, Kate. "AI Will Shape Your Soul: But how is up to us," Christianity Today, 9-11-23, https://www.christianitytoday.com/ct/2023/october/artificial-intelligence-robots -soul-formation.html.

177 Grant, Rebecca. "Artificial intelligence and US nuclear weapons decisions: How big a role?" Fox News, 11-7-23, https://www.foxnews.com/opinion/artificial-intelligence -us-nuclear-weapons-decisions-how-big-role.

178 Raasch, Jon Michael. "AI gives birth to AI: Scientists say machine intelligence now capable of replicating without humans - 'Self-evolving AI': Scientists explain ground-breaking new tech discovery," Fox News, 12-15-23, https://www.foxnews.com/science /ai-gives-birth-ai-scientists-say-machine-intelligence-capable-replicating-without-humans.

179 The Powers of the Heavens:

(1) Pulpit Commentary

"**The powers of the heavens**" are the **hosts of the prince** of the power of the air, "the **spiritual wickedness** in high places [unseen realms]." (Emphasis and brackets added). https://biblehub.com/commentaries/matthew/24-29.htm.

180 (2) Thayer's Greek Lexicon

(An army, a host); strength, ability, power...power consisting in or resting upon **armies, forces, hosts**...2 Peter 2:11; of the **power of the devil and evil spirits**, 1 Corinthians 15:24; i. e. of **the devil**, Luke 10:19; Revelation 13:2; **angels, as excelling in power**...Romans 8:38; 1 Peter 3:22. universally, **the power of God**: Matthew 22:29; Mark 12:24; Luke 22:69; Acts 8:10; Romans 1:20; Romans 9:17; 1 Corinthians 6:14. (Emphasis added). https://biblehub.com/greek/1411.htm.

(3) "Of the Heavens" – Thayer's Greek Lexicon

These **heavens are opened** by being cleft asunder, and from the upper heavens, or **abode of heavenly beings**, come down upon earth...the things and **beings in the heavens** (i. e. angels) and on the earth...The **region above the sidereal heavens**, the seat of an order of things eternal and consummately perfect, where **God dwells** and the **other heavenly beings**...(Emphasis added). https://biblehub.com/greek/3772.htm. Humans will die of sheer terror in the last days...

(1) Ellicott's Commentary For English Readers

Men's **hearts failing them for fear.**—The verb so rendered is used by St. Luke only in the New Testament. **Its literal meaning is to breathe out the soul**, [they will die] and it was, therefore, a word which would naturally enter into the vocabulary of a physician, both in its primary and figurative sense. The mental state which it expresses exactly agrees with that described in Acts 27:20, in connection with the tempest. (Emphasis added). https://biblehub.com/commentaries/luke/21-26.htm.

(2) Barnes' Notes On The Bible

Men's hearts failing them - This is an expression **denoting the highest terror.** The word rendered "failing" **commonly denotes to "die,"** and here it means that **the terror would be so great** that people would faint and be **ready to die** in view of the **approaching calamities.** (Emphasis added) https://biblehub.com/commentaries/luke/21-26.htm.

181 A great deception...

(1) Bengel's Gnomen

Matthew 24:24. Signs affect the intellect; prodigies, one class of which is **fearful sights** (see Luke 21:11, and cf. Acts 2:19), **trouble the mind.—**, if [it were] possible). (Emphasis added). https://biblehub.com/commentaries/matthew/24-24.htm.

(2) Pulpit Commentary

Paul testifies that such should be the action of the antichrist, "whose coming is after the working of Satan, with all power and signs and lying wonders" (2 Thessalonians 2:9; comp. Revelation 13:13, 14). Many of these wonders may have been **effectuated by natural forces unknown to the majority of men**, and therefore **considered as superhuman**; others may have been **derived from the spiritual world**, but necessarily from that realm thereof which is **under the control of demons.** (Emphasis added). https://biblehub.com/commentaries/matthew/24-24.htm.

182 A 2006 analysis put it this way: "The fastest increasing quantity on this planet is the amount of information we are generating. It is (and has been) expanding faster than anything else we create or can measure...Information is accumulating faster than any material or artifact in this world, faster than any by-product of our activities. ...Two economists at UC Berkeley calculated our total global information production for one year...[Hal] Varian and [Peter] Lyman estimate that the total production of new information in 2000 reached 1.5 exabytes. They explain that is about 37,000 times as much information as is in the entire holdings Library of Congress. For one year! Three years later the annual total yielded 3.5 exabytes. That yields a 66% rate of growth in information per year. See: "The Speed of Information," The Technium, Accessed Feb. 18, 2022, http://www.kk.org/thetechnium/archives/2006/02/the_speed_of_in.php.

183 WEF. "The Power of Digital Intermediaries: Insight Report," World Economic Forum, February 2022 Edition, Accessed, March 6, 2022, https://www3.weforum.org/docs/WEF_Advancing_towards_Digital_Agency_2022.pdf.

"The report, called **Advancing Digital Agency**: The Power of Data Intermediaries describes a digital ID system that would collect personal data about your online behavior, purchase history, network usage, medical history, travel history, energy uses, health stats, and more. This data would then be used to determine who could open bank accounts, conduct financial transactions, access insurance, health care treatment, book trips, cross borders, and more." See: Staff, Blaze TV. "World Economic Forum unveils new 'Digital ID' plan—and it's TERRIFYING: 'Nothing is beyond the realm of possibilities'" The Blaze, March 3, 2022. https://www.theblaze.com/amp/wef-digital-id-plan-2656835686?fr=operanews.

184 See the United Nations document:

"United Nations Strategy for Legal Identity for All: Concept note developed by the United Nations Legal Identity Expert Group." Especially see the subsections (16, 19,

37a-b) titled, "Population register, Implementation – General Norms, Digital Identity, and Biometrics". https://unstats.un.org/legal-identity-agenda/documents/UN-Strategy-for-LIA.pdf.

185 Inconceivably, several of today's relatively "conservative" online resources flatly claim that the Bible nowhere addresses the issue of a futuristic burgeoning of technology. Below are a few examples.

(1) Compelling Truth.org

"In summary, **the idea of technology increasing** as a sign of the end times is a popular one, but is also **often exaggerated**. Daniel 12:4 simply speaks of an increase in knowledge, offering no additional details. We are only promised knowledge will be increased in the final days, **without any predictions regarding today's technologies**." (Emphasis added). https://www.compellingtruth.org/Bible-technology.html.

(2) GotQuestions.org

Many passages of Scripture refer to what will happen at the end of the age, but no… passage seems to deal with increasing knowledge or technology as a sign for us. (Emphasis added). Got Questions. "Does the Bible say that an increase in technology is a sign of the end times?" Accessed Feb. 17, 2022. https://www.gotquestions.org/Bible-technology.html.

186 However, there are renowned scholars, even from hundreds of years ago, who clearly understood the biblical implications of exponentially increasing technological wonders as a distinctive biblical sign of the "end times." Francis Bacon lived from the mid-1500s through the early 1600s. He was a renowned English philosopher and statesman who served as Attorney General and as the Lord Chancellor of England. His works are widely acknowledged as the nascent development of today's modern scientific method. His treatises remained influential throughout the entire systematic knowledge revolution. His writings and tangible advancements in the various fields of scientific discovery and methodology are still central points of scholarly debates to this day.

Even Sir Francis Bacon saw the meaning and the importance of the prophecy of Daniel 12:4, "Many shall run to and fro, and knowledge shall increase." Following are Francis Bacon's own prophetic words. This is only one example of his prescient explanations of Daniel 12:4. We find various, but equal, restatements of this postulation throughout his other important works as well:

"And this **Proficiency in** Navigation, and discoveries, may plant also an expectation of the further proficiency, and **augmentation of all Sciences**, because it may seem **they are ordained by God to … meet in one Age**. For so the Prophet Daniel **speaking of the latter times** foretelleth: as if the openness and through passage of the world, and **the increase of knowledge were appointed to be in the same ages**, as we see it is **already performed** in great part. (Emphasis added)

The above quote is from - Dr. Fleming, James D. "At the End of the Days, Francis Bacon: Daniel 12," 3-7-19, (p. 27), https://journals.openedition.org/cahierscfv/pdf/635.

187 In this and the following several chapters about the prophecies of Yeshua, Daniel, and Revelation that speak to an explosion of technological advancements in the last days, much of the material comes from my last book Yeshua Protocol (Defender Publishing, 2023). I have reduced that material to an edited version here, because the

truths represented are absolutely vital to our continued study of our prophetic times. Therefore, if you desire an even deeper study of these facts, I urge you to read Yeshua Protocol as well.

188 Following are six more scholars confirming what I have stated in this chapter.

(1) The Pulpit Commentary (On Matthew 24:14)

The truth is that the gospel will be everywhere offered, but not everywhere received. And then, when all these signs…shall have appeared, shall the end come…of this world or this age. (Emphasis added), Matthew 24:14, https://biblehub.com/commentaries/matthew/24-14.htm.

(2) Ellicott's Commentary on the Entire Bible (On Matthew 28:20)

Even unto the end of the world.—Literally, of the age. The phrase is the same as that in Matthew 13:39-40; Matthew 13:49; Matthew 24:13-14. In Hebrews 9:26 it is used of the time of the appearance of Christ in the flesh, as the beginning of the last age of the world. (Emphasis added) See: https://biblehub.com/commentaries/matthew/28-20.htm.

(3) Gaebelein's Annotated Bible

"The end of which the Lord speaks…will be the visible manifestation of the Son of Man in power and in glory out of the opened heavens." (Emphasis added). https://www.studylight.org/commentaries/eng/gab/matthew-24.html#verse-1-51.

(4) Myer's New Testament Commentary

Jesus' declaration] must not be limited to the Roman Empire (Luke 2:1), but should be taken quite generally: over the whole habitable globe. https://biblehub.com/commentaries/matthew/24-14.htm

(5) Expositor's Greek Testament

Matthew 24:14 asserts the same thing with regard to the preaching of the gospel of the kingdom: time for preaching it in the whole world, of all nations, before the end. (Emphasis added) https://biblehub.com/commentaries/matthew/24-14.htm.

(6) Dr. Constable's Expository Notes (Matthew 24:24)

"Jesus proceeded to give His disciples a general picture of conditions just before He will return to end the present age and inaugurate His kingdom." (Emphasis added). https://www.studylight.org/commentaries/eng/dcc/matthew-24.html#verse-1-3.

189 Expositor's Greek Testament

Matthew 24:14 asserts the same thing with regard to the preaching of the gospel of the kingdom: time for preaching it in the whole world, of all nations, before the end.…Jesus wished to ensure that all Israel should hear the gospel before the end came; therefore He emphasized the shortness of the time. Here He wishes to impress on the disciples that the end will not be for a good while; therefore He emphasizes the amount of preaching that can be done. https://biblehub.com/commentaries/matthew/24-14.htm.

190 End of the Age. John F. Walvoord, President, Dallas Theological Seminary, Editor, Bibliotheca Sacra.

"Having completed in Matthew 24:4-14 the itemization of the nine signs which will be fulfilled in the present age in general and which will be especially characteristic of the end of the age, Christ now gives specific signs, answering the disciples' original question. They had asked for the sign of the end of the age and of His coming into His kingdom." See: Walvoord. "Signs of the End of the Age," accessed Feb. 24, 2022, https://bible.org/seriespage/3-signs-end-age.

191 "The Book of Daniel is the apocalyptic book of the Hebrew Bible. Its sister book would be the Book of Revelation." Dr. James Tabor. Quoted by: PBS FRONTLINE. "The Book of Daniel", pbs.org, Accessed Feb. 17, 2022, https://www.pbs.org/wgbh/pages/frontline/shows/apocalypse/explanation/bdaniel.html.

192 Moody Bible Institute of Chicago
Christ Himself in Matthew 24:15 predicted the abomination of desolation of Daniel 12:11 as future, not past. Prophecies of the book of Revelation written late in the first century also anticipate as future the fulfillment of parallel prophecies in Daniel. For example, Revelation 13 parallels the final stage of Daniel's fourth empire. This could not, therefore, refer to events fulfilled in the second century B.C. [Daniel's own time]. See: Moody Bible Institute: "Daniel. The Key to Prophetic Revelation," accessed Feb. 26, 2022 (written 1971), https://bible.org/book/export/html/6551.

193 I am not claiming that our modern technological wonders that appear to approximate the "miracles" of Revelation are in fact the complete fulfilments of those prophecies. Rather, what we possess may only be the precursors to the ultimate realities of them... that are still yet to come.

194 Daniel's 4:2 is the Scroll of Revelation
(1) Dr. Gary Everett's Study Notes on the Holy Scriptures Daniel's vision comes to a close with a few brief remarks about the **last times** and the **coming of the Lord** and the final **Day of Judgment**. This lengthy vision that Daniel is given **takes biblical prophecy** up to the **Second Coming of the Messiah**. (Emphasis added). Everett's Study Notes on the Holy Scriptures, "Daniel 12" Studylight.org, https://www.studylight.org/commentaries/eng/ghe/daniel-12.html#verse-1-13.
(2) Beale, G. K. - Commentary on the Greek Text
"**The only other place in the Bible**, before Revelation 5, wherein a scroll is sealed, is in Daniel chapter 12...**There's only one place** in the future where a scroll is unsealed. It's found in **Revelation 5 and 6**. The metaphor of seals can be found outside Daniel elsewhere in the OT and Jewish apocalyptic, **but the seals in Rev. 5:1ff come from Dan. 12:4, 9**." (Emphasis added)G. K. Beale, The Book of Revelation: A Commentary on the Greek Text, New International Greek Testament Commentary (Grand Rapids, MI; Carlisle, Cumbria: W.B. Eerdmans; Paternoster Press, 1999) p.347.

195 Hebrew 7227. Rab. Biblehub.com, https://biblehub.com/hebrew/7227.htm.
196 Ibid.
197 Hebrew 7751. Shuwt. Biblehub.com, https://biblehub.com/hebrew/7751.htm.
198 Daath is used 95 times in the Old Testament.Hebrew 1847. Daath. https://biblehub.com/hebrew/1847.htm.
199 "By 330 BC, Aristotle coined the Greek term technologia and split **scientific knowledge** into three parts: theoretical science, practical science, and productive science (technology). According to Luna (1994), the earliest use of the word technology in the United States was found in a Harvard University course on the "application of the Sciences to the Useful Arts" in 1816. The 1832 Encyclopedia Americana defined technology as principles, processes, and nomenclatures." See: San Jose State University in San Jose, CA ."Introduction History of Technology" Accessed Feb. 22, 2022, https://www.sjsu.edu/people/patricia.backer/history/introduction.htm.

200 Hebrew 7235. Rabah. Biblehub.com, https://biblehub.com/hebrew/7235.htm.

201 Daniel 12. "Bell's Commentary on the Bible" Studylight.org, https://www.studylight.org
/commentaries/eng/cbb/daniel-12.html#verse-1-13.

202 Lode Star Solutions. "How Fast Is Knowledge Doubling?" Accessed Feb. 22, 2022,
"https://lodestarsolutions.com/keeping-up-with-the-surge-of-information-and-human
-knowledge.

203 "Within chapter 24, Jesus repeatedly quotes or alludes to Daniel, Zechariah and Isaiah.
It's important to remember that Jesus preached at a time when even ordinary people
memorized large portions of Scripture, so he could expect that people would hear his
many references to the OT."
      Dr. Manning, Jr. Gary. "No Stone Left Unturned: Solving a Minor Mystery," Biola
University, 5-21-13, https://www.biola.edu/blogs/good-book-blog/2013/no-stone-left
-unturned-solving-a-minor-mystery.

204 Greyman-Kennard, Danielle. "Israel is only the first target, warns Hamas commander,"
The Jerusalem Post, 10-09-23, https://www.jpost.com/middle-east/article-765304.

205 "On October 7, 2023, the Palestinian Sunni Islamist group Hamas (a U.S.-designated
foreign terrorist organization, or FTO) led surprise attacks against Israel by land, sea,
and air. The assault came on a Jewish holiday, 50 years after the Egypt-Syria surprise
attack that sparked the 1973 Yom Kippur War." https://crsreports.congress.gov/product
/pdf/download/R/R47754/R47754.pdf.

206 Israel News Staff. "Israeli Investigators Document Cases of Sexual Violence," Newsmax,
11-16-23, https://www.newsmax.com/world/globaltalk/israel-women-sexual-violence
/2023/11/16/id/1142494.

207 Worse than September 11 attacks in U.S.
"By latest count, the attacks by Hamas—the Arabic acronym for the Islamic Resistance
Movement—killed more than 1,300 Israelis and third-country nationals, including at
least 29 Americans, in a country whose population is less than 10 million. In America,
that would be equivalent to killing nearly 40,000—13 times more than the number of
Al Qaeda victims on 9/11."
      Satloff, Robert. "Why 10/7 Was Worse for Israel Than 9/11 Was for America," The
Washington Institute, 10-15-23, https://www.washingtoninstitute.org/policy-analysis
/why-107-was-worse-israel-911-was-america.

208 Klein, Joshua, "'Moderate' Palestinian Authority Calls to Murder Jews: 'Fight the Jews'
and 'Kill' Them All", Breitbart.com, 10-22-23, https://www.breitbart.com/politics
/2023/10/22/moderate-palestinian-authority-calls-murder-jews-fight-jews-kill-all.

209 Greyman-Kennard, Danielle. "Israel is only the first target, warns Hamas commander,"
The Jerusalem Post, 10-09-23, https://www.jpost.com/middle-east/article-765304.

210 "Generally, order is collapsing and is being replaced by chaos. This has been happening
for the past five to 10 years. We see it in more and more places now," Israeli writer and
historian Yuval Noah Harari.
      Achom, Debanish. "Could Lead To Third World War If...": Israeli Author's Caution
On Gaza War," NDTV, 10-16-23, https://www.ndtv.com/world-news/world-war-3
-annihilation-of-humankind-israeli-historian-yuval-noah-hararis-caution-4486123.

211 Seligman, Lara and McLeary, Paul. "Attacks on U.S. troops in Middle East ramp up

as Israel conflict escalates: The episodes add a dangerous new element to the fighting in Gaza and deepen fears that Iran might take a more regional approach to fomenting violence," Politico, 10-19-23, https://www.politico.com/news/2023/10/19/american-forces-thwart-drone-strikes-bases-syria-00122507.

212 Ladden-Hall, Dan. "Iran Threatens to Drag the U.S. Into Regional Holy War," The Daily Beast, 10-17-23, https://www.thedailybeast.com/iran-threatens-to-drag-the-us-into-regional-holy-war.

213 Sorace, Stephan. "Iran threatens Israel over looming ground offensive in Gaza: report - Iran FM warns Israel of 'huge earthquake' should Lebanon's Hezbollah get involved," Fox News, 10-15-23, https://www.foxnews.com/world/iran-threatens-israel-looming-ground-offensive-gaza-report.

214 NYP Editorial Board. "As Iran threatens preemptive strike, Biden must deter with total force," New York Post, 10-17-23, https://nypost.com/2023/10/17/after-iran-threatens-preemptive-strike-biden-must-deter.

215 Szuba, Jared. "Iran's Khamenei threatens US as Pentagon readies 2,000 troops for region," Al-Monitor, Oct. 17, 2023, https://www.al-monitor.com/originals/2023/10/irans-khamenei-threatens-us-pentagon-readies-2000-troops-region.

216 "Iran issues stark warning to U.S. over arms shipment to Israel: Suggests that there may be adverse consequences or tensions resulting from such actions." KITV, 10-17-23, https://www.youtube.com/watch?v=53opNmoQcnc.

217 Reuters. "Putin cautions Israel against using tactics in Gaza like Nazi siege of Leningrad," Reuters, 10-13-23, https://www.reuters.com/world/putin-israeli-ground-operation-gaza-will-result-civilian-losses-2023-10-13.

218 Gehrke, Joel, Washington Examiner. "Israel war: Kremlin threatens nuclear war after Biden compares Russia to Hamas," Gazette.com, Oct 20, 2023, https://gazette.com/news/wex/israel-war-kremlin-threatens-nuclear-war-after-biden-compares-russia-to-hamas/article_a83387f4-8805-5aab-ae14-e658c3b5b8fe.html.

219 Staff. "Turkey's Erdogan says Israel's operations in Gaza 'amounting to genocide': After slow rapprochement with Jerusalem, president appears to reverse course, accuses Israel of 'attacks against civilians,'" Times of Israel, 10-20-23, https://www.timesofisrael.com/turkeys-erdogan-says-israels-operations-in-gaza-amounting-to-genocide.

220 Herskovitz, Jon. "North Korea Threatens US for Sending Aircraft Carrier to South," Bloomberg.com, 10-13-23, https://www.bloomberg.com/news/articles/2023-10-13/north-korea-threatens-us-for-sending-aircraft-carrier-to-south#xj4y7vzkg.

221 Kim, Hyung-Jin. "North Korea raises the specter of nuclear strike over US aircraft carrier's arrival in South Korea," AP News, 10-13-23, https://apnews.com/article/north-korea-nuclear-weapons-us-aircraft-carrier-be56e91daba9eeeaf2edefdccf3c9133.

222 Cook, Ellie. "China Warns Israel Has 'Gone Beyond' Self-Defense in War," Newsweek, 10-15-23, https://www.newsweek.com/israel-hamas-china-gaza-strip-idf-air-strikes-1834790.

223 Reuters. "Analysis: China and Russia find common cause in Israel-Hamas crisis," Reuters, 10-20-23, https://www.reuters.com/world/china-russia-find-common-cause-israel-hamas-crisis-2023-10-20.

224 Magdy, Samy and Krauss, Joseph. "Gaza carnage spreads anger across Mideast,

alarming US allies and threatening to widen conflict," AP News, 10-18-23, https://apnews.com/article/israel-gaza-hospital-jordan-egypt-protests-590f24d154fb3cb256ec1707ec78b816.

225 Pollack, Joel. "Hamas Official: We Will Repeat October 7 Terror Attack Until Israel is Annihilated," Breitbart, 11-1-23, https://www.breitbart.com/middle-east/2023/11/01/hamas-official-we-will-repeat-october-7-terror-attack-until-israel-is-annihilated.

226 I am referring to events like the first Gulf War with Saddam Hussein launching Scud Missiles into Israel and threatening to bring the "Mother of All Wars" to the planet, the first Gulf War, the subsequent September 11, 2001, terrorist attacks on the United States; the U.S. coalition led war in Iraq and Afghanistan (the longest war in U.S. history), Arab Spring, consistently launched Hamas and Hezbollah missile attacks against Israel, Iran's continual calling of Israel's annihilation, and the like.

227 "46 Bible Verses about Rebirth Of Israel," Bible.Knowing-Jesus.com, accessed 10-24-23, https://bible.knowing-jesus.com/topics/Rebirth-Of-Israel.

228 For example – Isaiah 49, Ezekiel 37, Ezekiel 38, and Ezekiel 39 – among others.

229 As one implicational example of Israel's return, consider the following. There are several prophecies about the vast armies of a coalition of cooperating nations that will surround Jerusalem in the last days in order to take it back, and/or defeat the people that are holding it. We find those prophecies in both the Old and New Testaments (i.e. Luke 21:20, Zechariah 12 and 14). But why would a World War scenario start over that one city...unless it were somehow occupied again by the Jewish people who had in fact returned and reoccupied it? The answer is that if one knows the entirety of the Word of God, then they would also know of the black and white biblical prophecies proclaiming Israel's last days resurrection in the Middle East. With that return, it would stand to reason that the fallen world, under Satan's control, would be livid concerning the Hebrew people possessing that territory again, and especially their possession of the Holy City of Jerusalem.

230 "On May 14, 1948 Israel was reborn as a nation after 2,000 years. No one can deny that this was truly a unique event in human history. Never have a people who lost their statehood later become a nation after such a long period of time."

See: JJ Travel In Israel. "After 2,000 years, how did Israel once again become a nation?", JJ Travel In Israel, 2-3-20, https://www.jjtravelinisrael.com/after-2000-years-how-did-israel-once-again-become-a-nation.

231 When Was Deuteronomy Written?
(1) "Although Deuteronomy is presented as an address by Moses, scholars generally agree that it dates from a much later period of Israelite history. An early edition of Deuteronomy as it exists today has been identified with the book of the Law discovered in the Temple of Jerusalem about 622 BC (2 Kings 22:8; 2 Chronicles 34:15)."

Britannica. "Deuteronomy," Accessed Oct. 28, 2023, https://www.britannica.com/topic/Deuteronomy.
(2) "There are competing views about the authorship of Deuteronomy. The traditional view, held by many religious Jews and Christians, is that the prophet Moses wrote Deuteronomy and the entire Torah. Modern scholars, however, argue that Moses could not have been the author of the entire text due to...repetitions, and stylistic differences.

Instead, they suggest that an unknown author or authors wrote Deuteronomy and the Torah as a whole, which was later compiled from a variety of sources. Although the story in **Deuteronomy is set during** the Israelites' time in the wilderness, **the text was written much later, probably around the 7th century BCE** after the priesthood, Temple, monarchy had been well-established. Therefore, the author of Deuteronomy could work in some of these ideas into the text." (Emphasis added)

Study.com. "Book of Deuteronomy: Overview & Purpose," Accessed 11-1-23, https://study.com/learn/lesson/book-deuteronomy-summary-overview-author.html.

232 Keil and Delitzsch Biblical Commentary on the Old Testament
The history of all times since the creation of man, and of all places under the whole heaven, can relate no such events as those which have happened to Israel. https://biblehub.com/commentaries/deuteronomy/4-32.htm.

233 Jamieson-Fausset-Brown Bible Commentary
The words may be **interpreted either wholly in a spiritual sense** (Joh 11:51, 52), or, as many think, **in a literal sense** also (Ro 11:1-36). They will be recalled from all places of the dispersion to their own land and enjoy the highest prosperity. [When the authors wrote this, there was not yet a literally returned Israel!] (Emphasis and brackets added), https://biblehub.com/commentaries/deuteronomy/30-3.htm.

234 Enduring Word Commentary – David Guzik (Deuteronomy 30), https://enduringword.com/bible-commentary/deuteronomy-30.

235 Symes, Kenneth, B.A., S.T.M. (Master of Sacred Theology) was a pastor in Baltimore, MD for almost twenty years. After serving almost eleven years as the Executive Director of Jewish Awareness Ministries, Inc., Ken is now the National Field Representative for J.A.M. https://www.xulonpress.com/bookstore/bookdetail.php.

236 Symes, Kenneth. "The Regathering of Israel," Israel My Glory Magazine, April/May 1991, https://israelmyglory.org/article/the-regathering-of-israel.

237 Deuteronomy 30. "Dr. Constable's Expository Notes: The possibility of restoration 30:1-10,: StudyLight.org, https://www.studylight.org/commentary/deuteronomy/30-6.html.

238 The modern prosperity of Israel and the technological advancements that this tiny and very young nation has brought to the entire planet – especially in the fields of medicine, digital tech, business and finance industry, farming tech, and engineering technologies are indisputable and well documented.
See: "Economy of Israel," Accessed Oct. 30, 2023, (Highly documented and referenced with reliable sources) https://en.wikipedia.org/wiki/Economy_of_Israel.

239 Israel population stats.
Barkat, Amiram. "Study Traces Worldwide Jewish Population From Exodus to Modern Age," Haaretz, 4-29-05, https://www.haaretz.com/2005-04-29/ty-article/study-traces-worldwide-jewish-population-from-exodus-to-modern-age/0000017f-e7d1-d97e-a37f-f7f53ba50000.
"Historical Jewish population comparisons," Wikipedia (Heavily referenced from ancient sources as well as modern), accessed Oct. 30, 2023, https://en.wikipedia.org/wiki/Historical_Jewish_population_comparisons.

240 Zechariah's prophecy of the latter days returned Israel. (The last one of the Old Testament).

(1) Pulpit Commentary
God **promises to bring his dispersed people home again** - a promise only yet partially fulfilled. My people. A title of honour (Hosea 2:23). From the east country, and from the west country. Two regions are named, **symbols of the whole world** (comp. Psalm 50:1; Malachi 1:11). The return of the captives from Babylon was a prelude of the future restoration of the dispersed, when all Israel shall be saved (Romans 11:26). (See a similar promise, Isaiah 43:5, 6; comp. John 11:52.) Zechariah 8:7. [When the authors wrote this, there was not yet a literally returned Israel!] (Emphasis and brackets added), https://biblehub.com/commentaries/zechariah/8-7.htm.
(2) Jamieson-Fausset-Brown Bible Commentary
I will save my people from…east…west—that is, **from every region** (compare Ps. 50:1; the "West" is literally, "the going down of the sun") to which they are scattered; they are now found especially in countries west of Jerusalem. The dispersion under Nebuchadnezzar was only to the east, namely, to Babylonia. **The restoration, including a spiritual return to God (Zec 8:8), here foretold, must therefore be still future** (Isa 11:11, 12; 43:5, 6; Eze 37:21; Am 9:14, 15; also Zec 13:9; Jer 30:22; 31:1, 33). [When the authors wrote this, there was not yet a literally returned Israel!] (Emphasis and brackets added), https://biblehub.com/commentaries/zechariah/8-7.htm.

241 Ellicott's Commentary for English Readers
Though Israel be not gathered.…The Servant falls back upon the greatness of the work committed to him, that **of restoring Israel**, and **is certain that sooner or later it will be accomplished.** Comp. the argument of Romans 9-11. [When the authors wrote this, there was not yet a literally returned Israel!] (Emphasis and brackets added), https://biblehub.com/commentaries/isaiah/49-5.htm.

242 Zechariah 8:8. "Keil and Delitzsch Biblical Commentary on the Old Testament," Biblehub.com, https://biblehub.com/commentaries/zechariah/8-8.htm.

243 "Commentary on the Old by Carl Friedrich Keil (1807-1888) and Franz Delitzsch (1813-1890) began publication in 1861 in German and 1863 in English. The translation into English was completed in 1891."

   Mansfield, Richard. "A Closer Look at Keil & Delitzsch: Commentary on the Old Testament," Accordance Bible, 7-1-21, https://www.accordancebible.com/k-and-d."

244 Zechariah 10. "Zechariah 10 – A Promise To Regather Israel," Guzik Commentary, https://enduringword.com/bible-commentary/zechariah-10.

245 **James M. Rochford** graduated Magna Cum Laude from Trinity Evangelical Divinity School with his Masters in Theological Studies.

   James Rochford's work is endorsed by: Dr. Robert C. Newman—Emeritus Professor of New Testament & Christian Evidences—Biblical Seminary— PhD Theoretical Astrophysics, Cornell University. Dr. Eric Tully—Professor of Old Testament and Semitic Languages—Trinity Evangelical Divinity School. Pat Reeder–PhD Philosophy, Ohio State University. Lee Campbell–PhD Neurosciences. See: https://www.evidence unseen.com/articles/preview-of-evidence-unseen.

246 Zechariah 10. "The Regathering of Israel," Evidence Unseen, accessed November 9,2023, https://www.evidenceunseen.com/articles/prophecy/the-regathering-of-israel.

247 Zechariah 10:8-10. "Gills' Exposition on the Bible," https://www.studylight.org /commentary/zechariah/10-8.html.

248 Gaebelein, Arno C.. "A True Biblical-Prophetic Belief," Accessed November 4, 2023, https://www.wholesomewords.org/etexts/gaebelein/meat2.html

249 Cloud, David. "Testimonies That Israel Will Return," Way of Life Literature: Publisher of Bible Study Materials, 8-25-22, https://www.wayoflife.org/reports/testimonies_that _israel_will_return.html.

250 John F. Walvoord (May 1, 1910 – December 20, 2002), was a Christian theologian, pastor, and president of Dallas Theological Seminary from 1952 to 1986. He earned AB and DD degrees from Wheaton College, an AM degree from Texas Christian University in philosophy, a ThB, ThM, and ThD in Systematic theology from Dallas Theological Seminary, and a LittD from Liberty Baptist Seminary. https://www.blue letterbible.org/commentaries/walvoord_john.

251 Dr. Walvoord, John F. "Chapter VII The Glorious Restoration Of Israel," accessed November 14, 2023, https://walvoord.com/article/288.

252 Dozens of scholars have seen the return of Israel in the last days as being clearly prophesied in the scriptures.
(1) At the following site is a chart listing dozens of scholars and their commentary statements on the return of Israel, as prophesied in the Bible.
See: Dr. Garland, Tony (Th.D.). "Did Early Students of the Bible Predict the Reestablishment of Israel?" Accessed 11-4-23. https://www.spiritandtruth.org/questions/232 .htm?x=x.
(2) For another lengthy list of scholars see:
Cloud, David. "Testimonies That Israel Will Return," Way of Life Literature: Publisher of Bible Study Materials, 8-25-22, https://www.wayoflife.org/reports/testimonies_that _israel_will_return.html.

253 "**No single intellectual voice contributed more** to the development of modern biblical prophecy **than Dr. John F. Walvoord**. During his six-decade-long career as an author, pastor, teacher, and educator, Dr. Walvoord articulated a comprehensive view of biblical prophecy that was based on his rock-solid belief that all the prophecies in the Bible either have been, or will be, literally fulfilled.
Dr. Walvoord began his teaching career as a professor of theology at Dallas Theological Seminary in 1936. In 1952, after the death of Dr. Lewis Sperry Chafer, the seminary's founder and first president, In 1986, after serving Dallas Theological Seminary for 50 years, Dr. Walvoord became chancellor.
From the beginning of his professional career, Dr. Walvoord spoke and wrote about **biblical prophecy** in light of **current world events.** Even **before the world believed** there could be a Jewish return to the Holy Land or a nation of Israel, **Dr. Walvoord insisted that a new Jewish state would emerge** and that no one, whether it be the British, the Palestinians, or the Arab nations, could stop this **inevitable fulfillment of biblical prophecy.**
He saw God's plan for the end-time begin to unfold as the Palestinian-Israeli conflict became the focus of NATO and Western leaders. He taught that soon **all the nations of the world** would be **embroiled in conflict** leading to the events prophesied in the books of Daniel and Revelation." (Emphasis added). See: About The Author – John F. Woodward: https://www.amazon.com/dp/0882078127?ref_=cm_sw_r_apan _dp_RGVP576MK27EKZ87HQV4&language=en-US.

254 I've written a book called Gods of Ground Zero that explains the entire Garden of Eden affair in great biblical detail. That book contains a number of shocking disclosures. I highly recommend you also read that study in your quest for even deeper biblical knowledge. See: Gallups, Carl. "Gods of Ground Zero: The truth of Eden's iniquity, why it still matters, and the mystery of what's coming next," (Defender Publishing – 2018).

255 SPUC. "Abortion leading cause of death around the world, killing more people than cancer and disease in 2022," Society for the Protection of Unborn Children, 1-5-23, https://www.spuc.org.uk/Article/385407/Abortion-leading-cause-of-death-around-the -world-killing-more-people-than-cancer-and-disease-in-2022.

256 For an example of the prophecy of Satan's last-days attack on Israel, see Ezekiel 37–39. For Satan's onslaught aimed at the Church and the Seed of womb, see Revelation 12.

257 Galatians 3:16.

258 See my book Gods of the Final Kingdom (Crane, MO: Defender Publishing, July 2019) for a thorough study of this biblical truth.

259 "Is Mary's Lineage in One of the Gospels?" Bible.org, accessed Jan. 2, 2019, https:// bible.org/question/mary%E2%80%99s-lineage-one-gospels.

260 Herod's Satan-led treachery.
(1) Cambridge Bible for Schools and Colleges:
[Herod's treachery] symbolizes the enmity of the serpent against the seed of the woman...including also the malice that pursued [Jesus] through life, the temptation, and at last the Cross. (Emphasis and brackets added) https://biblehub.com/commentaries /revelation/12-4.htm.
(2) Gill's Exposition of the Entire Bible: Just as the dragon Pharaoh lay in the midst of his rivers, in the river Nile, Ezekiel 29:3; to slay the male children of Israel as soon as born; and as the dragon Herod sought to take away the life of Jesus quickly after his birth; and as Satan is like a roaring lion, seeking whom he may devour, so the Pagan empire, or the Pagan emperors, took every opportunity to stifle the kingdom of Christ in embryo. (Emphasis added) https://biblehub.com/commentaries/revelation/12-4.htm.

261 Jamieson-Fausset-Brown Bible Commentary
The remnant of her seed—distinct in some sense from the woman herself. Satan's first effort was to root out the Christian Church, so that there should be no visible profession of Christianity. Foiled in this, he wars (Re 11:7; 13:7) against the invisible Church, namely, "those who keep the commandments of God, and have the testimony of Jesus". These are "the remnant," or rest of her seed, the Church, in her beauty and unity (Israel at the head of Christendom, the whole forming one perfect Church)... https://biblehub.com/commentaries/revelation/12-17.htm.

262 See all of Genesis 17
"And Abraham said to God, "If only Ishmael might live under your blessing!" Then God said, "Yes, but your wife Sarah will bear you a son, and you will call him Isaac. I will establish my covenant with him as an everlasting covenant for his descendants after him." (Genesis 17:18-19; NIV)

263 From the Virtual Jewish Library:
"In the biblical tradition about the origin of the Edomites or, more precisely, in accounts about the eponym "Esau who is Edom" (Gen. 36:1), the Edomites are related

to the Hebrews. Esau was the grandson of Abraham the Hebrew and the son of Isaac. The close relationship of Esau to Israel is especially emphasized in the narratives which point out his closeness with Jacob-Israel, and describe their birth as twins.

In the accounts of Esau's marriages...it is told that Esau married **Canaanite-Hittite** women (Gen. 26:34; cf. 36:2). It is likewise told that he **married Ishmaelite** women (Gen. 28:9; cf. 36:3). He also took Hivite wives (Gen. 36:2). These parenthetical narrative remarks...confirm the contents of the genealogical lists of Edom. The ethnic composition appears to be even more heterogeneous when in addition to the **Canaanite-Hittite**, Hivite, and Ishmaelite elements, Kenazite (Gen. 36:15), **Amalekite** (36:16), and especially Horite (36:20, 21, 29, 30) elements are found in the genealogical list of Esau's descendants and in the list of the chiefs of Esau." https://www.jewishvirtuallibrary.org/edom.

264 NBC News. "Obama Attends EU Meeting During Netanyahu's Speech," March 3, 2015, https://www.nbcnews.com/politics/barack-obama/president-obama-attends-eu-meeting-during-netanyahus-speech-n316346.

265 Garver, Rob. "Here's what's in Iran's $100 billion in assets that will become unfrozen by the nuclear deal," Business Insider, 7-14-15, https://www.businessinsider.com/whats-in-irans-100-billion-in-frozen-assets-2015-7.

266 Krishnadev Calamur. "In Speech To Congress, Netanyahu Blasts 'A Very Bad Deal' With Iran," NPR, 3-3-2015, https://www.npr.org/sections/thetwo-way/2015/03/03/390250986/netanyahu-to-outline-iran-threats-in-much-anticipated-speech-to-congress.

267 Williams, Dan, Spetalnick, Matt. "Israel's Netanyahu draws rebuke from Obama over Iran speech to Congress," Reuters, March 3, 2015, https://www.reuters.com/article/us-usa-israel/israels-netanyahu-draws-rebuke-from-obama-over-iran-speech-to-congress-idUSKBN0LZ0BS20150303.

268 Ibid.

269 Washington Post Staff. "The complete transcript of Netanyahu's address to Congress," The Washington Post, 3-3-2015, https://www.washingtonpost.com/news/post-politics/wp/2015/03/03/full-text-netanyahus-address-to-congress.

270 "The pact came after an all-night work session that extended well past the talks' original deadline of March 31."
Eilperin, Juliet. "Obama announces outlines of a nuclear deal: 'If Iran cheats, the world will know'" Washington Post, 4-2-2015, https://www.washingtonpost.com/news/post-politics/wp/2015/04/02/u-s-iranian-officials-expected-to-speak-on-nuclear-deal.

271 White House – Office of the Press Secretary. "Statement by the President on the Framework to Prevent Iran from Obtaining a Nuclear Weapon," 4-2-15, https://obamawhitehouse.archives.gov/the-press-office/2015/04/02/statement-president-framework-prevent-iran-obtaining-nuclear-weapon.

272 Google Question: What was April 2, 2015, on the Hebrew calendar? Google Answer: April 2, 2015 / Gregorian Calendar...13 Nisan 5775 / Hebrew Calendar.

273 Here's an example of that fact. "Critics have highlighted that the text in the Hebrew Bible which addresses revenge on the Amalek constitutes a narrative of 'genocide'."
See: Middle East Monitor, "Netanyahu declares holy war against Gaza, citing the Bible," 10-29-23, https://www.middleeastmonitor.com/20231029-netanyahu-declares-holy-war-against-gaza-citing-the-bible.

274 Giatti, Ian M.. "'Remember what Amalek has done to you': Netanyahu compares Hamas to rival of the Israelites," Christian Post, 11-31-23, https://www.christianpost.com/news/netanyahu-compares-hamas-to-amalek-rival-of-the-israelites.html.

275 The Washington Post published the following, on Oct. 8, 2023 – the day after the Hamas attack on Israel: **Washington Post Headline:** "Iran Helped Plot Attack on Israel Over Several Weeks: The Islamic Revolutionary Guard Corps gave the final go-ahead last Monday in Beirut."

"Iranian security officials helped plan Hamas's Saturday surprise attack on Israel and gave the green light for the assault at a meeting in Beirut last Monday, according to senior members of Hamas and Hezbollah, another Iran-backed militant group. Officers of Iran's Islamic Revolutionary Guard Corps had worked with Hamas since August to devise the air, land and sea incursions—the most significant breach of Israel's borders since the 1973 Yom Kippur War—those people said." (Emphasis added). See: Said, Summer, Faucon, Benoit, and Kalin, Stephen. "Iran Helped Plot Attack on Israel Over Several Weeks," Washington Post, updated Oct. 8, 2023, https://www.wsj.com/world/middle-east/iran-israel-hamas-strike-planning-bbe07b25.

276 Jewish News Syndicate. "Iranian president calls to eliminate the Jewish state," JNS, 11-11-23, Ebrahim Raisi called for Israel to be replaced by a Palestinian state "from the river to the sea." https://www.jns.org/iranian-president-calls-for-the-destruction-of-israel.

277 "From the river to the sea" - New York Times (2023)
"The phrase "from the river to the sea"—or in Arabic, "min al-nahr ila al-bahr"—**dates to the dawn of the Palestinian nationalist movement** in the early 1960s, about a quarter century before Hamas came into existence. **It gained popularity within the Palestine Liberation Organization**, or P.L.O., as a call for returning to the borders under British control of Palestine, where Jews and Arabs had both lived before the creation of Israel as a Jewish state in 1948. **The slogan reflects the geography of that original claim: Israel spans the narrow stretch of land between the Jordan River and the Mediterranean Sea."**

Demirjian, Karoun and Stack, Liam. "In Congress and on Campuses, 'From the River to the Sea' Inflames Debate," New York Times, 11-9-23, https://www.nytimes.com/2023/11/09/us/politics/river-to-the-sea-israel-gaza-palestinians.html.

278 Hebrew. Strong's 2001. "Haman". https://biblehub.com/hebrew/2001.htm.

279 Aramaic. "Semitic language of the Northern Central, or Northwestern, group that was originally spoken by the ancient Middle Eastern people known as Aramaeans. It was most closely related to Hebrew, Syriac, and Phoenician and was written in a script derived from the Phoenician alphabet. Aramaic dialects survived into Roman times, however, particularly in Palestine and Syria. Aramaic had replaced Hebrew as the language of the Jews as early as the 6th century BCE. Certain portions of the Bible—i.e., the books of Daniel and Ezra—are written in Aramaic, as are the Babylonian and Jerusalem Talmuds. Among the Jews, Aramaic was used by the common people, while Hebrew remained the language of religion and government and of the upper class. Jesus and the Apostles are believed to have spoken Aramaic." Britannica. "Aramaic language," accessed Nov. 14, 2023, https://www.britannica.com/topic/Aramaic-language.

280 Esther 3:5, "Interlinear", Biblehub.com, https://biblehub.com/interlinear/esther/3-5.htm.

281 HELPS Word-studies in the Greek
When 2372 /thymós ("expressed passion") is **used of people** it indicates **rage (personal venting of anger**, worth). This flaw is completely absent of the Lord expressing (inspiring) intense anger. Accordingly, 2372 (thymós) is used of God's perfect, holy wrath in Revelation (Rev 14:10,19,15:1, etc.). This anger is directed against sin with intense opposition and without sin. (Emphasis added) https://biblehub.com/greek/2372.htm.

282 "'Hamas,' the Arabic terrorist group acronym moniker of Harakat al-Muqawama al-Islamiya (Islamic Resistance Movement), is also a chilling homophone in the Bible: violence." See: Jeremiah J. Johnson. "'Hamas' is in the Bible - and the terrorist group lives up to the name," Washington Times, 10-18-23, https://www.washingtontimes.com/news/2023/oct/18/hamas-bible-and-terrorist-group-lives-name.

283 Hebrew. Stong's 2555. "Hamas" (Pronounced Chamas – Ch – being spoken in Hebrew with a guttural sound for "H") https://biblehub.com/hebrew/2555.htm.

284 Jewish News Syndicate. "Iranian president calls to eliminate the Jewish state," JNS, 11-11-23, Ebrahim Raisi called for Israel to be replaced by a Palestinian state "from the river to the sea." https://www.jns.org/iranian-president-calls-for-the-destruction-of-israel.

285 Messianic Bible. "Purim: From Haman to Hamas and the Role of the Righteous," Accessed November 15, 2023, https://free.messianicbible.com/holiday/purim-haman-hamas-role-righteous.

286 Stanage, Niall. "Five things to know about the $6 billion Iran deal now back in spotlight," The Hill, 10-12-23, https://thehill.com/homenews/administration/4251092-iran-deal-6-billion-hostages-five-things-know.

287 The word of the LORD came to me: Son of man, set your face toward Gog, of the land of Magog, the chief prince of Meshecha and Tubal, and prophesy against him and say, Thus says the Lord GOD: Behold, I am against you, O Gog, chief prince of Meshechb and Tubal. And I will turn you about and put hooks into your jaws, and I will bring you out, and all your army, horses and horsemen, all of them clothed in full armor, a great host, all of them with buckler and shield, wielding swords. **Persia, [Iran]** Cush, and Put are with them, all of them with shield and helmet; Gomer and all his hordes; Beth-togarmah from the uttermost parts of the north with all his hordes—many peoples are with you. (Ezekeil 38:1-6, emphasis and brackets added)

288 I am, of course, referring to Noah's ark of Genesis 6ff. When the flood (God's wrath) came upon the unbelieving world, Noah and his family were safe inside the ark and spared. Yet the Bible says that God Himself shut the doors to the ark as the flood came down upon the earth. It was God's way of saying "You didn't repent when you had the chance. Now it's too late." Today, the preaching of the Gospel of Jesus Christ is the "ark." But there's coming a day of another act of God's wrath. This time it will be global. The door (the way to salvation through Jesus – who is "The Door" John 14:1-6) will be shut. Also by God Himself.

289 Weigmann, Katrin. "The code, the text and the language of God," National Library of Medicine, February 2004, https://www.ncbi.nlm.nih.gov/pmc/articles/PMC1298980.

290 Cold Spring Harbor Laboratory. "The Human Genome Project," Accessed April 2, 2022, https://www.cshl.edu/archives/guide-to-hgp/.

291 See: National Human Genome Research Institute home webpage. Genome.gov, accessed March 22, 2022, https://www.genome.gov/human-genome-project.

292 Landau, Elizabeth. "DNA project interprets 'book of life'," CNN, 9-5-12,https://www.cnn.com/2012/09/05/health/encode-human-genome/index.html.

293 National Human Genome Research Institute. "Deoxyribonucleic Acid (DNA) Fact Sheet," Accessed Nov. 12, 2023, https://www.genome.gov/about-genomics/fact-sheets/Deoxyribonucleic-Acid-Fact-Sheet.

294 "June 2000 White House Event," (Remarks Made by the President, Prime Minister Tony Blair of England (via satellite), Dr. Francis Collins, Director of the National Human Genome Research Institute, and Dr. Craig Venter, President and Chief Scientific Officer, Celera Genomics Corporation, on the Completion of the First Survey of the Entire Human Genome Project) Genome.gov., Accessed April 23, 2022, https://www.genome.gov/10001356/june-2000-white-house-event.

295 In the "Depths of the earth," is a Hebrew expression for something along the lines of: In an unseen place that is nearly impossible to plumb. The deepest depths.
Barnes' Notes on the Bible
   Wrought in a place as dark, as obscure, and as much beyond the power of human observation as though it had been done low down beneath the ground where no eye of man can penetrate. https://biblehub.com/commentaries/psalms/139-15.htm.

296 Brookhaven National Laboratory. "Researchers find surprising similarities between genetic and computer codes," Phys.org, 3-29-13, https://phys.org/news/2013-03-similarities-genetic-codes.html.
(1.) "Computational biologist Sergei Maslov of Brookhaven National Laboratory worked with graduate student Tin Yau Pang from Stony Brook University to compare the frequency with which components "survive" in two complex systems: bacterial genomes and operating systems on Linux computers. Their work is published in the Proceedings of the National Academy of Sciences."
(2.) Also see: Service, Robert R. "DNA could store all of the world's data in one room: New algorithm delivers the highest-ever density for large-scale data storage," Science.org, March 2, 2017, https://www.science.org/content/article/dna-could-store-all-worlds-data-one-room.
   "Humanity has a data storage problem: More data were created in the past 2 years than in all of preceding history. And that torrent of information may soon outstrip the ability of hard drives to capture it. Now, researchers report that they've come up with a new way to encode digital data in DNA to create the highest-density large-scale data storage scheme ever invented. Capable of storing 215 petabytes (215 million gigabytes) in a single gram of DNA, the system could, in principle, store every bit of datum ever recorded by humans in a container about the size and weight of a couple of pickup trucks."
(3.) Also see: USA. (Video). Scientists Found Proof of GOD in DNA Code - Evidence of God - The God Code - God DNA," Uploaded Nov. 28, 2019, https://www.youtube.com/watch?v=XuUR7v7hkOQ.

297 A Number of Renowned Scientists Do Not Believe Evolution is Scientifically Accurate or Plausible:
(1.) "A Scientific Dissent from Darwinism," dissentfromdarwin.org, accessed April 23, 2022, https://dissentfromdarwin.org/.
(2.) The List. "A Scientific Dissent from Darwinism," Accessed April 23, 2022. To see

the actual signed list of each renowned scientist (update 20210 see: https://www.discovery .org/m/securepdfs/2021/07/Scientific-Dissent-from-Darwinism-List-07152021.pdf.

298 Lawrence Berkeley National Laboratory. "Researchers identify new mechanism for keeping DNA protein in line," 6-29-17, https://phys.org/news/2017-06-mechanism-dna -protein-line.html.

299 Leslie A. Pray, Ph.D. "Major Molecular Events of DNA Replication," 2008 Nature Education 1(1):99, Accessed 3-25-24, https://www.nature.com/scitable/topicpage/major -molecular-events-of-dna-replication-413.

300 King Abdullah University of Science and Technology. "Enzyme follows a two-step verification system before cutting and repairing DNA damage," Phys.org, 4-3-17, https:// phys.org/news/2017-04-enzyme-two-step-verification-dna.html.

301 Video described in this chapter: Animation by Drew Berry at the Walter and Eliza Hall Institute of Medical Research. Studio filming by Raquel Nuno. The Entire Transcript can be found at the video's location on YouTube. Quoted video: Veritasium. "Your Body's Molecular Machines," Last accessed Nov. 12, 2023, https://www.youtube.com /watch?v=X_tYrnv_o6A. Also see: "DNA animation (2002-2014) by Drew Berry and Etsuko Uno," https://www.youtube.com/watch?v=7Hk9jct2ozY.
   Also see: "Drew Berry: Animations of unseeable biology" TED. 2012, https://www. youtube.com/watch?v=WFCvkkDSfIU.

302 Veritasium. "Your Body's Molecular Machines," Last accessed Nov. 12, 2023, https:// www.youtube.com/watch?v=X_tYrnv_o6A.

303 Read the full transcript at this YouTube link – located in the drop down section under the actual video. Quoted video: Veritasium. "Your Body's Molecular Machines," Last accessed Nov. 12, 2023, https://www.youtube.com/watch?v=X_tYrnv_o6A.

304 Veritasium. "Your Body's Molecular Machines," Last accessed Nov. 12, 2023, https:// www.youtube.com/watch?v=X_tYrnv_o6A.

305 Googolplex
   Written out in ordinary decimal notation, it is 1 followed by 10100 zeroes. To put this in perspective, the mass of all books required to write out a googolplex of zeroes would be vastly greater than the masses of the Milky Way and the Andromeda galaxies combined (by a factor of roughly 2.0 × 1050), and greater than the mass of the observable universe by a factor of roughly 7 × 1039. See: https://en.wikipedia.org/wiki/Googolplex.

306 Host: Shelley Quinn and Dr Tim Standish…Guest: Dr. Ryan Hayes.
   Three Angels Broadcasting Network (3ABN). "DNA and Design: - The Creator Revealed," YouTube, 3ABN, 2019, accessed November 12, 2023, https://www.youtube .com/watch?v=Lx1ZiQyYdHM.

307 Ibid.

308 Ibid.

309 Ibid.

310 Ibid.

311 Piper, Kirstie. "I thought I was pro-life until I saw an ultrasound," Focus on the Family, 9-30-21, https://www.focusonthefamily.com/pro-life/abortion/i-thought-i-was-pro-life -until-i-saw-an-ultrasound.

312 "Scientists Found Proof of God in DNA Code - The God Code," YouTube Channel - Engineering Made Easy, accessed November 15, 2023, https://www.youtube.com/watch ?v=tF86T0N316c.

313 Ibid.

314 Paulson, Steve. "The believer: Francis Collins -- head of the Human Genome Project -- discusses his conversion to evangelical Christianity, why scientists do not need to be atheists, and what C.S. Lewis has to do with it," August 7, 2006, https://www.salon.com /2006/08/07/collins_6.

315 Freeland, S J 1, and Hurst, L D. "The genetic code is one in a million." Published Sept. 1998, https://pubmed.ncbi.nlm.nih.gov/9732450.

316 Definitions from Oxford Languages
non·ran·dom, adjective, adjective: non-random: "Determined by or resulting from factors other than chance." "a nonrandom distribution pattern." Google: what does non-random mean.

317 Ibid.

318 Merriam-Webster Dictionary
Intelligence
(1) the ability to learn or understand or to deal with new or trying situations : REASON, also : the skilled use of reason.
(2): the ability to apply knowledge to manipulate one's environment or to think abstractly as measured by objective criteria (such as tests). https://www.merriam-webster.com/dictionary/intelligence.

319 Koonin, EV, Novozhilov, AS. "Origin and evolution of the genetic code: the universal enigma." February 2009, https://pubmed.ncbi.nlm.nih.gov/19117371.

320 Giulio, Massimo Di. "Arguments against the stereochemical theory of the origin of the genetic code," November 2022, https://pubmed.ncbi.nlm.nih.gov/35970477.

321 Host: Shelley Quinn and Dr Tim Standish...Guest: Dr. Ryan Hayes.
Three Angels Broadcasting Network (3ABN). "DNA and Design: - The Creator Revealed," YouTube, 3ABN, 2019, accessed November 12, 2023, https://www.youtube .com/watch?v=Lx1ZiQyYdHM.

322 Torgerson, Adam,. "Coevolution and Darwin's 'abominable mystery,'" Willamette University, November 04, 2016, https://willamette.edu/news/library/2016/11/smith-coevo -mystery.html.

323 Diffuse **coevolution** (or 'guild' coevolution) refers to **reciprocal** evolutionary **responses between suites of species.**
From: Encyclopedia of Ecology, 2008. Science Direct, "Coevolution," accessed November 12, 2023, https://www.sciencedirect.com/topics/agricultural-and-biological-scienc-es/coevolution.

324 Massey, Steven E. "A neutral origin for error minimization in the genetic code," November 2008, https://pubmed.ncbi.nlm.nih.gov/18855039.

325 Koonin, Eugene V and Novozhilov, Artem S. "Origin and Evolution of the Universal Genetic Code," November 2017, https://pubmed.ncbi.nlm.nih.gov/28853922.

326 Caldararo, Franco, Di Giulio, Massimo. "The genetic code is very close to a global optimum in a model of its origin taking into account both the partition energy of amino acids and their biosynthetic relationships," January 2022, https://pubmed.ncbi.nlm.nih .gov/35085754.

327 Concluding Statements: "Our **hypothesis** is that **life on Earth** as we know it today, was developed **when all natural amino acids were already present.**" (Emphasis added)

Rosandić, Marija, Paar, Vladimir. "Standard Genetic Code vs. Supersymmetry Genetic Code – Alphabetical table vs. physicochemical table," Science Direct, August 2022, https://www.sciencedirect.com/science/article/pii/S030326472200082X.

328 "Watson and Crick proposed that the DNA is made up of two strands that are twisted around each other to form a right-handed helix, called a double helix. Base-pairing takes place between a purine and pyrimidine: namely, A pairs with T, and G pairs with C." Molnar, Charles and Gair, Jane. "9.1 The Structure of DNA," Accessed November 22, 2023, https://opentextbc.ca/biology/chapter/9-1-the-structure-of-dna.

329 2023 Jul 27;24(15):12029. doi: 10.3390/ijms241512029.
The Evolution of Life Is a Road Paved with the DNA Quadruplet Symmetry and the Supersymmetry Genetic Code. Marija Rosandić 1 2, Vladimir Paar 2 3. https://pubmed.ncbi.nlm.nih.gov/37569405.

330 Ryugu. (Japanese - Dragon Palace), a magical underwater palace in a Japanese folktale. https://en.wikipedia.org/wiki/162173_Ryugu.

331 Ashley Strickland (22 March 2023). "RNA compound and vitamin B3 found in samples from near-Earth asteroid". CNN. Retrieved 22 March 2023. https://edition.cnn.com/2023/03/21/world/ryugu-asteroid-organic-molecules-scn/index.html.

332 He served under Joe Biden, Barack Obama, and Bill Clinton. See the following resources for more background info on Dr. Collins.
(1) Sellers, Stead. "Leadership During Crisis with Francis S. Collins, MD, PhD". Washington Post. 12-17-21, https://www.washingtonpost.com/washington-post-live/2021/12/17/leadership-during-crisis-with-francis-s-collins-md-phd.
(2) Secretary Sebelius Announces Senate Confirmation of Dr. Francis Collins as Director of the National Institutes of Health Archived September 21, 2012, at the Wayback Machine 7-Aug-09, Accessed November 22, 2023, http://www.hhs.gov/news/press/2009pres/08/20090807d.html.

333 "Gene Therapy Cures Cystic Fibrosis In Lab". Tribune Digital-Chicago Tribune, accessed November 21, 2023. http://articles.chicagotribune.com/1990-09-21/news/9003190188_1_cystic-fibrosis-healthy-genes.

334 Paulson, Steve. "The believer: Francis Collins -- head of the Human Genome Project -- discusses his conversion to evangelical Christianity, why scientists do not need to be atheists, and what C.S. Lewis has to do with it," August 7, 2006, https://www.salon.com/2006/08/07/collins_6.

335 Ibid.

336 Ibid.

337 Dr. Collin's biblical and public declaration of faith.
"TRANSCRIPT: Bob Abernethy's interview with Dr. Francis Collins, Director of the Human Genome Project at the National Institutes of Health," PBS, June 16, 2000, https://www.pbs.org/wnet/religionandethics/2000/06/16/transcript-bob-abernethys-interview-with-dr-francis-collins-director-of-the-human-genome-project-at-the-national-institutes-of-health/15204.
You can also see Dr. Collins in person in a 2016 presentation of his personal testimony at a Cal. Tech. auditorium.
The Veritas Forum. "My Journey from Atheism to Christianity | Francis Collins at Cal Tech." YouTube, 9-6-16, https://www.youtube.com/watch?v=HaEQyNeaFZs.

338 Proto-Sinaitic
   Proto-Sinaitic, the North Semitic alphabet, or Early Alphabetic is considered the
   earliest trace of alphabetic writing and the common ancestor of both the Ancient South
   Arabian script and the Phoenician alphabet. These are the scripts that led to many
   modern alphabets of the world.
   (1) Garfinkel, Yosef; Golub, Mitka R.; Misgav, Haggai; Ganor, Saar (May 2015). "The
   'Išba'al Inscription from Khirbet Qeiyafa". Bulletin of the American Schools of Oriental Research. 373 (373): 217–233.
   (2) "North Semitic alphabet". Encyclopedia Britannica. Accessed, 2-12, 2022. https://
   www.britannica.com/topic/North-Semitic-alphabet.
   (3) Rollston, C. (2020). The Emergence of Alphabetic Scripts. In R. Hasselbach-Andee
   (Ed.), A Companion to Ancient Near Eastern Languages (1st ed., pp. 65–81). Wiley.
   (4) "Sinaitic inscriptions | ancient writing". Encyclopedia Britannica. Accessed 3-14-
   22, https://www.britannica.com/topic/Sinaitic-inscriptions.
   (5) "Earliest Known Hebrew Text in Proto-Canaanite Script Discovered in Area Where
   'David Slew Goliath'". Science Daily. November 3, 2008, https://www.sciencedaily.com
   /releases/2008/11/081103091035.htm.
   (6) Wikipedia. "Proto-Sinaitic script," Accessed 3-22-22, https://en.wikipedia.org/wiki
   /Proto-Sinaitic_script.
339 Paleo-Hebrew
   (1) Ngo, Robin. "Computer Program Learning to Read Paleo-Hebrew Letters," Biblical
   Archeology, 4-30-15, https://www.biblicalarchaeology.org/daily/biblical-artifacts
   /inscriptions/computer-program-learning-to-read-paleo-hebrew-letters.
   (2) "Paleo-Hebrew Alphabet," https://en.wikipedia.org/wiki/Paleo-Hebrew_alphabet.
   "Palaeo-Hebrew, Proto-Hebrew or Old Hebrew, is the writing system found in Canaanite inscriptions from the region of biblical Israel and Judah. **It is considered to be the
   script used to record the original texts of the Hebrew Bible** due to its similarity to the
   Samaritan script, as the Talmud stated that the Hebrew ancient script was still used by
   the Samaritans."
   (3) Modern Hebrew Development
   Between the 6th and the 2nd century BCE, Classical, or Square, Hebrew gradually
   displaced the Aramaic alphabet, which had replaced Early Hebrew in Palestine. Square
   Hebrew became established in the 2nd and 1st centuries BCE and developed into the
   Modern Hebrew alphabet over the next 1,500 years. It was apparently derived from
   the Aramaic alphabet rather than from Early Hebrew but was nonetheless strongly
   influenced by the Early Hebrew script.
   Britannica. "Hebrew Alphabet," Accessed 2-21-22, https://www.britannica.com/topic
   /Hebrew-alphabet.
   (4) Shurpin, Yehuda. "What Is the Authentic Ancient Hebrew Alphabet?: Ketav Ivri vs.
   Ketav Ashurit," Chabad.org, accessed 3-13-22, https://www.chabad.org/library/article
   _cdo/aid/3582435/jewish/What-Is-the-Authentic-Ancient-Hebrew-Alphabet.htm
        "[The currently used Hebrew script], ketav Ashurit ("Assyrian script"), is the one
   we know today as the Hebrew alphabet."
340 There are, however, experts in the ancient languages of the world that believe the Hebrew

alphabet may prove to be the oldest of all known alphabets. That would include, they claim, even those that are presently dated to have preexisted the Hebrew. Of course those discoveries are also disputed by a bevy of other renowned experts, but it's still a fascinating possibility to consider. Is Hebrew The Oldest Language? See the following:

(1) Fox News. Bonner, Walt. "Hebrew may be world's oldest alphabet," Foxnews.com, 12-5-16, https://www.foxnews.com/science/hebrew-may-be-worlds-oldest-alphabet.

(2) Bower, Bruce. "Oldest alphabet identified as Hebrew," Science News, 11-19-16, https://www.sciencenews.org/article/oldest-alphabet-identified-hebrew.

(3.) Times of India. "[Hebrew] Oldest language of the world," 5-13-20, https://timesofindia.indiatimes.com/readersblog/whatsup-university/oldest-language-of-the-world-19460.

341 Rabbi Raskin, Aaron L.. "Ayin: The sixteenth letter of the Hebrew alphabet," Chabad.org, accessed 4-12-22, https://www.chabad.org/library/article_cdo/aid/137088/jewish/Ayen.htm.

342 Some Hebrew names have mystical-spiritual meanings:

"Each letter in the Hebrew alphabet (Aleph-Bet) has both a literal and mystical [spiritual/transcendent] meaning. This means that each name has a mystical [spiritual/transcendent] significance, based on the letters which form the name."

Tzadka, Yigal. "The Book of Hebrew Letters, hebrewtoday.com, accessed May 3, 2022, https://hebrewtoday.com/product/the-book-of-hebrew-letters. Also See: Study Light.org. "Language Studies Hebrew Thoughts https://www.studylight.org/language-studies/hebrew-thoughts.html?article=599?article=599.

343 It is a scholastically verified fact that the ancient Semitic/Hebrew language did have meanings attached to each letter, and that those ancient meanings are still used and studied by a number of Hebrew people today. For further study of this factual attestation, see the following resources:

Handelzalts, Michael. "In the Beginning: The Origins of the Hebrew Alphabet," Haaretz, 8-4-13, https://www.haaretz.com/jewish/.premium-why-hebrew-should-be-called-jewish-1.5316745.

"The names of the Hebrew letters have meaning in the Hebrew language. That doesn't actually matter when writing or reading, but it is nice to know."

(2) Dr. Benthien, George W.. "The Hebrew Language And Way of Thinking," January 2013, accessed 2-23-22, https://gbenthien.net/assets/docs/Hebrew.pdf.

(3) Hebrew Alphabet Letter Meanings

Based upon the notes and understandings from studying with Kabbalist Samuel Avital. "Hebrew Alphabet Letter Meanings," Accessed 3-12-22, http://www.walkingkabbalah.com/hebrew-alphabet-letter-meanings.

(NOTE: While I do not put stock in the mystical Kabbalistic practices of Orthodox Judaism, I include this reference as attestation that the "letter meaning" phenomenon is widely recognized even among the most conservative orthodox Jews and has been studied, interpreted, and practiced for well over a 1,000 years. This is an important refutation to some detractors who claim there is no such phenomenon attached to the Hebrew alphabet, modern or ancient.)

(4) Bible Lexicons: Ancient Hebrew Alphabet.

Study Light Bible Study Site: "Ancient Hebrew Alphabet," Accessed https://www.study
light.org/lexicons/eng/hebrew/ahl_alphabet.html.

Copyright: © 1999-2013; Ancient Hebrew Research Center. Old Testament
Hebrew Lexical Dictionary developed by Jeff Garrison for StudyLight.org. Copyright
1999-2022. All Rights Reserved, Jeff Garrison, Gdansk, Poland.

(5) Rabbi Cohn-Sherbok, Dan. "Creation Mysticism: Fashioning the World from
Letters," My Jewish Learning publication, accessed 3-13-22, https://www.myjewish
learning.com/article/creation-mysticism-fashioning-the-world-from-letters. (My Jewish
Learning was launched in 2003 and is now a part of 70 Faces Media, the largest non-
profit, nondenominational Jewish media organization in North America.)

(6) Waltke, Bruce K.; O'Connor, M. (1990). An Introduction to Biblical Hebrew
Syntax. Winona Lake, Indiana: Eisenbrauns: 83.

(7) Wilson-Wright, Aren M.. "On Origin of Alphabetic Writing," Radboud University,
Nijmegen. November 2019, https://bibleinterp.arizona.edu/sites/bibleinterp.arizona.
edu/files/images/On%20the%20Origin%20of%20Alphabetic%20Writing.pdf.

344 (8) Hebrew Today. "The Hebrew Alphabet -The Letter Shin (שׁ)." Accessed 4-8-22,
https://hebrewtoday.com/alphabet/the-letter-shin-%D7%A9/

(9) Freeman, Tzvi. "KabAlefBet! The Kabbalah of every one of the letters of the Hebrew
alphabet," accessed April 2, 2022, https://www.chabad.org/multimedia/video_cdo/aid
/829340/jewish/KabAlefBet.htm. This site details the modern interpretations of the
ancient Hebrew letter meanings, studied for generations among the Orthodox Hebrew
people.

(10) Chadwick, Jonathan. "Has the 'missing link' in the history of the ALPHABET
been discovered?" U.K. Daily Mail, 4-14-22 https://www.dailymail.co.uk/sciencetech
/article-9470949/Archaeologists-missing-link-early-alphabet.html. SEE this image of
the archeologically confirmed ancient Semitic languages with attached letter meanings...and the evolution of the Alphabet. https://i.dailymail.co.uk/1s/2021/04/15
/08/37731400-9470949-Detailed_the_process_that_she_thinks_the_Canaanites
_used_to_get_-a-61_1618470347913.jpg.

(11) Freeman, Tzvi. "The Kabbalah [mystical meaning] of every one of the letters of
the Hebrew alphabet," https://www.chabad.org/multimedia/video_cdo/aid/829340
/jewish/KabAlefBet.htm.

Haaretz is an Israeli newspaper. It was founded in 1918, making it the longest
running newspaper currently in print in Israel, and is now published in both Hebrew
and English in the Berliner format. See: https://en.wikipedia.org/wiki/Haaretz.

345 Handelzalts, Michael. "In the Beginning: The Origins of the Hebrew Alphabet,"
Haaretz, 8-4-13, https://www.haaretz.com/jewish/.premium-why-hebrew-should-be
-called-jewish-1.5316745.kyeoj

346 Hebrew Today. Who We Are.

"Hebrew Today is a reputable publication house, specializing in the highly professional
and unique fusion of linguistics and journalism. Our products are developed and written by professionals in the fields of education, linguistics, and the Hebrew language....
Many teachers use our newspapers to teach Hebrew both in classes and in private
lessons, because they find that we offer an easy and effective way to learn the Hebrew

alphabet and grammar." See: "Who We Are," HebrewToday.com, accessed 4-21-22, https://hebrewtoday.com/company-overview.

Also see: https://hebrewtoday.com/content-our-approach-learning-hebrew.

347 Tzadka, Yigal. "The Book of Hebrew Letters, HebrewToday.com, accessed May 3, 2022, https://hebrewtoday.com/product/the-book-of-hebrew-letters.

348 Poltorak, Alexander. "History and Customs," Chabad.org, accessed April 12, 2022, https://www.chabad.org/library/article_cdo/aid/310887/jewish/History-and-Customs.htm.

349 "Mezuzah also spelled Mezuza (Hebrew: "doorpost"), plural Mezuzoth, Mezuzot, Mezuzahs, or Mezuzas, small folded or rolled parchment inscribed by a qualified calligraphist with scriptural verses (Deuteronomy 6:4–9, 11:13–21) to remind Jews of their obligations toward God. The parchment is placed in a metal, wooden, or glass case so that the word Shaddai ("Almighty") can usually be seen on the back of the parchment. After a special blessing is recited, the mezuzah is firmly fixed to the main doorpost of the home (to the right as one enters). It is a custom with some Jews to kiss the mezuzah as they pass it."

Encyclopedia Britannica. "Mezuzah: Judaism," Accessed 4-8-22, https://www.britannica .com/topic/mezuzah.

350 Hebrew Today. "The Hebrew Alphabet -
The Letter Shin (ש)." Accessed 4-8-22, https://hebrewtoday.com/alphabet/the-letter -shin-%D7%A9.

351 Cross, Frank Moore Jr." Yahweh and the God of the Patriarchs," The Harvard Theological Review, Vol. 55, No. 4 (Oct., 1962), pp. 225-259. Published by: Cambridge University Press on behalf of the Harvard Divinity School. https://vdocuments.site /yahweh-and-the-god-of-the-patriarchs.html?page=34.

352 Studylight.org. "Ancient Hebrew Alphabet," (Al-Aleph), Accessed June 23, 2018, https://www.studylight.org/lexicons/hebrew/ahl_alphabet.html.

353 Editors. Britannica. "The Hebrew Alphabet," Britannica.com, accessed May 2, 2022, https://www.britannica.com/topic/Hebrew-alphabet.

354 See: Psalm 22:16-18, Zechariah 12:10, and Isaiah 53:5-6.

355 Quarterly Statement - Palestine Exploration Fund" - 1869, https://archive.org/details /quarterlystateme11pale/page/237/mode/1up.

See also: https://en.wikipedia.org/wiki/Siloam_inscription#cite_ref-5.

356 This photograph of the Siloam Inscription is found on the website of Dr. David Graves, PhD - Archeologist. https://biblicalarchaeologygraves.blogspot.com/2014/12 /figure-19.html.

357 O.T. 853. "Eth," Biblehub.com, https://biblehub.com/hebrew/853.htm.

358 Depending upon the font used, there are about 1,200 pages of the Old Testament in modern English translations. But the word eth is found almost 11,000 times in the Old Testament. Averaging being used about ten times for every single page of the Old Testament.

359 **Accusative Case:** The accusative case is a grammatical case whose main function is to show the direct object of a verb. (Most people will encounter the term "accusative case" when studying a language other than English.) One can find the direct object by finding the verb and asking "what?" (or "whom?").

For example: The dog ate our turkey. The verb is "ate". Now ask what? The direct object (accusative case) is our turkey. See:Grammar Monster. https://www.grammar-monster.com/glossary/accusative_case.htm.

360 Bible Resources. "What are the two Hebrew words, Aleph and Tav existing in Hebrew manuscripts at the beginning of thousands of Scriptures, which are not translated into English language Bible translations?" 7-15-2020, https://bibleresources.info/what-are-the-two-hebrew-words-aleph-and-tav-existing-in-hebrew-manuscripts-at-the-beginning-of-thousands-of-scriptures-which-are-not-translated-into-english-language-bible-translations-india.

361 A Hebraic Explanation of the word Eth.
Oxford Jewish Thought - Essays by Rabbi Eli Brackman: Rabbi Eli Brackman. "An extra word in the Bible: finding the mystical in the simple," OxfordChabad.org, 8-27-09, https://www.oxfordchabad.org/templates/blog/post.asp?aid=708481&PostID=14343&p=1.

Also see: Goldtmann, Harry. Biblical Word Studies. ""Eth (את) and the three crosses," accessed March 23, 2022, https://goldtmann.wordpress.com/2016/02/11/eth-%D7%90%D6%B5%D7%AA-and-the-three-crosses.

Bio for Harry Goldtmann: A Chemical Engineer with a Masters in Lean Six Sigma. A born again believer and student of Hebrew. https://goldtmann.wordpress.com/author/zachariah28/

Harry Goldtmann: "I have learned the use of this word in Hebrew may have had more meaning in the primitive Hebrew language, and that over time as languages improved, the meaning lost its significance. Today, eth, is generally used to point out more definitely the object of a verb or preposition. Reading through the scholars on the linguistics of this word, they struggled to define a use. One states, "This word by degrees lost much of its primitive force, so that as set before nouns and pronouns already definite, it scarcely increases the demonstrative power. What I gathered from reading the scholars, basically, this is a Hebrew word that doesn't belong in the Bible today, for its use was in the primitive times....I've been told every word of the Bible is precious and has a purpose. I have also been told how God can take the littlest of things and turn them into something big. Is there a message in this little word, which linguistically no longer applies? Was this a primitive method of placing emphasis on the noun, in today's world, putting a word in BOLD font?"

362 Ibid. A Hebraic Explanation of the word Eth.
Oxford Jewish Thought - Essays by Rabbi Eli Brackman. Rabbi Eli Brackman. "An extra word in the Bible: finding the mystical in the simple."

From the article: "We will therefore approach this question from an exegetical point of view first followed by a mystical perspective, which ultimately proves most satisfactory in our case."

"This interpretation is found in a Jewish mystical text of 1905 by Rabbi Sholom Dov Ber of Lubavitch (Sefer Hamamorim 5665 p. 15). Rabbi Sholom Dov Ber analyses the word 'Eth' in the context of love of G-d, whereby he resolves the question posed at the beginning of this essay. In the simple interpretation of this word it emphasizes a deep mystical meditation that all of existence is nullified before G-d's existence...." (Emphasis added)

363 Got Questions. "What is the biblical significance of the number seven/7?" Accessed 4-8-22, https://www.gotquestions.org/number-7-seven.html.

364 See Colossians 1 and John 1.

365 See Messianic Rabbi Zev Porat's book "Unmasking the Chaldean Spirit," (Defender Publishing) for an in-depth and stunning presentation of the actual place of the crucifixion and the Hebrew/biblical meaning of the word Golgotha.

366 Hebrew Resources Admin. "The Extra Large "BET" in the First Letter of the Hebrew Bible," 4-3-09, https://hebrewresources.com/the-extra-large-bet-in-the-first-letter-of-the-hebrew-bible.

367 Ibid. (Last paragraph of the article)

368 Ibid.

369 "The letter RESH," Gabriel Levy, accessed Nov. 24, 2023, https://gabrielelevy.com/pages/the-letter-resh.

370 "The letter ALEPH," Gabriel Levy, accessed Nov. 24, 2023, https://gabrielelevy.com/pages/the-letter-aleph.

371 Your Jewish Journey. "SHIN (HEBREW LETTER)," Accessed November 24, 2023, https://bje.org.au/knowledge-centre/jewish-languages/hebrew-alphabet/shin.

372 Rabbi Raskin, Aaron L.. "Yod -The tenth letter of the Hebrew alphabet," Accessed November 25, 2023, https://www.chabad.org/library/article_cdo/aid/137082/jewish/Yod.htm.

373 "Meaning 1. Truth 2. **sign** 3. life or death…. also found pertaining to the "**Covenant** between the Parts,"12 when G-d caused Abraham to fall into a deep slumber and told him that his children would reside in a foreign land (the land of Egypt) for four hundred years and afterwards go out with great wealth and an outstretched arm."

Rabbi Aaron L. "Tav- The twenty-second letter of the Hebrew alphabet," Accessed November 25, 2023, Raskinhttps://www.chabad.org/library/article_cdo/aid/137287/jewish/Tav.htm.

374 Bollinger, Hope. "Interesting Facts about the Meaning & Importance of the Number 12 in the Bible," Crosswalk.com, 1-22-21, https://www.crosswalk.com/faith/bible-study/12-interesting-facts-about-number-12-in-the-bible.html.

375 If an angelic encounter is given to us, it is not so that we can convince others of how "spiritual" we are. Apparently there were false teachers in the early church who engaged in this type of practice. Attempting to "conjure" this kind of experience could easily result in demonic infiltration into the event, or, at the very least, a dangerous psychological delusion that plays upon our fallen sin nature. The rule is: Follow only the Lord Jesus Christ, by faith. If He determines to assist us by sending an angelic messenger, not only will we not be required to ask him for it – but ample evidence of the genuineness of the visitation will be given to us as well.

Do not let anyone who delights in false humility and the worship of angels disqualify you. Such a person also goes into great detail about what they have seen; they are puffed up with idle notions by their unspiritual mind. (Colossians 2:18)
Expositor's Greek Testament

[In reference to these false teachers] "The Worship of Angels" - This should probably be explained with reference to the invisible world, with which they professed to hold communion, but which really was closed to them.

Jamieson-Fausset-Brown Bible Commentary

Plainly the [manifestations] were actually seen…whether of demoniacal origination (1Sa 28:11-20), or phenomena resulting from natural causation, mistaken…as if [it were] supernatural. Paul, not stopping to discuss the nature of the things so seen, fixes on the radical error…https://biblehub.com/commentaries/colossians/2-18.htm.

376 See: Matthew 18:15-17, 1 Corinthians 5:1-13.

377 "The first recognizable social media site, in the format we know today, was Six Degrees – a platform created in 1997 that enabled users to upload a profile and make friends with other users."
Ortiz-Ospina, Esteban (2019) - "The rise of social media" Published online at Our WorldInData.org. Retrieved from: https://ourworldindata.org/rise-of-social-media.

378 The moment I heard the man say, "I am a fellow minister with you," the following passage came to mind. However, the truth of it did not fully register with me, until several days later: [The angel said to John – do not worship me!] I am a fellow servant with you and with your fellow prophets and with all who keep the words of this scroll. Worship God!" (Revelation 22:9, brackets added for context).

379 **Sons of God** (i.e. Job 1:6). A Hebrew expression used in the Old Testament for angels - the members of God's divine court and thus members of the obedient realm of God's creation.
Pulpit Commentary
By "the sons of God" it is generally admitted that, in this place [Job 1:6], the angels are meant (so again in Job 38:7). https://biblehub.com/commentaries/job/1-6.htm.

380 See: Hebrews 13:2, Acts 12:3-19, and especially Genesis 18:1-2; 19:1-2
Regarding the account of "three men" in Genesis 18, who were only later to be revealed as angels – observe the following:
Cambridge Bible for Schools and Colleges
The sudden appearance of the three men before the tent is especially recorded. Their approach had not been observed. As in the case of Genesis 32:24, Joshua 5:13, Judges 13:10-11, the **angelic visitants are not distinguishable from ordinary men.** (Emphasis added). https://biblehub.com/commentaries/genesis/18-2.htm.

381 Got Questions. "Could an alien deception be part of the end times?", Gotquestions. org, accessed 12-13-23, https://www.gotquestions.org/alien-deception.html.

382 See Zechariah 4.
Practically all the renowned scholars understand this passage to be ultimately speaking of the birth of the church – coming out of the prophecies given to Israel, and Yeshua Himself, who also came "out" of Israel. For verification of this fact, see: https://bible hub.com/commentaries/zechariah/4-6.htm.

383 Charles Haddon Spurgeon. "Spurgeon remains highly influential among Christians of various denominations, to some of whom he is known as the "Prince of Preachers". He was a strong figure in the Reformed Baptist tradition, defending the 1689 London Baptist Confession of Faith, and opposing the liberal and pragmatic theological tendencies in the Church of his day." https://en.wikipedia.org/wiki/Charles_Spurgeon.

384 Spurgeon, Charles, Haddon. "The Healing of One Born Blind," August 11, 1872, https://www.spurgeon.org/resource-library/sermons/the-healing-of-one-born-blind /#flipbook.

Printed in the USA
CPSIA information can be obtained
at www.ICGtesting.com
JSHW031548240824
68559JS00013B/18